CEYLON LECTURES

CEYLON LECTURES

[Delivered as Extension Lectures in Ceylon in March, 1944]

BY

BENI MADHAB BARUA

GYAN

Published by

Gyan Publishing House
5, Ansari Road
Daryaganj, New Delhi-110002
Phone: 011-47034999, 9811692060
E-mail: books@gyanbooks.com

Distribution Network
gyanbooks.com
India, USA, Canada, UK, Australia

ISBN: 978-93-6280-412-9 (PB)
First Published, 1945

2nd Impression 2024

Printed at: Gyan Press, Delhi.

CEYLON LECTURES
Author: BENI MADHAB BARUA

CEYLON LECTURES

[Delivered as Extension Lectures in Ceylon in March, 1944.]

BY

Tripiṭakācārya

BENI MADHAB BARUA, M.A., D.LIT. (Lond.)

PROFESSOR, CALCUTTA UNIVERSITY.

Published by

SATIS CHANDRA SEAL, M.A., B.L.

Hony. General Secretary,

Bhāratī Mahāvidyālaya

1, Gour Laha Street,

Calcutta.

1945

PREFACE

In this preface to my Ceylon Lectures printed at last in a book form, it may not be out of place briefly to narrate the story of their origin and development.

It was on a joint invitation from Mr. Ranasinha, the Public Trustee acting on behalf of the Dona Alpina Ratnayake Trust, and Prof. G. P. Malalasekera acting on behalf of the Buddhist Brotherhood of the University of Ceylon, to deliver two public lectures on Buddhism that I decided to go across to Ceylon last year, in the second week of March. There could be no inducement from any material gains, since no such prospects were held out to me by either. My object was purely cultural. I hit upon a plan for at least six lectures, three in History and three in Religion series so that I might adequately express my thoughts about the people and civilization of the island. Accordingly, I communicated my wishes to Prof. Malalasekera, Prof. H. C. Ray and Rev. Rahula, and here to Sir Baron Jayatilaka, all of whom were sincerely interested in the matter. Subsequent correspondence revealed that I had acted wisely, as I was required by other societies and institutions, including the University of Ceylon, to deliver lectures under their auspices.

The eight lectures presented in the following pages have been retouched here and there. Three of them are provided with appendices. The chronological order in which the lectures were delivered has not been preserved.

Lecture V, *Buddhism as Buddha's Personal Religion,* has provoked a good deal of discussion in Ceylon. Among the adverse critics, Mr. H. D. Ratnatunga has proved the most eloquent on the *anatta* or 'no-soul' doctrine of Buddhism.

In Lecture VI the subject of 'Buddhism as an Institutional religion' has been discussed at some length. A distinction has been made between Buddhism from Buddha's personal point of view and Buddhism from the point of view of his disciples and followers. I have clearly stated that institutional religions have scope also for personal ones. But, historically speaking, I shall be the last person to mistake a Sāriputta or Moggallāna for the Buddha himself.

As for the question of *reality,* I am at a loss to understand the difference between *actuallty* and *reality.* If *Paṭiccasamuppāda,* which is the basic concept of Buddhism, has no bearing on 'actuality' or 'factual reality', then what is that on which its bearing lies? If Buddhism stands for truth, what is that truth? By truth we must understand a statement of some 'fact', 'actuality' or 'factual reality' which we have got to face without any haggling. In Buddha's own words, it is that element (*sā dhātu*) which exists by its own right, independently of the advent or non-advent of all truth-finders and path-finders, that is to say, independently of all ideal constructions.

Some persons professing to be staunch followers of Buddhism are very touchy when a modern critical scholar proposes to consider the philosophical position of Buddhism in the historical context of the *Upaniṣads* or the *Great Epic.* But, what better contexts can really there be suggested? Buddhism as a system of thought, or of ethics, or as a faith, stands or falls only when its position is correctly ascertained in these contexts. Those who have carefully read the two sets of texts and kept the concordances before them, will certainly bear me out when I say that there is hardly an utterance of the Buddha, either in the *Nikāyas* or in the *Jātakas,* which has not a direct or indirect reference to some point of the doctrine in the *Upaniṣads,* or in the *Mahābhārata,* the per-Pāṇinian epic. Yet that does not mean that I have foisted any soul-theory on the Buddha or Buddhism.

Religious orthodoxy, I admit, has its own place and importance. But it becomes intolerable when it crosses its own boundary, and blurs our vision. There is a point of distinction between the five *khandhas* as constituents of existence and the five *upādāna-khandhas* where the mental factor of attachment or craving for establishing ownership over those constituents or aggregates (C. D. Chatterji, in *Bhārata-Kaumudī*, i, pp. 161-181).

Similarly there is a point of distinction between *ātmavāda* alias *satkāyadṛṣṭi* meaning the doctrine of a permanent being, and *ātmabhāva* meaning a living individuality in the biological sense of the term. The fact that Buddha sharply criticises and opposes the *Upaniṣad* idea of *attā* in the sense of a permanent entity or an element of reality (not necessarily soul) which is above the law of change or becoming, does not mean that he denied the factual reality of living individualities. In the *Sangīti Suttanta*, for instance, Buddha says, "There is (biologically speaking) the attainment of four kinds of living individuality : one in which dawns the consciousness of one's own self, *sañcetanā*, as well as that of others ; one in which there dawns the consciousness of other's but not that of one's own self ; one in which there dawns the twofold consciousness ; and one in which there dawns neither of the two" (Dīgha iii, p. 231). The word *sañcetanā* admits also of an interpretation in terms of the conative action of the will.

The interesting points of inquiry raised by Mr. D. B. Jayasinghe have been appropriately discussed in the footnotes under Lectures IV and V.

It was indeed much encouraging to me that such a fastidious man as the late lamented Mr. Jogendra Lal Barua, Founder President of the Jogendra Rupasibala Tripitaka Trust, was not only not displeased that I cautiously treated Buddhism as an epoch-making product of the evolution of the *adhyātma-sādhanā* of India through the *Vedas*, the *Upaniṣads* and other texts, but welcomed with a warm heart the mode of argument followed.

I received an equally cheering letter from my esteemed cousin, Mr. Birendra Lal Mutsuddi, the able exponent in Bengali of Anuruddha's *Compendium of the Abhidhamma system*.

The opinions will differ as they are bound to. The criticisms are welcome if they are constructive and suggestive. We are not yet out of the wood. We are still groping in the dark as to the real historical and philosophical position of Buddhism. To put the matter in the significant words of Mr. Jayasinghe, "Where then are the Buddha's views on reality? I reply that they have been staring at us (in our face) for the last 2500 years or so. If we do not recognize them it is because we are lost in a welter of controversy and in such an embarrassing wealth of exegetic detail that we cannot see the wood for the trees".

The manuscript of the lectures was handed over to the press in March, 44, and I even hoped to see them in print before June following. Lecture I was printed off in the fourth week of March last year. The main difficulty which stood in the way was that of procuring paper by the press at controlled rates. The printing could be expedited only since this difficulty was got over through the earnest effort of Mr. S. C. Seal, M. A., B. L., Honorary General Secretary to the Bhāratī Mahāvidyālaya. I owe him sincere thanks for this.

The lectures which were dictated could not have been made ready so soon if I had not Mr. D. L. Barua, my pupil and colleague, to act as the amenuensis. A similar assistance was received from my nephew-in-law, Hemendra Bikas Barua, M.A., in preparing Lecture VII. I must express my indebtedness to them for this, as also to my esteemed friend Dr. Wijesekera who kindly assisted me in completing Lecture III in Colombo. I am equally indebted to my esteemed colleague, Mr. Sailendra Nath Mitra, Secretary to the Councils of Post-Graduate Teaching in Arts and Science, Calcutta University. The Index is prepared with the kind assistance of Mr. Amites Banerjee, M.A., Professor of History, Hindu Academy, Daulatpur.

Dated, Calcutta, *B. M. Barua.*

May 26, '45.

TRAVELS AND REMINISCENCES

My stay in Ceylon was rather too short and my programme too heavy to enable me to visit all the places I would like to, especially those in northern and southern parts.

However, Rev. Rahula and Prof. Malalasekera would not have me leave the shores of the island without seeing Anurādhapura, Mihintāle, Polunnaruva, Sigiriya, Mātale and Kandy. Both, as my guardian angels, accompanied me wherever I moved, and made the best possible arrangements beforehand for my safety and comfort with the kind assistance of Mr. Gunasekera, the son-in-law of Mrs. Dona Alpina Ratnayake and Mr. Ratnatunga of the Ceylon Civil Service. But this pleasant and romantic tour through the ancient sites could not have been so instructive and profitable but for the invaluable company of Dr. Parana Vitana, Commissioner of Archaeology. In him we found a man with versatile interests and information. Full of humour, energy and vigour, he was frightfully shy of public appearance. His whole being was permeated by the spirit of an antiquarian and an archaeologist. With the heart of a poet and lover he seemed identified with all the glorious antiquities of the island. The Mahayana foundations discovered and the traces of Mahāyāna in the literature of Ceylon are things of his deepest interest and regard.

I left Calcutta by the Madras Mail train on the 8th March, 1944, to reach Colombo on the 12th, accompanied by my old pupil Mr. Satadal Kar, M. A. At Madras we had little difficulty to face as Mr. Sabhasan Chaudhuri, Asstt. Engineer of the South Indian Railway and Mrs. Chaudhuri were there to look after us. An Indian bound for Ceylon begins to feel the strangeness of the situation from the Mandapam Camp Station. Immediately after his arrival at Colombo, he has to report himself personally at the Health Office almost from day to day. Though all this is done in the name of health and safety, it does not require much intelligence to understand what is actually behind the show. Professors Malalasekera and Ray were, however, there to save us all unnecessary troubles within the operation of the law.

Rev. Rahula arranged with Mr. and Mrs. Pedris of 8 Alfred Place, Colpetty, Colombo, to play the part of our generous hosts. They were rich enough in land and money, but richer far in cordiality and generosity.

We were invited to dinner at the houses of Mr. Dhanapala of Kelaniya, Mr. Julius Lenarolle, Dr. Mendis, Prof. Ludobyke and Dr. Wijesekera. Everywhere the ladies of the house would not allow us to feel that we were strangers, so frank and sweet and homely were their dealings. Mrs. Dhanapala, educated at Allahabad and Santiniketan,, was from a Tamil Hindu family, whereas Mr. Dhanapala, an artist and educationist, was by his religion a Buddhist. But they made a happy home with everything delightfully simple and artistic about it. It was in their house that we were served with purely Sinhalese dishes. Elsewhere these were half Sinhalese and half European.

At Kandy we passed a quiet night on a fine hill-top, under the roof of the Hon'ble Mr. George E. de Silva, the Minister of Public Health, and Mrs. de Silva. Here was another matrimonial alliance between a Buddhist and a Dutch Christian.

As we travelled from Mātale to Kandy we felt as if every house on the roadside was eager to welcome and entertain us. Such a genial atmosphere prevailed all over the island.

My joy knew no bounds when I met my old friends, the Venerable Devarakkhita, the Venerable A. P. Buddhadatta and others. The Venerable Dr. Baddegame Piyaratana Nāyakatthera, the present head of the Vidyodaya Pariveṇa, and the Venerable Paṇḍita Welivitiye Sorata Nāyakatthera, the Vice-Principal of the same great Buddhist institution, did me great honour, indeed, by their unexpected courtesy in coming personally to invite me to pay a visit to their Pariveṇa. They were very pleased to learn that I was a pupil of Prof. S.C. Vidyābhusana. Principal of the Sanskrit College, Calcutta, and Prof. Rhys Davids, Founder President of the Pali Text Society, since both these Professors read Pali with the Most Venerable Siri Sumangala, Founder Principal of the Vidyodaya College. Thus I could claim some relation with this great institution of Ceylon through my revered teachers whose memory was lovingly cherished there.

I also remember with joy my meeting with my old beloved pupil, Brahmachari Devapriya Walisinha. The only person I sadly missed was my esteemed colleague, Rev. Professor Siddhartha, who died prematurely after his return from Europe.

In the University I had the honour of meeting Dr. Jennings, the present Vice-Chancellor, and all the Professors and Lecturers, including Mr. (since Dr.) Hettiaratchi of whom we all his teachers in Calcutta are proud for his intellectual acumen and erudition.

I availed myself of a kind invitation from the Hon'ble Minister Mr. D. S. Senanayake, Leader of the Council of State, to meet him with all his worthy colleagues, particularly the Hon'ble Dr. Kannangara and the Hon'ble Mr. George E. de Silva, to both of whom I am greatly beholden for many a personal reason. The leader of the House kindly took me into the gallery of the Council of State just to have an idea of the manner in which the deliberations and proceedings of the House were carried on. The members of the House seemed more disciplined and Parliamentarian in their habits than those in Bengal. The beauty of the assembly seemed a bit marred by the presence of three stately figures in the centre of the Hall, who were there to watch what was going on inside.

In the social circle Professor Malalasekera, President of the Buddhist Congress, offered me an opportunity to meet the representatives and leading workers of various Buddhist societies at an afternoon tea-party. The cordiality of feelings expressed on this occasion will ever be remembered with a feeling of gratitude.

Mr. M. S. Anne, Representative of the Government of India, ungrudgingly lent his ever-helping hand and spared no pains to bring me into personal contact with the leading personages, official and non official, among the Indians, the Ceylonese and the Europeans.

The Ceylon Press as a whole did their very best to give a

wide publicity to the gist of the lectures, thereby laying me under obligation.

But there are two solemn occasions to record, one when I faced the august assembly of the Theras of Ceylon headed by the Venerable Dhammānanda Nāyakatthera, appearing in their shining yellow robes at the peaceful and sombre *Sāl* grove of the Vidyālankāra Pariveṇa to receive the honorary diploma of *Tipiṭakācariya,* just the day after my arrival at Colombo, and the other when subsequently I had to confront even a larger congregation headed by the Venerable Dr. Baddegame Piyaratana Nāyakatthera and Dr. Paravahere Vajirañāṇa, Ph.D. (Cantab.), President of the Ceylon Mahābodhi Society, to receive its blessings.

Equally solemn was the occasion when Swāmi Siddhātmānanda of the Rāmkrishna Mission took me round the Rāmkrishna *āśrama* and temple in a quiet vicinage in the suburb of Colombo.

When I met Sir Baron Jayatilaka in Calcutta on the eve of my journey, we had a discussion regarding the present literary output in Sinhalese. He was definitely of the opinion that although there were a good many writers, none of their writings, wheher poems, novels or dramas, had attained an appreciable degree of excellence ; these were rather below the par. Out of curiosity I went to a theatre in Colombo when the play called *Mahāwanse* was staged. It made indeed a very poor show ; the stage was in a primitive condition. I strongly felt that an impetus should come from India to the development of Sinhalese literature, and wired to that effect to Dr. B. C. Law who, as is usual with him whenever a good case is made out for cultural advancement, promptly responded agreeing to found two prizes to be awarded annually, each of the value of Rs. 150|-, one for the encouragement of Sinhalese literature and the other of that of researches in Buddhism.

A traveller from India is bound to feel as he goes from north to south as though the two chains of rocky hills, *viz.,* the Eastern and Western Ghats, are moving with him guarding the island against the encroachments of the ocean that surrounds it and displaying throughout their abundant riches in wood and timber, tea gardens, rubber plantations and cocoanut groves. The Ratnapura area (Ratnadvīpa of old) is noted to this day for its wealth consisting in precious stones. The people in countrysides keep to their old habits; generally they live in indolence and contentment. The rubber trees were subjected then to 'high tapping' for yield which was regarded by the planters themselves as 'suicidal tapping for war purposes'.

There is ample living space for the existing population, half of which are Buddhists. A considerable portion of the island is still lying fallow. It is a pity that the island should be dependent for rice on other countries. I did not come across any forest which was not noted for its durable and glossy ebony wood and other varieties of timber, but the soil seemed congenial also for *mahogini*. I observed that Burma teak was in great demand in preference to Ceylon's own ebony wood.

The island is provided throughout with motorable roads, and it is absolutely free from dust. The cocoanut groves are cool and pleasant and kept up neat and clean. The natural sceneries are the most charming and incomparable. On all sides, as far as the eyes can see, lies the ocean with its blue sheet of water and rolling waves breaking upon the shores, and meets the blue sky which hangs over it as a canopy, forming a horizon (*cakravāla*) of infinity within which the sun and moon rise and set. An Indian, being thus faced with the panoramic view of the ocean and the hills, cannot help being constantly reminded of the following lines of Kālidāsa :

.... *Pravṛttamātreṇa payāṁsi pātum āvartavegād bhramatā ghanena*
ābhāti bhūyiṣṭham ayaṁ samudraḥ pramathyamāno giriṇeva bhūyaḥ||
Dūrādayaś cakranibhasya tanvī tamāla-tāla-vanarāji-nīlā/
ābhāti velā lavaṇāmburāśer dhārānibaddheva kalanka-rekhā||

The salt-water lagoons, good for fishery, appear like sleepy lakes and offer a sad contrast to the ocean proper with their faded colour and jaded look, maintaining around the least impressive population of the island consisting mostly of fisher-folk. The ancient cities of Anurādhapura, Polunnāruva and the rest contain the lake-like tanks (*vĕvas, vāpīs*), some of enormous sizes, that stand as lasting monuments to the piety and fame of the former kings of the island when it was an independent country. It is, however, sad that the interior of the island is still full of malaria, and this breaks out periodically in an epidemic and malignant form, taking a heavy toll of human lives.

There still exists a National Congress Party in the island with its adherence to the noble creed of non-violence preached by Mahātmā Gandhi. But it is not politically the strongest one, nor is there any clear sign of its activity. The people of Ceylon do, however, hold Mahātmāji in their high esteem and cherish with pride the memory of his gracious visit. Śrī Lankā had also a chance to welcome Pandit Jahawarlal Nehru in the rôle of a peace-maker when a tension arose between Indian labour and local workmen. Nehru's decisive opinion was that the people of Ceylon being bits of us, the Indians in Ceylon had no right whatsoever to be there as mere exploiters without any active sympathy with the joy and sorrow, prosperity and adversity of the dwellers of the island. The same was, *mutatis mutandis*, his advice to the Indians in Burma when a similar trouble arose there and he went across with a peace mission.

The sad event which happened after my return to India was the death of Sir Baron Jayatilaka which seemed all too sudden and unexpected. Sad it is that he was not spared longer to see two things completed, each dear to his heart, namely, the compilation of the Sinhalese Dictionary and the erection of the relic temple in the premises of the Vidyālankāra Pariveṇa. As for the first, happily he leaves behind him his worthy lieutenant, Mr. Julius Lanerolle, to continue the work, and as for the second, the whole Buddhist populace.

I must remain ever grateful to Rev. Nelluwe Jinaratna and other Ceylon friends at whose instance the local Mahābodhi Society held a public meeting to express felicitations to me. The kind words of appreciation expressed on the occasion by Professors S. N. Das Gupta and D. R. Bhandarkar, Drs. B. K. Sirkar, Kalidas Nag and Nihar Ranjan Roy were really more than what I deserved.

In connection with his journey to Ceylon Professor S. C. Vidyabhusana recorded with pride that he had received addresses from all the important monasteries including the Totogamawa (Tīrthagrāma), in which the Bhikkhus observed that for more than 450 years after the demise of Rāmacandra Kavibhāratī, no learned Pandit had gone from India. But I have not personally been an aspirant throughout my life for an honour of this kind. The best endeavour of my life consists in groping in the dark in order to find a new way of looking at things, taking nothing on absolute trust, and unsettling, if possible, all settled ideas. For me the best compliment was indeed one which came from the Hon'ble Dr. Kannangara, the Minister of Education, and which purported to saying that my heart was filled with genuine love for Ceylon. This was quite natural to me since my boyish fancies about the island were aroused at an early age, and what was precisely expected from me by my children who knew something about my real feelings. Under a false apprehension due to the general impression among my Calcutta friends that my attitude towards Ceylon was antagonistic, my wife implored me to take care that I had not hurt the feelings of any section of the people of Lankā. The eight lectures were delivered respectively on 17-3-44, 22-3-44, 23-3-44, 15-3-44, 14-3-44, 16-3-44, 22-3-44 and 21.3.44.

I cannot conclude this account of my travels in Ceylon without gratefully mentioning the kind letter received from Mr. Frederick Grubb, General Secretary to the Anglo-Indian Temperance Association, London, in warm appreciation of my lecture tour. To Mr. and Mrs. Grubb under whose roof and affectionate care I was privileged to spend at Wimbledon Park the third year of my stay in England I ever owe a personal debt which is irrepayable. So there is no astonishment that the press report of my tour in Ceylon induced him to write this letter enclosing a copy of his own instructive article—*Ceylon's place in the New World Order,* published in the "Ceylon Daily News" of 13th April, 1944. Mr. Grubb as former London correspondent of the "Ceylon Daily News" and as one keenly interested in the welfare of India and Ceylon, political or otherwise, pleads forcibly for the same cause when he poignantly observes : "Whatever the ultimate relations of India and Ceylon may be, it is manifestly to the advantage of both that a good understanding should exist between them. No one would care to contemplate the possibility of Ceylon becoming one of the cockpits of this or another war, but some unforeseeable realignment of world forces in days to come might even cause her to become a bone of contention amongst rival Powers. In any case, the establishment of Ceylon as a connecting link between those who have been for so long antagonised by conflicting interests would be no unworthy mission for her forward-looking people, and it would be an unmistakable service to the cause of international amity."

TABLE OF CONTENTS

A. In History Series

B. In Religion Series

ERRATA

P. 12, l. 1—Read *sky-going* for *sky-koinf.*
P. 36, l. 15— " *Chronicles* for *Chrnoicles.*
P. 38, l. 14— " *abundant* for *aboundant.*
P. 39, l. 6— " *induced* for *indeed.*
P. 40, l. 23— " *Ratnapura* for *Ratanpura.*
P. 44, l. 27— " *in* for *on.*
P. 56, l. 12— " *in Ceylon* for *as in Ceylon.*
P. 72, l. 4— " *-vibhanga* for *-vibhaga.*
P. 73, l. 18— " *Netti-* for *Neti-.*
P. 90, l. 7— " *Negāpaṭam* for *Nāgapaṭam.*
P. 220, l. 8— " *religion in* for *religion. In.*
P. 247, l. 22— " *demands* for *demnads.*
P. 262, l. 30— " *Milinda* for *Mlimda.*
P. 265, l. 22— " prajñā).[2] for prajñā 2.
P. 274, l. 6— " *eightfold* for *eightfold.*
P. 279, ll. 24-25—read *The Persian poet says, "Walk gently, better walk not, for innumerable lives are under your feet"* for *The great Persian poet and teacher Sa'di says: "Walk gently, because many ants are under your feet."*

ADDENDA

P. 13, ll. 3-4; Read *"The trade connection of Ujjayinī with Siṁhala"* for *'The trade connection of Bengal with Siṁhala."*

P. 13, ll. 5-6; Read *"Śrīmanta, son of Dhanapati Saodāgar"* for *"Śrīmanta, son of Chānd Saodāgar."*

P. 191, ll. 24-26 : Add the following note to the statement concerning the fate of the individuality *(attabhāva)* of an Arahant after death :

There must have been a vital reason for which Bhikṣu Yamaja was taken to task for his bold statement, that as far as he could construe the Master's teaching, an Arahant becomes extinct as an individual with death, and after death he does not undergo any further process of rebirth : *khīṇāsavo bhikkhu kāyassa bhedā ucchijjati vinassati, na hoti parammaraṇā.* According to Buddhaghosa, the reason for it was that Yamaja's representation of Buddha's teaching tended to make it endorse the annihilationistic doctrine standing for the end of individual existence at death : *yasmā pan'assa satto ucchijjati vinassatī' ti ahosi tasmā diṭṭhigataṁ nāma jātaṁ.* In the Pali scholiast's opinion, if Yamaja had said, "The formations come-to-be and cease to be, the occurrence of fresh formation (of lower tendencies) does no longer occur", his statement would have been a correct one : *sace hi'ssa evaṁ bhaveyya—"Saṁkhārā uppajjanti c'eva nirujjhanti ca, saṁkhārappavattam eva appavattaṁ hotī' ti diṭṭhigataṁ nāma na bhaveyya.* By *Saṁkhāras* Buddhaghosa invariably understands the formations belonging to the three lower planes of existence and the three lower levels of consciousness *(tebhūmikā saṁkhārā).* If Buddha were certain that the process of further becoming is at an end for an Arahant or perfect saint with the complete destruction of the three unwholesome roots *(akusalamūlā),* from which spring up all forms of ultimately painful individual existence *(bhavas),* he ought to have stated it in the clearest possible terms.

In the *Udāna*, I. 10, when the question was pressed as to the destiny (*gati*) of the Arahant Bāhiya after his death, Buddha's significant reply was *Nirvāṇa*, better *Nibbāna-dhātu*, *Nirvāṇa* as the element of reality which he described evidently in terms of the *Upaniṣad* description of *Brahmadhāma*, the realm of Brahman the Absolute :

Yattha āpo ca paṭhavī tejo vāyo na gādhati |
na tattha sukkā jotanti, ādicco na-ppakāsati |
na tattha candimā bhāti, tamo tattha na vijjati ||
Yadā ca attanā vedi muni monena brāhmaṇo |
atha rūpā arūpā ca sukhadukkhā pamuccati ||

Cf. *Muṇḍaka Up.*, ii. 2. 10 ....

Na tatra sūryo bhāti, na candra-tārakaṁ,
nemā vidyuto bhānti, kuto'yaṁ agniḥ |
tam eva bhāntaṁ anubhāti sarvaṁ,
tasya bhāsā sarvam idaṁ vibhāti ||

In Buddha's dictum, precisely as in that of the *Upaniṣad*, a cosmical or ontological stamp is given to a purely psychical state reachable through the highest state of *dhyāna* or *samāpatti*, the ninth state called *saññā-vedayita-nirodha*, in which the five aggregates cease to be the objects of consciousness and, therefore, of attachment, and *Nirvāṇa* becomes the object of the *bhavāṅga-citta* freed from all its limiting conditions. For an Arahant this may be a daily experience like the periodical natural state of sleep. One thing, however, is certain, namely, that the release spoken of is one from the three *bhavas* of *kāma*, *rūpa* and *arūpa*, all of which are rooted in *avijjā*. But as indicated in the appendix, when the course of life follows the upward trend, *pasāda* takes the place of *taṇhā* and *adhimokkha* that of *upādāna*, while on the *lokottara* level, *pasāda* or *saddhā* assumes the form of *sammādiṭṭhi* and *adhimokkha* that of *sammāsankappa*, and the wholesome states follow one another along with the neutralization or cessation of the unwholesome ones.

P. 199. ll. 67 : Add the following note to the clause "*If negatively nirodha and positively pāripūri be held out as the final goal of life's efforts*"—

Śāriputra appears to have correctly represented the purport of Buddha's main doctrine when he points out : *Dasa nijjaravatthūni. Sammādiṭṭhissa micchādiṭṭhi nijjiṇṇā hoti, ye ca micchādiṭṭhi-paccayā aneke pāpakā anusalā dhammā sambhavanti te c'assa nijjiṇṇā honti, sammādiṭṭhipaccayā ca aneke kusalā dhammā bhāvanā-pāripūriṁ gacchanti sammāvimuttissa micchāvimutti nijjiṇṇā hoti, ye ca micchāvimutti-paccayā aneke pāpakā akusalā dhammā sambhavanti te c'assa nijjiṇṇā honti, sammāvimuttipaccayā ca aneke kusalā dhammā bhāvanā-pāripūriṁ gacchanti.*

Here Buddha's chief disciple carefully brings out the signification of Buddha's fourfold aim of religious efforts. He uses the Jaina term *nijjarā* (neutralization, *lit.* wearing out) for *nirodha* (cessation). At the rise of the right view (*i.e.*, all-round view), the wrong view (*i.e.* one-sided view, *ekanga-dassanaṁ*) is neutralized, which is to say, many sinful and unwholesome states that arise from the wrong view get neutralized, and, on the other hand, many wholesome states which arise from the right view proceed to development and fulness. Same as to the remaining nine steps to *Nirvāṇa* and their opposites. Thus at each step the negative concept of neutralization or cessation of unwholesome states is supplemented by the positive concept of development and fulness of wholesome states, without which the doctrinal position of Buddhism becomes reduced to that of Jainism and Sāmkhya-Yoga, apart, however, from the question of the existence of soul as an abiding entity. The only positive thesis to be upheld by Buddha by way of logical escape from the grip of eternalism and annihilationism, both of which were regarded as extreme positions in thought within the definition of soul theories was the idea of *kamma-santati* or *sankhāra-santati* (continuity of craving induced karmic forms, which makes for pain and leads to degradation of nature) followed by *dhamma-santati* (continuity of the series of wholesome states, which makes for progress and leads to elevation of nature), both implying the succession of *attabhāvas* in one form or another.

LECTURE I

INDIA AND CEYLON

Ceylon is a dreamland of my boyhood. It is very strange indeed that I went across the Bay of Bengal four times for travels over Burma but had not had the opportunity heretofore of seeing this seagirt and pear-shaped island which roused up my boyish fancy. I shall fall short of language, therefore, to express the overwhelming feeling of gratitude to the Buddhist Brotherhood of the University of Ceylon and the Dona Alpina Ratnayake Trust for their kind invitation to deliver some public lectures in this magnificent city, and no less to my esteemed friends the Rev. Bhikkhu Rahula, Professor Malalasekera, Professor H. C. Ray and Sir Baron Jayatilaka who must have been instrumental in my being in your midst to-day.

Since my young friend Mr. P. P. Siriwardhana, the General Secretary to the Mahabodhi Society of Ceylon, then a worker of the Mahabodhi Society in Calcutta, promised, half in jest half in earnest, to offer me a freehold of five acres of land if I would settle in this beautiful island of yours, since I met in Calcutta the keen-minded Rev. Rahula, B. A. (Lond.), a research scholar of your

* This is the first lecture of the History series delivered on March 17, under the auspices of the Mahabodhi Society of Ceylon in the meeting hall of the Vidyodaya Parivena, Colombo.

young University, and since Professor Ray sounded me if I would like to come over to this ancient land where Buddhism is still a living faith, I paused for a while to think over the matter, wavering between 'yes' and 'no'.

You are not to think that this wavering on my part was due to any personal or national prejudice against Ceylon. It was rather due to the trepidation of heart I then felt at the magnitude of the task I would have to face, had I agreed forthwith, especially when flashed across my mind the vivid recollection of the stalwarts who went before me from India and Bengal to establish an eternal bond of love and fellowship between the two countries. Unworthy as I am, I felt that with me was somehow or other bound up the honour of two great seats of learning, that with me were inseparably linked the unbroken cultural heritage of Bhāratavarṣa, the enviable cultural past and present of Bengal, and no less. the *sādhanā* of my native district—Chittagong, and the pathetic story of the struggle of my people for keeping burning the lamp of the *Sadharma* in secluded corner against tremendous odds.

I got over this wavering on a second thought that I might be sure of that warm reception which is the characteristic of the tropical fervour of you all, inasmuch as you were all bits of us and virtually the same people, inhabiting the same land, speaking the same language, thinking the same thought, and having the same heritage of racial genius and culture, although placed in a somewhat different local environment. The following stanza from the Dhammapada came naturally into sweet recollection:

Cirappavāsiṃ purisaṃ dūrato sotthim āgataṃ /
ñāti-mittā suhajjā ca abhinandanti āgataṃ / /

"The kinsmen, friends and comrades welcome one who is come safe amongst them from distance, after a long separation."

I am then here to-day to claim you back all as our kith and kin, to remind all the ties of close relationship that have lasted through all the vicissitudes of time, clime and fortune to which we both have been subjected, to feel the same throb of life in every fibre of our being, to try to awaken you to a new consciousness of our racial affinity, and to invite you, last of all, to join us in the immediate task of solving our common problems which so imperiously demand a solution for the right guidance of our steps to an all-round progress and for the guidance as well of misguided humanity.

Devānaṃpiya Piyadasi Asoka of Jambudvīpa truly said : "There is no such gift as the gift of the *Dhamma,* no such assosciation as one through the *Dhamma,* no such distribution as one of the *Dhamma* and no such connection as one through the *Dhamma*" (R. E. XI). The essence of the *Dhamma*" he spoke of is love, the basis is the agreement in the fundamentals of human understanding and conduct, the spirit is that of rendering service to the country *(desāvuti)* and doing good to the whole world *(sarva-loka-hita),* the strength is concord *(samavāya)* through the interchange of each other's thoughts and the genuine appreciation of each other's aspirations, the guiding principle is ceaseless action with fortitude, ardent faith and indefatigable energy (*parā-krama),* and the expression is winsome cordiality.

But I may confidently state that in the present case, the age-long connection between India and Ceylon is not only cultural. It is geological, geographical, racial, political, commercial, industrial, palæographic, linguistic, literary, religious, artistic, philanthropic, administrative, and educational as well. It was established not only through the exchange of worldly and spiritual goods, colonisation and religious mission, the migration of tribes and fusion of races, common contributions to various aspects of civilization, not only through University affiliations and administrative incorporation, not only through matrimonial alliances and interchanges of ideas and good will, but through occasional exchanges of arms, invasions and forcible occupations, diplomatic strategies, military co-operations, ruthless plunders and acts of vandalism and royal discourtesy as well.

Taking a retrospective view, however, we may not be a little amazed to find how all these factors, good and evil, combined to form different episodes in the grand drama of our common national life, a few select pictures of which I will ask you to witness with me, in the first course of lectures. And whatever our comment on particular acts and judgement on individual actors, viewing as a whole the historical situation of the two countries, intelligently, sympathetically and dispassionately, none, I believe, can honestly reject the finding of Dr. Mendis, that "every great change in India—political, religious, social or economic—had its repercussions in this island,

and every wave of Indian civilization up to the end of the fifteenth century made its way to this land and left its mark on the life and thought of its people."[1]

The whole of the island of Ceylon, like the whole of the Deccan peninsula to which it was most probably once joined and portions of Northern India, is to be included in what the geologists call the "Gondwanaland."[2] It is geologically but a part and parcel of the Indian peninsula, the mountains of Ceylon consisting of 'the same old, hard, crystalline rocks as the Deccan.' The regional strike of the rocks in all but its southern portion indicates a southerly continuation of the Eastern Ghats, its southern portion being only a 'continuation of the rocks of Travancore and southernmost portion of Madras.' In other words, the rocks in Ceylon may justly be regarded as southerly extensions of the Mahendra, Malaya and Sahya mountains of South India, now 'interrupted by the sea encroaching on and covering the intervening portion.'[3]

Jambudvīpa, which was claimed by Aśoka as the sphere of his cultural influence, comprised not only the whole of India but also Tambapaṃṇī in the extreme south, five Mediterranean countries in the west, and Southern Asia around India. As a matter of fact, it coincided more with Jambudvīpa as described in the *Great Epic* and the *Purāṇas* than with that of Pali tradition.[4]

1 *The Early History of Ceylon*, p. 1.
2 M. C. Stopes, *Ancient Plants*, p. 173.
3 M. S. Krishnan, *Geology of India and Ceylon*, p. 101 ff.
4 Barua, *Asoka And His Inscriptions*, *loc. cit.*, Pt. I, Ch. III.

To the early Buddhists, Jambudvīpa was one of the four sub-continents of the then known portion of the earth.[1] It was known as extended on the north and shaped like a bullock-cart with its face towards the south.[2] It was situated to the south of Mount Sumeru (Pali Sineru).

As defined in the *Great Epic* and the *Purāṇas,* Jambudvīpa comprised all the four sub-continents of the Buddhists, and Bhāratavarṣa was just one of its seven or nine constituent countries. Bhāratavarṣa or India proper was the great peninsula bounded on the north by the mighty Himalayas, and on the remaining three sides by the seas. Its length from south to north was konwn as 1,000 *yojanas,* and the outline of its topography was compared to a vertically-set half-moon,[3] or, as in the Great Epic, to a bow *(dhanusaṃstha)* with its string stretched to a point to from an apex,[4] which is now known as Dhanuṣkoṭi.

The island of Ceylon called Tāmravarṇa or Tāmraparṇa was counted among the eight *upadvīpas* or adjoining minor islands of Bhāratavarṣa, the remaining seven being Indradvīpa, Kaśeru, Gabhastimat, Sāgara, Sauma, Gandharva, and Vāruṇa.[5]

---

1 *Dīgha,* ii, p. 235: *uttarena āyataṁ, dakkhiṇena sakaṭamukhaṁ* :cf. Beal, *Buddhist Records of the Western World,* i. p. 70.

2 B. C. Law, *India As Described in Early Texts of Buddhism and Jainism,* p. 2; Malalasekera, *Dictionary of Pali Proper Names,* i, *sub voce* Jambudīpa.

3 Beal, *op. cit.* i, p. 70.

4 *Mbh.,* vi. 6. 38.

5 *Mārkaṇḍeya Purāṇa,* lvīi. 2-3; *Viṣṇu P.,* iii.

Megasthenes, the Greek ambassador to the court of Candragupta Maurya, grandfather of Aśoka, did not visit Tāmraparṇī, which was described by him in his *Indika* under the name of *Taprobanē*. His account was undoubtedly based on the local information in Pāṭaliputra, according to which *Taprobanē* was a large, mountainous island in the sea, separated from the mainland only by a river.[1] It was rich in palm-groves, abounded with wild beasts and large tortoises.

The Periplus of the Erythrean Sea, written in the 1st Century A.D., applied to the *Taprobanē* of Megasthenes the name of *Paleisimundu* which Professor Raychaudhuri has identified with Pārasamudra, the Sanskrit name met with in the *Arthaśāstra* (II. 11), ascribed to Kauṭilya Viṣṇugupta. This name is suggested also in Vālmīki's *Rāmāyana*, which locates Lankā on the other side of the sea *(sthite pāre samudrasya)*.[2]

In the *Arthaśāstra*, Pārasamudra finds mention as a place noted for precious gems *(maṇi)* and the export of *agaru* (resin of aloe) of variegated colour and smelling like cascus or *navamallikā* flower *(Jasminum)* and is distinguished from Tāmraparṇī and Pāṇḍyakavāṭa (Gate of Pāṇḍya), the two regions in South India, opposite to Ceylon, which are said to have been noted for their pearls. In the *Rāmāyaṇa*, too, Laṅkā or Pārasamudra is distinguished from Tāmraparṇī, which is connected, pre-

---

1 McCrindle, *Ancient India*, pp. 60, 61, 178 ff.

2 *Rāmāyaṇa*, vi. 3.21. Raychaudhuri, *Political History of Ancient India*, 4th Ed., p. 278.

cisely as in the Arthaśāstra, with Pāṇḍyakapāṭa, noted for gems and pearls.[1] Here Tāmraparṇī is described "as a large river, which went to meet and traverse the sea *(samudram avagāhate)*, containing the row of islands, coverd with the beautiful sandal woods."[2] The *Rāmāyaṇa;* too, mentions the Malaya mountain, to which the *Mārkaṇḍeya Purāṇa* traces the origin of the Tāmraparṇī river, as the rocky elevation of the Deccan region.[3] What interests us most here is to note that Malaya, which was the name of a mountainous region in South India,[4] denoted alike the central mountainous part of Ceylon, known as the home of the Pulindas.[5]

The trade connection of India with Ceylon goes back indeed to a very early date. India's trade may be broadly classified under three heads, *viz.*, (1) inland, (2) coastal, and (3) overseas. The inland trade was carried on partly in country boats plying along the rivers navigable with them, and mainly in bullock-drawn wagons that moved to and fro along two main land-routes, one, the Southern or South-Western Road *(Dakṣiṇāpatha)*, extending from Rājagṛha, the old capital of Magadha, down to Pratiṣṭhāna, the capital of Mūlaka, on the upper bank of the Godāvarī, *via* Pāṭaliputra, Vaiśālī, Kapilavastu, Śrāvastī, Kauśāmbī, Vidiśā and Ujjayinī, and the other, the Northern or North-Western Road

1 *Ibid,* iv. 18 : *Muktā-maṇi-vibhūṣitam.*
2 *Ibid,* iv. 41. 16-17 : *yuktaṁ kapāṭaṁ pāṇḍyānām.*
3 *Ibid,* iv. 41. 15.
4 *Mbh.* vi. 7. 56 : *Tāmraparṇa-śilā śrīmān Malaya-parvataḥ.*
5 *Mahāvaṁsa,* vii. 68.

(Uttarāpatha) from Śrāvastī, Kauśāmbī, or some such halting place on the Southern Road to as far north-west as Takṣaśilā, Puṣkarāvatī, and Puruṣapura (Peshāwar). These were connected with various other branch routes, *e.g.*, some connecting Benares with Śrāvastī towards the north-west, with Gayā, Tāmralipti and Kaliṅga (Orissa) towards the east and south-east, some connecting Ujjayinī with such western sea-ports as Surāṣṭra, Bhṛgukaccha (Bharukaccha) and Śūrpāraka, and some leading to Sindhu and Sauvīra in the Lower Indus Valley across the desert of Rājputānā.[1]

The coastal trade was carried on in the sea-going sailing merchant vessels of different sizes and patterns[2] touching at such sea-ports as Tamali, Vaṅga, Tāmralipti on the east coast, Tāmraparṇī (Tambapaṇṇī) in the south, Śūrpāraka, Bhṛgukaccha and Surāṣṭra on the western coast. The coastal trade was extended to Further India and China, the vessels touching at such ports as Takkola, Suvaṇṇakuḍḍa, Kālamukha, Suvaṇṇabhūmi, Vesuṅga and Java.

The over-seas trade of India with China followed sometimes the route which lay from Tāmralipti to Java *via* Ceylon, and that of India and Ceylon with Babylon and Mediterranean countries followed generally the route which lay from Śūrpāraka (modern Sopārā) and Bhṛgukaccha (modern Broach).

---

1. Rhys Davids, *Buddhist India,* p. 105. ff.; B. C. Law, *India as Described,* p. 68 ff|
2. The subject is exhaustively dealt with by Radhakumud Mookerji in his *Indian Shipping.*

A rough list of the places, countries, and ports to which Indian traders and merchants went is given in the Pali Canonical work called *Mahāniddesa* (pp. 154, 415), and from it one can have a fairly clear idea of the land, river and sea-routes then followed.[1] The traders from different parts of India and from outsisde, including a distant country like China, who came to the Upper Punjab for business are mentioned in the Pali book of *Apadāna* (II, pp. 358-59).[2] The *Periplus of the Erythrean Sea* was written as a guide to merchants interested in the coastal trade with India, Ceylon and Persia. The *Indika* of Megasthenes, the *Geography* of Ptolemy, the *Arthaśāstra* of Kauṭilya, and the Buddhist *Jātakas and Avadānas* are of no less help as reliable sources of information about India's trade-relations with Ceylon. *Taprobanē*, as we learn from the *Indika* of Megasthenes, was known in the 4th century B.C. as a sea-girt island, situated to the south of India and noted for its large tortoise-shells, large-sized elephants of much superior breed that were exported to Kalinga in large boats constructed for the traffic. It was also known as the country which produced more gold and larger pearls than India.

In the *Arthaśāstra,* as we noted, Pārasamudra enjoyed its importance as a place, which was noted for its precious gems and finest kind of *agaru*. Among the elephants

---

1 Sylvain Lévi, *Etudes Asiatiques,* ii, pp. 1-55, 431.

2 R. C. Majumdar, *Suvarṇaadvīpa,* p. 56 ff. ; B. C. Law, *India As Described,* p. 70 ff. ; Barua, *Asoka And His Inscriptions, loc. cit.*, Pt. I, Ch. 3.

then available in India, it speaks of those bred in Kaliṅga, Aṅga, Karūṣa, and Eastern India as being the best.[1]

There is nothing astonishing then, that the *Periplus* should say 'that pearls, precious stones, muslins and tortoise-shells were exported from Ceylon and that its chief town was *Palæsimundu*', or that Ptolemy writing his geography in the 2nd century A.D. should meniton 'rice ginger, beryl, sapphire, gold, silver and elephants' as its chief products.

Let us see if any further light can be thrown on India's trade-connection with Ceylon from the *Jātakas* and *Avadānas*. In the Pali *Valāhassa Jātaka* (No : 196), as you, perhaps, all know, Ceylon, or at least its western province, is called the island of Tambapaṇṇī, and in it is located a Yakkha city called Sirīsavatthu, meaning 'the Abode of the Lord of Luck, *i.e.*, of Viṣṇu.' Some five hundred sea-going merchants from Northern India 'were cast on the shore from the river Kalyāṇī to Nāgadīpa'. In the Mahāvaṃsa, where, too, Sirīsavatthu is mentioned as a prosperous Yakkha city, it is distinguished from the island of Tambapaṇṇī. The merchants found on their landing the Yakkhiṇis welcoming them, and, what is more, wanting to use them as their husbands on the plea that they were sea-faring merchants like their husbands whose whereabouts were not known ever since. Half of them managed to escape from their clutches and return to their own country, being carried by the *valāhassa*, a

1. *Arthaśāstra*, ii. 2 : *Kaliṅgāṅga-gajāḥ śreṣṭhāḥ, Prācyāś ceti Karūśajāḥ.*

sky-koing horse of the cloud race. Half of them remained behind in the enchantment of the she-demons, only to perish.

The Sanskrit version of this story in the *Divyāvadāna* has somewhat a different tale to tell. Here the island is called Tāmradvīpa, and its dwellers are said to have been the *rākṣasis* subduing whom the adventurous Siṃhala, son of an Indian merchant, became eventually the ruler of the land.

The Pali version of the story is particularly important, for here we are introduced to the Yakkhas who were really the daring sailors and merchants to whose enterprising spirit the prosperity of the city of Sirīsavatthu in Tambapaṇṇī was due. It narrates, morever, the vicissitudes of life under which the womenfolk of the place, like those of Kerala or Mālābār, had to fare free in their dealings with men. It states the circumstances in which the traders from India became settlers in Ceylon.

The trade-relationship of Ceylon with the ports on the eastern coast of India is evident from the account given in the Pali Chronicles and Buddhaghosa's Vinaya-Commentary of the voyage of Devānampiya Tissa's envoys to Pāṭaliputra and return to Ceylon *via* the port of Tāmralipti in Lower Bengal, and a similar account left by the earlier Chinese pilgrim, Fa Hian, of his boat journey from Pāṭaliputra to Tāmralipti and his sea-voyage from Tāmralipti to Ceylon.[1] Similarly the coastal trade of your island with Suppāraka and other ports on

1. Beal, *op. cit.*, i, p. lv. ff.

the western coast is borne out by the *Mahāvaṃsa* description of Vijaya's arrival at Laṅkā from the country of Lāḷa *via* Broach and Sopārā. The trade connection of Bengal with Siṃhala up till a comparatively modern date is proved by the Bengali legend of Śrīmanta, son of Chānd Saodāgar, describing the romance of his perilous sea voyage.

That the countries of India that lay nearest and just opposite to Ceylon were Pāṇḍya, Coḷa and Kerala is equally borne out by the inscriptions of Aśoka (R. E. II, R. E. XIII) and the long and eventful history of Ceylon. The easiest land-route from South India lay through Madourā (Dakkhiṇa-Madhurā) and Pāṇḍya-kapāṭa. It was by this route that Thera Buddhaghosa went across to Anurādhapura from Kāñcīpura. But as indicated in the *Rāmāyaṇa*[1] and the Tamil account of the Maurya invasion of South India, there existed a land-route from Central India to Pāṇḍya, which lay partly through Aparānta and Karṇāṭa, and in the lower part through southern Mysore along the banks of the Kāverī.[2] The reality of this route is confirmed by the testimony of Hwen Thsang[3] and that of the Mahābhārata.[4]

As for political connection, I may begin by stating that the great Ceylon contemporary of Devānaṃpiya

1 *Rāmāyaṇa,* iv. 41. 12-14.

2 S. K. Aiyangar, *Beginnings of South Indian History,* p. 891; H. C. Raychaudhuri, *op. cit.,* p. 219; "The invaders (*i.e.,* Vimba Moriyar (Maurya upstarts) advanced from the Konkan, passing the hills Elilmalai, about sixteen miles north of Canamore, and entered the Kongu (Coimbatore) district ultimately going as far as the Podiyil Hill (in the Tinnevelly district".

3 Beal, *Buddhist Records,* ii, p. 253.

4 *Mahābhārata,* iii. 118. 3-8.

Asoka of India, son of Bindusāra, was Devānampiya Tissa, son of king Muṭasiva. The dynasty to whcih he belonged is traced back in your Chronicles to Prince Vijaya from India, though not in a direct line. Whether Vijaya, the founder of the dynasty and king eponymos of Ceylon, was a prince from Bengal or some other part of India, is still a debatable question, which I would like to reserve for discussion in my next lecture. One thing, however, is certain that, as stated in your Chronicles, the position of this royal family was strengthened by a matrimonial alliance with the royal House of Pāṇḍya. The Pāṇḍya princess form Madourā was not sent over alone, but with her went seven hundred daughters of the Pāṇḍya nobility less by one. With her were sent over also the eighteen guilds of artisans (*seṇis*). Thus indeed was formed the first social aristocracy in the island, and the way was paved for the development of practical arts and crafts. It is also certain that the language of this royal family and nobility was an Aryan speech, as we shall see more of it later on. The fact of this marital connection with the Pāṇḍya royal family and nobility may explain how this speech came to be punctuated with the Dravidian accents.

Your Chronicles have sought to establish a definite synchronism between the dynastic succession of the kings of Ceylon from Vijaya to Devānampiya Tissa on the one hand, and that of the kings of Magadha from Ajātasattu, son of Bimbisāra, to Devānaṃpiya Asoka on the other. This synchronism was made doubly significant by being worked out in two lines of succession, namely, *Rāja-*

paramparā and Thera-paramparā; Royal and Pontifical. Thereafter we lose the thread of synchronism, although the historian has the opportunity of establishing the synchronism occasionally in individual cases which are, however, few and far between, and linking together the kings and events of the two countries.

Behind the connection which came to be established between the two countries since the advent of Mahinda and Saṃghamittā with their great message and mission of love during the reign of Devānaṃpiya Tissa and Devānaṃpiya Aśoka, there was a political relationship, which began with the Maurya invasion of the South. That Tambapaṇṇī, the farthest of the independent countries in the South, came within the diplomatic sphere of the Maurya sovereignty, along with Coḷa, Pāṇḍya, Satiyaputra and Keralaputra and the intervening territories, is manifest from Aśoka's inscriptions. The Indian inscriptions and your Chronicles both bring out the fact that there was an exchange of emissaries between the two states, but that which went from Aśoka, either in the form of coronation presents or in that of humanitarian works and message of piety and good will, was far deeper in its appeal and effect than the mere mechanical relationship of royal diplomacy. The deputation and response received from your great king was no less remarkable in its far-reaching effect. The great edifice of civilization of which you are justly proud was reared up on this joint result of action and reaction, appeal and response. Thenceforth Buddhism truly became the guiding and moulding factor of your entire civilization and national outlook, and, above all, laid the unshakable foundation of our mutual understanding and appreciation.

After Devānaṃpiya Tissa and while the Śuṅgas were the ruling power in Āryāvarta, particularly Magadha, Duṭṭhagāmaṇi was the great and most powerful king whom you rightly reckoned as your national hero, the saviour of your faith and of your civilization. The religious monuments that were built about this time in your land may be shown to have borne resemblance, in both technique and execution, to those great monuments in India, particularly the *stūpas* at Bharhut, better Berhut (Vīrahotra), and Sāñcī (Kākanāva). How the knowledge of the architectural art, with sculpture and painting as its handmaids, travelled over to your country is not definitely known. But your tradition avers that when these monuments were being consecrated, Duṭṭhagāmaṇi sent out his invitation to all the Buddhist brothers of the Theriya school, and many distinguished Theras from different parts of India came to Ceylon and took part in the grand celebration, enhancing its importance. The places and centres of Theravāda Buddhism represented by them included Rājagaha, Isipatana, Jetavana, Mahāvana at Vesālī, Ghositārāma at Kosāmbī, Dakkhiṇāgiri at Ujjenī, Pupphapura (Pāṭaliputra), Kasmīramaṇḍala, Pallavabhogga, Yona city, Viñjhāṭavī (the Vindhyan Forest), Bodhimaṇḍavihāra (the Bodhgayā monastery), Vanavāsī, and Kelāsa-mahāvihāra.[1]

---

1 *Mahāvaṁsa*, xxiv. 29-43.

The list which is supplied in the *Great Chronicle* is typical only, and not exhaustive. From the mention of Pallavabhogga (the Pallava territory) you may incline to take it as an anachronism from the fact that the history of the Pallavas of Vengi was of a much later date, but the doubt is at once set at rest, if by the Pallavas we understand, as we should, the Pahlavas or Parthians who had their satrapy in Surāṣṭra and its neighbourhood, leaving aside the question of the Punjab and other parts.

Viewed in this light, the list is as it should be, and it tallies almost literally with the one we come across in one of the Nāgārjunīkoṇḍa inscriptions of the time of the Īkṣvāku rulers of the Kṛṣṇā region in South India, completed only with the addition of the representatives of the island of Tambapaṇṇī and a few other places including Tambapaṇṇa in South India.[1] In both the *Great Chronicle* and the *Nāgārjunīkoṇḍa inscription*, the representative Theras are introduced as those who were gladdeners of the island of Tambapaṇṇī.[1] Thus both the evidences unmistakably go to prove the frequent intercourse between the cultural representatives of India and Ceylon from the 2nd or 1st century B.C. to the 2nd or 3rd century A.D. I may also add that the earlier Bodhgayā railing still bears an inscription of the 1st century B.C. recording a donation from a Buddhist pilgrim called Bodhirakkhita from Tambapaṇṇī.

1 The additional places mentioned are Gandhāra, Cīna, near Maṇipur, Cilāta (Kirāta, near about Cīna), Tosali (Puri district in Orissa). Pālura (Dantapura, the old capital of Kaliṅga or Orissa), Aparanta (Pali Sunāparanta with Suppāraka as its sea-port, modern Konkan), Vaṅga (East Bengal), and Damila (Coḷa). *Epigraphia Indica*, xx, p. 22.

The reign of Samudragupta with which began the Augustan Age of Indian literature, philosophy and art synchronised with that of Kitti-Siri-Meghavaṇṇa with which commenced the second eventful and remarkable stage of the history and civilization of Ceylon. According to the Chinese writer called Wang Hiuen ts'e king Meghavarman (identified by Sylvain Lévi with Meghavaṇṇa) sent an embassy with gifts to Samudragupta for the latter's permission to erect a monastery, preferably at Bodhgayā for the residence of the monks from Ceylon, which was readily granted. The great Chinese pilgrim, Hwen Thsang, who saw this monastery in the full vigour of its life towards the middle of the 7th century A.D. has left a vivid account of it in his famous itinerary.[1]

This was the first Siṃhala Saṅghārāma erected in Northern India but certainly not the first monastic foundation of Ceylon in India, for we learn from the Nāgārjunīkoṇḍa inscription of Virapurisadatta that a spacious monastery called Sīhala-vihāra was built on the bank of the river Kṛṣṇā in South India at least a century earlier.[2] The foundation of the Mahābodhi Saṅghārāma still exists just outside the northern entrance of the Bodhgayā

1 Beal, *Buddhist Records*, ii, p. 133 ff.

Though Hwen Thsang does not mention the name of the two great contemporaries, his narration of the circumstances leading to the erection of the monastery confirms the veracity of the information supplied by Wang Hiuen ts'e. Barua, *Gayā And Buddhagayā*, i, p. 179 f.

2 *Epigraphia Indica*, Vol. XX, p. 22; D. C. Sircar, *Select Inscriptions*, i, p. 225.

temple, defying the ravages wrought by time and in spite of the neglect of centuries.[1]

The earlier Chinese pilgrim who is usually taken to have visited India and Ceylon during the reign of Candragupta Vikramāditya, the worthy son and successor of Samudragupta, had nothing particularly to say about the Ceylon monastery at Bodhgayā, although he found three monasteries in existence there, all liberally supported by the local laity.[2] That there was at least one monastery at Bodhgayā prior to the erection of the Mahābodhi Saṅghārāma is evident from the *Mahāvaṃsa* list to which your attention has already been drawn.

Since the erection of the Mahābodhi Saṅghārāma three distinguished pilgrims came over to Bodhgayā from Ceylon : (1) Silākāla the 'Mango-novice' who came with his kinsman Moggallāna during the reign of Kassapa I (460-478 A.D.) and returned to Ceylon with the hair-relic (kesadhātu) during the reign of the next king Moggallāna I (478-496 A.D.) ; (2) Mahānāman who came probably during the reign of Aggabodhi I (568-601 A.D) and donated a small shrine with a Buddha-image installed therein in *Saṃ* 269 (588-589 A.D.)[3] ; and (3) Śramaṇa Prakhyātakīrtti of royal descent who had his visit recorded in an inscription of unknown date.[4]

---

1 See the ground plan of this historic foundation of Ceylon in Cunningham's *Mahābodhi* and Barua's *Gayā & Buddhagayā*, ii.

2 Beal, *Buddhist Records*, i, p. lxiii.

3 Fleet, *Gupta Inscriptions*, p. 274 ff.

4 Bloch, *A. S. R.*, 1908-9, iv, p. 156 ; Panday, J.B.O.R.S., iv, p. 485 ff ; Barua, *Gayā & Buddhagayā*, ii, p. 71 ff.

With the stay of Fa Hian in Ceylon for two years a cultural link was established for the first time between the three countries of India, Ceylon and China. From the account of what he saw in the island, it would seem certain that his visit could not be earlier than the reign of Kitti-Siri-Meghavaṇṇa (334-362 A.D.) and later than that of Kitti-Siri-Megha (Kuḍā Kit Siri Mevan, 537-556 A.D.). Weighing carefully the evidences for and against, I cannot help connecting his sojourn in your island with the reign of the former. All that he states[1] with reference to the reigning king, the worship of the Tooth-relic brought over from (Dantapura in) Kaliṅga in the 9th regnal year of Meghavaṇṇa, and the king's affection for the Abhayagiri Vihāra, and the like admirably fits in with the Mahāvaṃsa account of the events of Meghavaṇṇa's reign.[2] That is to say, the synchronism between Meghavaṇṇa and Samudragupta may be established not only through the embassy sent by the former but by the itinerary of Fa Hian as well. The political relation between India and Ceylon during Samudragupta's reign is borne out by his Allahabad Stone-pillar inscription.

Fa Hian says that his journey to Ceylon was forestalled by 'a religious brother from India', and that he heard him one day when the latter, 'seated on a high throne, was reciting a sacred book' and exhorting the audience to lead a pious life, basing his discourse on the future

---

1 Beal, *op. cit.*, i, p. lxxiv ff.

2 *Mahāvaṁsa*, xxxvii, 53-99.

wanderings of the Buddha's alms-bowl'. Who was this eminent 'religious brother from India' held in such high esteem by the people of Ceylon? Wickramasinghe's identification of this *dharmakathika* with Dharmagupta rests on no solid ground; it is unconvincing in the opinion of Professor Malalasekera. Dr. B. C. Law is inclined to take him for the great Pali scholiast, Buddhaghosa.

This is still a great puzzle in the history of Buddhism in Ceylon and a much disputed question. Without meaning to detain you over it, I may just tell you that if we are to believe with Professor Malalasekera in the authenticity of the *Cūlavaṃsa* narrative,[1] there is no escape from the conclusion that there were at least two Buddhaghoṣas from India, or that Buddhaghosa, a contemporary of Mahānāma, was a different individual from Buddhaghosa, a contemporary of the king of Ceylon bearing or deserving the title of *Siri-kuḍḍa, Siri-pāla, Siri nivāsa.* The eloquent Indian preacher of Fa Hian's time may better be identified with Thera Kassapa or Kumāra Kassapa at whose instance Culla Buddhaghosa undertook to write his commentary to the *Dhammapada.*[2] After Fa Hian's visit, a monk of central India called Guṇabhadra passed through Ceylon on his way to China in 435 A.D.[3]

Buddhaghosa of the time of king Mahānāma was a highly gifted Pāli scholar connected with Buddhist

1 *The Pali Literature of Ceylon*, p. 80.
2 See Lec. III.
3 Nanjio, *Catalogue of the Chinese Tripiṭaka*, p. 415 f.

vihāras at Kāñcīpura and other places in South India. Buddhadatta, a native of Uragapura (modern Uraiūr on the Kāverī river), Dhammapāla of the Vadaratittha Vihāra, a native of Kāñcīpura, Anuruddha, a native of the same place, who was the author of the Paramattha-vinicchaya and Sāriputta, a Colian monk who was the author of the Padāvatāra,—all of them came across to Ceylon, wrote Pāli works of great authority, and have been honoured as celebrities of the Mahāvihāra School.

The repeated Damila (Dravidian) incursions, particularly those from the Coḷa territory, bringing depredation, plunder, ruthless destruction of life and property and desecration of shrines in their train and aiming at permanent or temporary occupation of your island since the days of Eḷāra, constituted a trying national struggle for your kings and people of which we shall see more in the next lecture. But in spite of these neighbourly jealousies and hostilites, the persons who made notable contributions to the development of the boasted Theravāda of Ceylon and maintained through centuries the cultural connection between the two adjacent countries were almost all Colians by their nationality.

Through political, military, as well as matrimonial alliances between the two royal Houses, there came to be established a durable connection between Ceylon and Pāṇḍya, the nearest Dravidian country. Another historical marraige deserving to be a fit subject of romance took place when king Vijayabāhu I (1055-1114 A.D.) married Princess Tilokasundarī, the handsome daughter of the then king of Kaliṅga, and made her his queen consort.[1] Trailokyasundarī, as noticed by Professor Ray, finds mention in a Bengal inscription as the daughter of Sāmalavarman of the royal dynasty of Siṃhapura (in Kaliṅga), which probably covered a part of Rāḍha or West Bengal.[2] This marital relation with the royal House of Siṃhapura was not without its further effect in that Niśśaṅkamalla and Sāhasamalla, sons of the Kaliṅga king, Goparāja, of Siṁhapura, ascended the throne of Ceylon, the second brother in 1200 A.D. even according to the Sinhalese inscriptions.[3]

As for the religious connection, you are all familiar with the far-reaching importance of the first Buddhist mission to this island led by Mahinda from Pāṭaliputta and Ujjenī *via* Malayakūṭa or Tāmraparṇī of South India[4] which resulted in the conversion of your royal House and people to the religion of Śākyasiṃha and the formation of the powerful Siṃhala Sangha, as well as of the arrival of Saṅghamittā which led to the foundation of the Bhikkhuṇī order. It will be a mistake, nevertheless, to think that the Buddhists were the first and only propagators of the Indo-Aryan religion here. Your Chronicles say in unequivocal terms that the Brāhmans, Tāpasas (Hermits), Niganṭhas (Jains), Ājīvakas, Temple-

---

1 *Cūlavaṁsa*, lix. 29-30.

2 *Dynastic History of Northern India.* Vol. I.

3 Hultzsch in *Epigraphia Indica*, XII, p. 4.

4 Beal, *Buddhist Records*, ii, pp. 231, 246, associating Mahendra's mission with Malayakūṭa, the country in South India below Drāviḍa as well as with Siṁhala. There can be little doubt that Hwen Thsang's Malayakūṭa with Mt. *Po-to-la-ka* (Vaidūryaka) is the same country as Tāmraparṇī of the *Mahābhārata*, iii. 88. 14-17.

priests (Devakulam), Paribbājakas (Wandering ascetics), in short, the recluses of various denominations (*nānā-pāsaṇḍakā samaṇā*) had obtained a foothold in Ceylon as precursors of the Buddhists, especially during the reign of Paṇḍukābhaya, grandfather of Devānampiya Tissa, even prior to the reign of the Nandas of Magadha. So far as your social and secular life is concerned, their influence is considerable. The same holds true in varying degrees of the social and secular life of other Buddhist countries.

There may still be a doubt in your mind if we belong to one and the same nation. To make one nation we need besides geographical unity the commonness of script, language, literature, race and culture. That the Sinhalese alphabet is just one of the many local variations from one and the same parent script called Brāhmī, or that the most ancient form of your alphabet goes to connect it with the Brāhmī of the inscriptions of Aśoka[1] and later on with that of the Śātavāhana inscriptions in the Nāsik, Kanheri and other West-Indian Buddhist caves is undoubted. Even the course of its still later development may be convincingly shown to have followed the process of change operating in the alphabets of Pāṇḍya, Coḷa, Andhra, Orissa and Burma. The ancient form of your language which became afterwards punctuated with the Dravidian accents goes undoubtedly to connect the island with the *hinter*-Indus region of the

1 One of the old Brāhmī inscriptions hitherto found in Ceylon takes us back to the reign of king Uttiya who was the immediate successor of Devānampiya Tissa.

Punjab below Mansehra, where a set of Aśoka's Rock Edicts was incised. The common features in the literatures, arts and crafts of the two countries are too well-known to need special mention. But we owe greatly our common national bonds to the mighty effort and far-reaching vision of Devānaṃpiya Asoka of whom it is truly said: "The missionary activity of Aśoka was a source of two boons. In his time, the whole of the country had become Aryanised. But the different provinces had their different dialects. Owing, however, to the stupendous efforts put forth by him for the diffusion of his faith, the communication between one province and another became more frequent and brisk, and the universal desire of having a common language was felt, a language which would be studied and understood in all provinces and became the medium of thought not only in secular but also religious matters. This led to the acceptance of Pali or monumental Prakrit as the *lingua franca* of India.... Here, *i.e.*, in common Aryan speech and mode of life were present the solvents that were required for the fusion of the diverse Indian races into one nationality or rather imperialism."[1]

Throughout your history you have resented and powerfully resisted all attempts from the Indian shore at territorial encroachments on your island. So there is nothing to grudge that you were all anxious to have your country separated from the administrative area of the mainland and succeeded in 1802 in seeing it formed into

1 D. R. Bhandarkar, Aśoka, Revised Ed., p. 251 ff.

a Crown Colony, provided that you do not mistake this separation for the alienation of our brotherly feelings and the breaking asunder of our age-long ties.

Speaking as a humble son of Bengal, I may mention that our relations have been the most cordial so far whether through the University or through comradeship in other spheres of activity. It was from Gauḍa (Bengal) that Paṇḍita Rāmacandra Kavibhāratī, a Brahman of high family, came to your island during the reign of Parākramabhuja, better Vīra-Parākramabāhu,[1] and wrote three works, the Bhaktiśataka, Vṛttaratnākara-pañcikā and Vṛttamālākhya, the first a devotional poem and the remaining two on prosody, each of high poetic merit. In all of them the Kavibhāratī has eulogised his royal patron who conferred on him the coveted title of *Bauddhāgama-cakravartin.* In his third work, the poet has left the following description of Lankā :

Asti hi navaratna-pūritā nagarī Lankā nāma viśrutā/
vilasac-caturabdhi-mekhalā vikhalā vibudhālaṅkṛto-darā//

"There is indeed the famous city called Lankā, filled with the Nine Gems, girdled with the four seas, bereft of wicked people, (and) adorned within by the wise."

The second great Brāhman of Bengal whom you have honoured with the title of *Sambuddhāgama-cakravartin* is the late Sir Asutosh Mookerjee, the greatest known Vice-Chancellor of the University of Calcutta and real builder of the edifice of higher education in India.

---

1 The king referred to is Präksamabāhu I.

He made ample provision for the teaching and study of the Sinhalese language, history and civilization.

When in the wake of the Theosophical movement under the leadership of Madame Blavatsky and Col. Olcot came the re-awakening of the religious consciousness of the Hindu and Buddhist worlds, India and Ceylon found in Swāmī Vivekānanda and Anāgārika Dharmapāla two lion-hearted, high-spirited and fearless youths to represent Hinduism and Buddhism at the Parliament of Religions held at Chicago in 1893. Imbued with the zeal for the revival of the lost glory of Mahābodhi, Dharmapāla founded the Mahābodhi Society and became a living bond of love and sympathy between Ceylon and India, particularly adopting Bengal as the field of his work when Mahāsthavir Kripāsharan of Chittagong founded the Bengal Buddhist Association in Calcutta in 1892 with the ambition of bringing about a regenaration of Buddhism in the land of its birth. At about this time were founded in Calcutta the now defunct Buddhist Text Society by Rai Sarat Chandra Das Bahadur of Chittagong, in London the Pāli Text Society by Professor T. W. Rhys Davids for a systematic publication of the Buddhist texts, and the Asiatic Society of Bengal undertook to collect and publish the Buddhist manuscripts from Nepāl. But the beacon light and dynamic force of the *Saddharma* was the Anāgārika who remains, especially by his demise at Isipatana Migadāva in the suburb of the Hindu holy city of Benares, as a perennial source of inspiration to the people of India and Ceylon.

Though I have taxed your patience enough, before I conclude this lecture, I must respectfully mention the inspiring name of Dr. Rabindranath Tagore who had always had a warm heart for Ceylon, just as for the whole of the Greater India the genius of Devānampiya Asoka sought to create.

Another high-souled person whom I should mention to you is Seṭh Jugal Kishore Birla, the eldest son of Rājā Baldeodas Birla of Jaipur, who is not only a business magnate but a saintly man with distant vision as well, a modern Anāthapiṇḍika who has by his open-hearted benefactions given strength to the Mahabodhi Society and strengthened thereby the bond of affection between India and Ceylon. After Rai Sarat Chandra Das Bahadur, among the younger generation of scholars and liberal donors for the cause of learning in general and Buddhism in particular, the name of Dr. Bimala Churn Law of Calcutta is certainly worthy of mention as one who has evinced a keen interest in the study of the Pali works of Ceylon and published at his own cost the English translation of some of them.

Since the demise of Sir Asutosh Mookerjee his second son, Dr. Syama Prasad Mookerjee, President of the Council of Post-Graduate Teaching in Arts, Calcutta University and President of the Mahabodhi Society, India, has been a living personal tie of love, good will and cultural fellowship between India and Ceylon. And since the demise of the Anāgārika his beloved successor in office, Brahmachāri Devapriya Walisinha, has been successfully carrying on the work of the Mahabodhi Society left unfinished by its great founder.

LECTURE II

A BIRD'S EYE VIEW AND PROBLEMS OF ANCIENT HISTORY OF CEYLON

In my lecture on India and Ceylon I took an outside view of some general aspects of the history and civilization of Ceylon, the aspects in which India's manifold relations with Ceylon might be envisaged. In the present lecture I propose to take an inside view touching those aspects in which a Ceylonese himself is likely to be interested.

The history of a country, as I understand it, is constituted by its collective life-movement, in both space and time, which gains in significance and value only in so far as it shapes the course and determines the character of a certain form of civilization. But for its intimate bearings on the diverse aspects of civilization it is blind, one-sided and fruitless. Its inner vitality consists not only in the nation's strength and resources for self-preservation and power of resistance but also when necessary, in the strength and will for self-assertion and self-expansion. Its inner beauty lies in the nation's power of creative

---

* This lecture was delivered on March 22, 1944 under the auspices of the Y. M. B. A., Ceylon, in the Town Hall of Colombo.

will, constructive imagination, moral sensibility, moral purity and broadness of outlook, while its outer beauty consists in a harmonious expression of the nation's mind and experience through its language, literature, religion, philosophy, arts, crafts, manners, customs, nay, through all its social, legal, political, commercial, religious and educational institutions. It must have some kind of idealism to create an urge from behind, some cherished objects or ends before it to inspire feelings, some pressing necessity to rouse up activity, and some obstacles to induce the will to overcome them. Stress must be laid on dynastic succession in matters of the state and on apostolic succession in matters of the church not only to be sure about the chronological setting of events which is the backbone of history but also for the reason that the king and the clergy are the powerful factors of a country's civilization or that the vital interests of the people centre somehow or other round them, they being looked upon as shapers of private and social life and custodians of public morality and property.

Certain problems are apt to arise, whether in connection with the nature of the materials collected, or in connection with the study and interpretation of the facts with their bearings on the collective life-movement or any aspect thereof.

The way to the construction and study of the ancient history and civilization of Ceylon has been made much easier now by the arduous labours of many a scholar. As regards its materials, you are in a most advantageous position for having a continuous national chronicle in your *Mahāvaṃsa* with its continuation and several other chronicles in prose and verse, Pali and Sinhalese. The inscriptions belonging to different reigns and supplementing, supporting or correcting the traditional accounts have also been rendered accessible, first by E. Müller and Bell and afterwards, in a more acceptable form, in the *Epigraphia Zeylanica.* The geological, artistic and other archæological finds are now well placed before us with their characteristics and meaning. The mature results of linguistic and literary researches are published to advance the cause of history. Similar finds, researches and publications in the surrounding countries, added to foreign accounts, have paved the way for a comparative study with a view to the understanding of the inter-connection and the nature of the influence of one civilization on another.

For a bird's-eye view of the early history and civilization of Ceylon, the little book of Dr. Mendis published in the Heritage of Ceylon Series is a boon alike to a man-in-the street and to a serious-minded reader. What I like in it especially is the fairness maintained in the statement of the entire position of the early history and civilization of the island.

The geographical position of Ceylon is rather easy to visualise. It is a large island, which is 'farther than any part of India', and which hangs like an eardrop (*kuṇḍala*) from a lobe or earlap of the mainland, the tapering ends of both confronting each other and being joined by a small chain, so to speak, of sandbanks and rocks. Whether you call this chain the Bridge of Rāma or prefer to give it the modern name of Adam's Bridge, the fact remains the same. Though the largest among the *upadvīpas* of Bhāratavarṣa, it is only 271½ miles from north to south, 137½ miles east to west, and 650 miles in circuit, it being in respect of its size, a little smaller than the State of Mysore. It was once known to the people of Northern India, as was pointed out, as an island, which was separated from the mainland only by a river.

To establish the general similarity between the physical features of Ceylon and the southernmost tableland of South India we need not quote any expert geological opinion. It was apparent even to a superficial or lay view, as may be gathered from Hwen Thsang's observation that the country of Siṃhala was 'the same as South India.'[1] Though probably based on hearsay, his remark was made with reference to Ceylon as a whole and what he then knew to be the country of Malakūṭa (Malayakūṭa) situated to the south of Drāviḍa meaning the Southern Coḷa kingdom with its capital at Kāñcīpura (Conjeeveram).

As regards the country of Malayakūṭa, the Malaya mountains, 'remarkable for their high peaks and precipices, their deep valleys and mountain torrents', abounding with sandal woods and having Mt. Po-ta-la-ka (Vaidūryaka) on the east, were situated on the south side and bordered the sea.[2] The Chinese pilgrim's Malayakūṭa was the same country as the Tāmraparṇī of the *Mahā-*

---

1 Beal, *Buddhist Records*, ii, p. 248.
2 *Ibid*, ii, p. 232.

bhārata (iii. 118. 3-8) with Mt. Vaidūryaka as its rocky landmark and situated below Pāṇḍya or Drāviḍa. In the case of Ceylon, the central region was and is occupied by the Malaya mass of high mountains, surrounded by the coastal plains. Though both the countries were noted for pearls, precious gems and large-sized elephants, Ceylon was and is more fortunate as regards its temperate climate throughout the year than South India which was and is considerably hot in summer. Referring to the deligtful climate of the island, Fa Hian noticed : "This country enjoys an agreeable climate, without any difference in winter or summer. The plants and trees are always verdant. The fields are sown just according to men's inclination ; there are no fixed seasons."

The 0° longitude was reckoned by the Indian astronomers from Ujjayinī,[1] which for that reason became the Greenwich of India. The meridian which passed through Ujjayinī was believed to have connected it with Ceylon in the south.

If you would look at the map, you may be sure to notice at once the striking resemblance in the general triangular shape of India, Australia, Africa and South America, your island being for all practical purposes the same to the Indian peninsula as what Tasmania is to Australia, Madagascar to Africa, or Falklands to South America. There is nothing astonishing then to imagine that Ceylon with South India was just a middle portion of a southern continent, which extended from Australia to South America. The original geological unity of the

1 Rapson, *Ancient India*, p. 175.

place just mentioned is now proved by the discovery in all of them of certain common plant and animal fossils. Though the size of the island as known to Megasthenes,[1] or as suggested in the *Periplus*,[2] or as given by Hwen Thsang,[3] was an exaggeration with regard to their times, it is not at all so, when judged by what it was or might be during the earlier geological periods. You must not think that your island is a geological formation of recent times, especially when archæological finds have brought to our notice the implements used by men in the *Neolithic* ("New Stone")[4] as well as the Palæolithic ("Old Stone") Age,[5] carrying back the beginning of your history and civilization to a hoary antiquity.

The history of Ceylon, precisely like that of any other country or island, presents at the outset the problem of the aborigines or primitive inhabitants. In offering a solution of this problem, we have to return satisfactory answers to the questions as to who they were, their origins, migrations, fusions, struggles for existence,

---

1 Megasthenes gives it 'a length of 7,000 stadia and a breadth of 5,000'.

2 The *Periplus* 'makes it almost touch Africa'. Mendis, op. cit., p. 50.

3 7,000 *li* (*i.e.*, nearly 1167 miles) in circuit. Beal, *op. cit.*, ii, p. 235.

4 The remnants of the Neolithic Age consist of the dolmens (Stone-chambers) and cists, the former found at Padiyagampola, near Rambukhana, and the latter in the Batticaloa district and in Nuvaragam Palata of the North Central Province.

5 The traces of the Plæolithic Age are 'a few tools, which consist of shells, cherts and quartz', are found near the cave-dwellings of the Veddas. See for details, John Pole's *Ceylon Stone Implements.*

persistence, extinction, expansion, transformation, habits of life, modes of livelihood, language, manners and customs, religious beliefs, the degrees of civilization attained, and modern identity.

As for your island, there is no means of ascertaining that the races who inhabited it in the Old or New Stone Age survived to so late a time as to come within the purview of your traditional history.

According to your *Chronicles,* the political history of Ceylon commenced just in the 5th century B.C., and that with the accidental conquest of the island by one prince Vijaya from some part of India and the foundation of a royal dynasty with him as its first king. Prior to this, the island was occupied and divided between two primitive peoples, broadly distinguished as Nāgas and Yakkhas. After the control of the island was taken out of the hands of the Yakkhas by Vijaya, a mixed race of Pulindas is said to have come into existence with the mountainous region of Malaya as its home. In the subsequent drama of the national life of the island the Nāgas and Yakkhas had no part to play except as mythical beings, the dreaded demons and demigods whose fury was to be appeased with sacrifice or offerings or checked by means of spells, incantations, the exercise of supernormal powers, and the like.

In comparatively modern times, we come across some wild tribes in the hilly portion of Ceylon who bear some aboriginal traits and are known by a generic name as Veddās. Dr. Saligmann who made a careful and wide investigation about the Veddās has written all that could perhaps be written about them as results of his panistaking anthropological research. And yet if the question be pressed as to the Veddās being precisely the modern descendants of the Palæolithic and Neolithic Ages, the scientific historian must always shrug his shoulder and be reluctant to accept the verdict of the anthropoligst as correct. To judge the past of the human race by the present is to put the cart before the horse. However interesting may be the stories of the lives of modern savages all over the world, these are not useful except as means of forming certain scientific hypothesis to account for the gradual emergence of human races into civilized life out of a state of comparative barbarity.

The manner in which the *Chrnoicles* set out the prehistoric chapter of your history hardly leaves room for doubt that the more powerful of the two main elements of the original population of Lankādīpa were the Yakkhas, and the weaker the Nāgas. Lankā, which came afterwards to denote the entire island as well as its capital city, was in earlier times just the name of one of the *dīpas* or divisions into which the inhabited portion of the island was divided. The three other divisions to which we are referred are called Nāgadīpa, Tambapaṇṇidīpa and Giridīpa, leaving out of account the Ojadīpa watered by the river Kadamba. The Nāgadīpa is located evidently on the north coast, the Tambanaṇṇidīpa on the western and south-western, the Lankādīpa on the eastern and south-eastern, and the Giridīpa in the central hilly region. The three main Nāga settlements are placed in Nāgadīpa, bordering the sea, on the banks of the river Kalyāṇī, which is to say, in Tambapaṇṇidīpa, and on the Kaṇṇāvaḍḍhamāna mountain,[1], which is to say, in Giridīpa. Thus they were broadly distinguished as those who were dwellers of hill-tracts *(pabbateyyā)* and those who dwelt on coastal plains. They are endowed with human speech and feelings and credited with social customs, such as that of giving dowry at the time of daughters' marriage. They knew the art of cooking and were being ruled by their own kings who were rich in precious gems. At the same time their human identity is made to vaninsh into the life of serpents, when they are distinguished also as aquatic and terrestrial *(jalaṭṭha-thalaṭṭā bhujagā)*[2] The legendary account may even be taken to divide the Nāgas into three physical types, *viz.*, the large-bellied *(Mahodara)*, the small-bellied *(Cūlodara)*, and the gem-eyed *(Maṇiakkhika)*, although these three occur as personal names of the three Nāga chiefs.

The Yakkha principalities, on the other hand, are sought to be located in two divisions, *viz.*, Tambapaṇṇidīpa, the Western Coastal Plain, and Lankādīpa, the Eastern Coastal Plain, the Sumanakūṭa or Adam's Peak at the south-west corner of the Malaya region being the rocky landmark of Tambapaṇṇidīpa, and Mount Lankā

1 Whether Kaṇṇāvaḍḍhamāna or simply Vaḍḍhamāna is the intended name of the mountain in the *Mahāvaṁsa*, i. 49, is a disputed question. I am inclined to treat Kaṇṇā as the name of Mahodara's younger sister, and Vaḍḍhamāna as the name of the mountain.

2 *Mahāvaṁsa*, i. 62.

at the south-east corner of the same region[1] being that of Lankādīpa. The Pulindas came to occupy later on the mountainous region of Malaya around Sumanakūṭa.[2]

As the *Valāhassa Jātaka* indicates, the Tambapaṇṇī division of Ceylon extended along the western sea-coast from the river Kalyāṇī in the south to Nāgadīpa in the north. Here was situated the prosperous Yakkha city called Sirīsavatthu, the "Abode of Śrīśa, *i.e.*, Viṣṇu." The place was being ruled by the *Yakkhiṇis* who were wily women of savage nature,—a veritable race of cannibals as they are described. According to the Sanskrit version of the birth-story, as narrated by Hwen Thsang, the name of this division was Ratnadvīpa because of its aboundant wealth in precious jewels and gems, and that of its capital, the "Iron City", while its female rulers were the *Rākṣasis*. The merchants seeking for gems frequently came to this island.[3] As known to Fa Hian, "This kingdom had originally no inhabitants but only demons and dragons dwelt in it. Merchants of different countries (however) came here to trade. At the time of traffic, the demons did not appear in person, but only exposed their valuable commodities with the value affixed. Then the merchantmen, according to the price marked, purchased the goods and took them away. But in consequence of these visits. . . men of other countries, hearing

1 According to Hwen Thsang, Mount Lankā stood at the south-east corner of the country, and its crags and deep valleys were occupied by the genii. Beal, *Buddhist Records*, ii, p. 251.

2 *Mahāvaṁsa*, vii. 67-68.
still reminds us of Ratnadvīpa.

3 Beal, *op. cit.*, ii, p. 239 ff. Ratnapura, near Adam's Peak,

of the delightful character of the place, flocked there in great numbers and so great a kingdom was formed."[1]

Thus from the earlier Chinese pilgrim we have a sober account of how through trade the people of the neighbouring countries came to know of the delightful character of the place, and were indeed to come and settle there in great numbers.

Its two versions taken together, the Valāhassa story tells us how the merchants who came to the island, whether due to ship-wreck or for trade, married the *Yakkhiṇis* and settled down, giving rise to a mixed race of men and increasing its population. The reason why they welcomed these merchants was that they were sea-faring merchants like their own men who were long absent from their midst and whose whereabouts were unknown since. Not that they were goblins living on human flesh, but they had to be represented so to warn the merchants from India against the folly of falling an easy prey to the wily arts of those women and not returning home.[2] The pauciy of men amongst them must have been the cause of a matriarchal system of society, which probably prevailed there, precisely as in Kerala or Mālābār.

It is interesting to note that Megasthenes mentioned the *Pandæ* (Pāṇḍyas) as "the only race in India ruled by women." Their territory was situated not far from the confluence of the five rivers of the Punjab,[3] which is to

1 *Ibid*, i. p. lxii.

2 The sailors from Chittagong composed a song in our days to warn their fellow men against going over to Burma, describing the wiles and guiles of the Burmese women.

3 McCrindle, *Ancient India*, p. 150.

say, from the Lower Indus Valley. Hwen Thsang called it the "Country of the Western Women" which was really an island in the sea. These women were the maidens of 'Persia *(Po-la-sse),* the abode of the western demons.[1] The *Mahāvaṃsa* applies the name of Mahilādīpa to the same island,[2] the appropriate Sanskrit name for which is Strīrājya.

The *Chronicles* that speak of two Yakkha principalities offer us altogether a different account of the social life of the Yakkhas. Here the systsem is patriarchal and marriage between a boy and a girl is arranged for by negotiation. The Yakkha city, Sirīsavatthu, is located outside the Tambapaṇṇī division, and it is distinguished from the other Yakkha capital called Lankāpura, Lankānagara. Marriage is said to have been solemnized with feast and festivity in the house of the bridegroom's parent. A Yakkha woman going with a person outside the society is severely punished.[3]

The historian will be much nearer the truth to connect the Veddās with the Pulindas and Śabaras of India rather than with any of the Palæolithic and Neolithic dwellers of the island whose whereabouts are only a matter of speculation. It need not astonish us at all that there should still be a village near Ratanpura and Sumanakūṭa, which bears the name of Habaragama to remind us of an ancient Śabara settlement (Sabaragāma) near the early home of the Pulindas. The Mārkaṇḍeya

1 Beal, *op. cit.,* ii. p. 240.
2 *Mahāvaṁsa,* vi. 43-45
3 *Ibid,* vi. 32-34, 62-64.

Purāṇa groups the Śabaras and Pulindas with the Āṭavyas (forest-dwellers) and places them all in South India, in a hilly region below the Mahānadī and Godāvarī. The Pulindas are mentioned as hill tribes who had their settlements also in Western India and the Midland. The *Mahāvaṃsa* has offered but a cheap explanation to account for the origin of the Pulindas of the Sumanakūṭa region from the two children of Vijaya by the Yakkhiṇī Kuveṇī instead of by the migration of them from the South, Central or Western India. Even with regard to the similar Neolithic finds of cists and dolmens in Ceylon and South India, this is precisely what would be expected in view of the original geological unity of the two places. The information supplied by Buddhaghosa goes to show that the pre-historic custom of preserving the bones of the dead in a house specially constructed for the purpose survived to his time,[1] if not to a still later period.

So far regarding the Nāgas, Yakkhas, Pulindas, Sabaras and Veddās. Now, as to the foundation of the first Indo-Aryan ruling dynasty or civilized rule, you are aware that your *Chronicles* and kings were all proud to trace its beginning from the conquest and colonisation of Ceylon by Prince Vijaya, son of Sīṁhabāhu, followed by his anointment as the first king. Here a difficult problem faces us and requires us to answer these three questions, each of great importance :

i How far can the *Mahāvaṃsa* account of Vijaya's advent be regarded as authentic ?

---

1 *Sumangala-vilāsinī*, i, p. 84 f. ; Barua, *Barhut*, i, p. 79.

ii From which part or country of India did he come, if he came at all?

iii What did his ascendancy to royal power actually mean to the historical process of development of the life and civilization of the island?

With regard to these questions, I may tell you at the outset that the *Mahāvaṃsa* story is just one of the four now available, and that out of the remaining three, one is narrated by Fa Hian and two by Hwen Thsang.

That which is sadly missed in the *Chronicles* is the previous trade-connection of India with Ceylon, which is to say, the important part played by Indian merchants and settlers in the historical process of colonisation and intermixture of blood. That which is missed in Fa Hian's account is the name of the first Indo-Aryan king of Ceylon.

According to the *Mahāvaṃsa* and other *Chronicles*, the founder of the first Indo-Aryan kingdom was Prince Vijaya, the eldest son of king Sīhabahu of Sīhapura in the kingdom of Lāḷa, situated between Kalinga and Vanga and to the east of Magadha (South Behār). The founder of Sīhapura, the capital of Lāḷa, was Sīhabahu who received his name from the circumstance of his having been begotten by a lion on his mother who was a princess of the then royal family of Vanga. The legend recorded by Hwen Thsang goes to represent rather Sīhabāhu himself as the prince who was banished by the then king of Southern India and accidentally landed on Ratnadvīpa and settled there to become the precursor and progenitor of the Indo-Aryan settlers by whom the kingdom was seized by force and the first king was elected together with his ministers. Here is effected a compromise between the *Mahāvaṃsa* story of Vijaya and Fa Hian's account of the development of an Indo-Aryan kingdom resulting from trade-relations and gradual settlements.

The second legend narrated by Hwen Thsang which is nothing but the *Divyāvadāna* version of the Pali Valāhassa story credits the merchant prince Siṃhala, son of Siṃha, a great merchant of Jambudvīpa, with the foundation of the first Indo-Aryan kingdom resulting from a military expedition which he had led from India. Before this he came to the island to trade at the head of 500 merchants, all of whom married the *Rākṣasis* and begot children. It is said that he destroyed the Iron City, broke down the iron prison, delivered the captive merchants, drove back the *Rākṣasis* to rocky islets in the sea, summoned the people to change their abodes, founded his capital, built towns, and so established himself as the first king.

It was nothing but a marvellous feat of ingenuity to invent the impossible story of a lion mating with a princess and begetting a son to account for the name of Sīhabahu, the founder of the city of Sīhapura named after him. Even in so late a record as the Belāva Copperplate inscription of Bhojavarman, the war-like princes of the royal House of Siṃhapura are praised as lion-like in their prowess :

bhejuḥ Siṃhapuraṃ guhām-iva mṛgendrāṇām[1].

1. *Epigraphia Indica*, Vol. XII, p. 37 f.

"they betook themselves to Siṃhapura, which was, as it were, a den to the lions."

Though the *Mahāvaṃsa* location of Sīhapura is fairly accurate, there still being a Siṃhapura in a jungle tract on the northern borderland of Orissa and in close proximity to the southern boundary of Rāḍha, it is difficult to reconcile with it other facts mentioned in connection with the banishment of Vijaya and his six hundred and ninety-nine men, the banishment of their wives, and that of their children. The Mahilādīpa on which their wives landed from the boat which carried them was an island, as I showed, almost below Persia, though not far from the mouth of the Indus. The Naggadīpa or Nāgadīpa, too, was an island in the Arabian sea, not far from the western sea-coast of the Deccan peninsula. Similarly the vessel in which Vijaya and his men were cast adrift carried them first to the port of Suppāraka (Sopārā, near Bombay) and then to that of Bharukaccha (Broach). It was from this western sea-port that they, going farther and farther south, accidentally arrived at the Yakkha city of Sirīsavatthu on the river Kalyāṇī.

To these may be added also the difficulty arising from the oldest known form of the Brāhmī alphabet in Ceylon and the oldest known form of the Sinhalese language.

Here we have to choose between three Siṃhapuras, one in the Punjab, one on the northern part of Orissa, and the third in the southern part of Orissa, near Chicacole. The first Siṃhapura which finds mention in the *Mahābhārata,* as well as in the itinerary of Hwen Thsang, was bounded on the west by the Indus and somewhat below Kāśmīra, and its capital lay at a distance of 700 *li* (about 140 miles) south-east from Takṣaśilā (Taxila). The city, about 2 to 3 miles in circuit, was enclosed by the crags and precipices. If Vijaya of the *Mahāvaṃsa* legend or Siṃhala, the merchant prince of the *Divyāvadāna* story, be connected with this Siṃhapura, it becomes easy to account not only for the vessels carrying their passengers to Mahilādīpa, Naggadīpa, and Suppāraka, but also for the oldest form of the Sinhalese language. This language, as may be judged from the oldest known inscriptions of Ceylon, retains the *r* sound, dispenses with such long vowels as *ā, ī,* and *ū,* has the first case singular ending in *e* instead of in *o,* as in Pali, or *aḥ,* as in Sanskrit, and uses all the three sibilants at random :

> *Devanapiya* (=*Devānaṃpiya*), *leṇe* (=leṇaṃ), *śaghaśa*[1], *sagaśa*[2], *ṣagaṣa*[3] (=*saṃghassa*).

The dialectical peculiarities of this language[4] are not fully explained by the dialect of the Mansehra version of Asoka's Rock Edicts in the Hazara district on the eastern

1. *Riṭigàla Inscriptions* in *E. Z.*, Vol. I, No. 10 a.
2. *Ibid,* Nos. 4, 7, 8, foll.
3. *Ibid,* No. 3. Wrongly read so far as *sagasa.*
4. The change of the genitive singular suffix *sa* (=Pali *ssa,* Sk. *sya*) into *ha, e.g.,* in *maharajaha,* is quite peculiar to old Sinhalese, without its exact parallel in any of the known inscriptions of India. The change of *ṣm* or *sm* into *mh* in Pali and Girnār dialect of Asoka's Rock Edicts does not meet the situation. The change of *sya* into *ha* is found to be a characteristic of the Dardic language in the Punjab proper. The change of the case-ending *sya* in *hyā* is one of the distinctive characteristics of the language of the inscriptions of the Achæmenian kings of ancient Persia..

side of the Indus, nor are these fully explained by the dialect of the Kalsi version in the district of Dehra Dun. We need a place somewhere below Mansehra on the one hand, and to the west of Kalsi on the other, and this requirement is exactly satisfied by the location of Siṃhapura by Hwen Thsang. The old Sinhalese dialect is found wanting in the traces of influence of the Sanskrit phonetics other than the three sibilants, and it equally lacks the long vowels, *ā, ī* and *ū* of the Kalsi dialect. So far as its tendency to dispense with such long vowels as *ā, ī, ū,* goes, it is the same as noticed in all the ancient inscriptions of India, whether of Aśoka or the Kuṣāṇas, written in Kharoṣṭhī characters. But these inscriptions found on the western side of the Indus are lacking in the Māgadhī first case-ending *e* instead of *o*.

Though the usual mode of Brāhmī alphabetic writing in Ceylon, precisely as in India, was from right to left, the Duwe Gala Cave inscription, No. 7, reverses the mode, thereby betraying the influence of the Kharoṣṭhī mode widely prevalent in the Punjab proper. The use of a bow string as a pointer to the inscription cannot but remind us of a very ancient device in some of the inscribed seals of the Indus Valley (Marshall's *Mohenjo-dāro,* iii, Pl. CIII. I).

The association of Siṃhapura with Lāḷa or Rāḍha or its proximity to Kalinga need not deter us from identifying it with Siṃhapura in Uttarāpatha. In the *Mahābhārata* (II. 27. 21), the countries of Siṃhapura, Suhma and Coḷa are associated together, and these are all located in Uttarāpatha. The Buddhist Sanskrit work called

Mahāvastu locates Utkala, later a part of Orissa, in Uttarāpatha. The Greeks mention the Pāṇḍyas among the autonomous tribes of the Punjab proper. Just like other ruling races, the Siṃhas of Siṃhapura may have migrated and founded territories elsewhere, *e.g.*, in the north and south of Kalinga. Probably the northern Siṃhapura in Kalinga was believed all along, due, no doubt, to the tradition in the *Chronicles*, to have been the homeland of Vijaya, and this weighed on the decision of your ministers even in offering in quick succession the throne of Ceylon to Niśśaṅkamalla and Sāhasamalla, two brothers and valiant princes from the royal family of Siṃhapura in the kingdom of Kalinga[1].

Geiger and Professor Suniti Kumar Chatterji incline to identify the Lāla country of your *Chronicles* preferably with Lāṭa above Gujarāṭ on the western coast of India. But their equation of Lāḷa with Lāṭa cannot be accepted as final until and unless they can show the connection of Lāṭa with some Siṃhapura in Western India with its dialect bearing these four distinctive characteristics of old Sinhalese: (i) the shortening of long vowels, (ii) the de-aspiration of consonants, (iii) the Māgadhī suffix *e* in 1st case, singular, and (iv) the random use of the three sibilants.[2]

It goes, however, without saying that neither the language nor the population of the island was the crea-

1 See the genealogical tree of the Ceylon rulers of the Kalinga dynasty in *E. Z.* Vol. II, p. 221.

2 See, *E.Z.*, Vol. I, p. 15 for comments on five characteristics.

tion of a day. Both were present there when the first Indo-Aryan dynasty was established, and the credit for the earlier development must at all events be given to the merchant settlers and other immigrants from India, the religious preachers included.

Though the *Mahāvaṃsa* says nothing about the previous trade-connection of India with Ceylon and the part played by Indian merchants and earlier settlers in the historical process of colonisation, it certainly suggests a few interesting points missed in other legends. It definitely mentions, for instance, Siṃhapura in Lāḷa or Kalinga as the royal capital from which the founder of the first Indo-Aryan dynasty came. It refers to the flourishing and guarded Yakkha city of Sirīsvatthu on the river Kalyāṇī, and speaks of the subterranean prison or fort, the passage to which lay through a tunnel *(suranga)*. It applies Indian names to the Yakkhiṇis of the place, *e.g.*, Kuveṇī (Kuverī, miscalled 'Kuvaṇṇā apparently for her dark complexion) and Kāḷī, just as your other *Chronicles* introduce the Yakkha king of the western territory under the name of Kāḷasena, and the Yakkha princess from Lankā and her mother under those of Posamittā and Koṇḍā[1]. The first person Vijaya met on landing is a *paribbājaka* or Brahmanical wandering ascetic who was really the Hindu god Uppalavaṇṇa (Viṣṇu) in disguise. Lastly, it presents Kuveṇī in the garb of a *tāpasī* or female hermit.

All the legends agree in stating that the foundation of the Indo-Aryan rule was accompanied by the building

1 Ṭīkā to *Mahāvaṁsa*, vii. 33.

of cities and towns, the planning of districts and rural areas, the location of the peoples according to the classes or castes to which they belonged, and the like. The king had to be formally anointed and his ministers elected or appointed. The *Mahāvaṃsa* credits Vijaya with the building of the city of Tambapaṇṇi, his chief minister Anurādha with that of the village Anurādhagāma on the bank of the river Kadamba, named after him, his Purohita called Upatissa with that of Upatissagāma to the north of the village of Anurādha, and three other ministers with those of Ujjenī, Uruvelā and Vijita,—all Indian place-names.

It is also in the fitness of things that the founder of the dynasty should, acting with foresight, think of strengthening his position in the island by establishing a matrimonial alliance with the neighbouring kingdom of Pāṇḍya on the Indian shore and forming a social aristocracy with the help of the Pāṇḍya princess and other maidens from the families of the Pāṇḍya nobles, brought over to the island for the purpose of marriage, as well as having the way for the future development of the arts and crafts of Ceylon by having the services of the eighteen guilds of craftsmen.

Both traditions and inscriptions prove the existence of a ruling dynasty in the island of Tambapaṇṇī before and after, as also at the time of, the reign of Devānaṃpiya Asoka. The *Chronicles* definitely state that this dynasty had not come into existence prior to the demise of the Buddha, for which the most workable date is 487-88

B.C.,[1] deducting 218 years from which we get 269-70 B.C. as the acceptable date of Asoka's consecration. This is not, however, to deny that 543-44 B.C., which is the current date of the Buddha's demise in your country, as also in Burma and Siam, is unmeaning. As Professor Raychaudhuri has aptly suggested, 543-44 B.C., is the date of accession of king Bimbisāra to power[2] which at a comparatively late period of the history of your island gained currency as the date of commencement of the Buddha Era.

According to the *Mahābhārata,* the *digvijaya* or military campaign undertaken by the fifth Pāṇḍava brother Sahadeva succeeded in subduing all the ruling peoples of South India including the Coḷas, the Pāṇḍyas, the Keralas, and the rest. Though the Siṃhalas are not mentioned exactly in the description of the *digvijaya,* in a subsequent chapter devoted to the *Rājasūya* sacrifice performed by the Pāṇḍavas at Indraprastha (Delhi), the king of the Siṃhalas is expressly said to have been represented along with those of the Ḍrāviḍas and

---

1 This agrees very nearly with that which is fixed by Takakusu, viz., 486 B.C., on the strength of the Chinese 'dotted recorid'. Fleet *(J.R.A.S.,* 1906, p. 984), Wickramasinghe *(Epi. Zeyl.,* iii, p. 46.) and John N. Senerveatne *(J.R.A.S.,* Ceylon Br., XXIII, p. 141 f.) seek to prove that the Buddha-era of 483 B. C. was in use in Ceylon up till the close of the 15th century.

2 This date is worked out by adding to 487-88 the total of years covering the period of the Buddha's ministry, that of his Enlightenment and the interval between Bimbisāra's accession and the Buddha's enlightenment (45+6+5=56).

Kāśmīrakas[1]. But the whole account being, more or less, an echo of the *digvijaya* on the part of Samudragupta who passes as the great Napoleon of India, we need not attach any undue importance to it. But it is certain that the ruling nation of Tambapaṇṇī came within the sphere of the foreign relation and moral influence of Aśoka, or that this was preceded by some sort of a political relationship of Tambapaṇṇī with the Maurya empire founded by Chandragupta, grandfather of Aśoka, in about 323 B.C. The veracity of Aśoka's statements in two of his famous edicts concerning the five southern powers cannot be doubted. The accuracy in the manner of introducing them presupposes a definite knowledge of the relative positions of their territories. In R. E. II, Pāṇḍya is placed below Coḷa, the Keralaputra territory below the Satiyaputra, and Tambapaṇṇī below all. In R.E. XIII, too, the country of the Tambapaṇṇīyas is correctly placed below Pāṇḍya, as Pāṇḍya below Coḷa. Even apart from the Tamil traditional account of the advance of the army of the Moriyan upstarts as far down as the Podiyil hill in Travancore, the knowledge of Taprobanē as an island, noted for its precious gems, larger elephants and pearls, and productive of more gold than India, is confirmed by the *Indika* of Megasthenes.

Aśoka in his R.E. II, claims to have arranged for two kinds of medical treatment *(duve cikīchā)*, one suitable for men and the other for animals, along with the

1 Mbh., II. 34. 12 : *Drāviḍā Siṁhalāś caiva rājā Kāśmīrakās tathā.*

supply and planting of medicinal herbs, roots and fruits throughout his empire, as also in the territories of his allies, Tambapaṇṇī included. In his R. E. XIII, on the other hand, he speaks of the *dūtas* (emissaries) going to them for the propagation of the principles of piety enunciated by him, as well as of the wide acceptance of them both by the ruler and the ruled. The name of the contemporary king of Tambapaṇṇī is not, however, mentioned.

The *Chronicles* of Ceylon, on the contrary, represent Devānaṃpiya Tissa, the second son and successor of king Muṭasiva, as a younger contemporary of Piyadassi Aśoka of India. They tell us that the latter sent his distant ally the valuable coronation presents which reaching late, the former was anointed for the second time[1], though only six months after the first ceremony. They also tell us that the first Buddhist mission under the leadership of Mahinda, son of Aśoka, arrived at Ceylon from Pāṭaliputta *via* Ujjenī in the 18th regnal year of Aśoka, more accurately, the 21st year . Mahinda's mission was quietly followed by the despatch of an envoy from the king of Ceylon to Aśoka duly returning with a graft from the Bo-tree and the Therī Saṃghamittā, daughter of Aśoka, leading a mission of Buddhist sisters. All the important events connected with the Buddhist mission, as also with the coronation of Tissa

1 Dr. Paranavitana has with strong reasons on his side sought to prove that the formal ceremony of consecration of kings was unknown in Ceylon before Devānampiya Tissa. Prior to his reign the kings as *gāmaṇis* were just elected by the people.

are very carefully dated so as to leave no room for suspecting their authenticity. But we are also particularly told that the reign of Muṭasiva, father and predecessor of Tissa, was considered unfavourable to the success of the Buddhist mission, although the reason is nowhere stated.

The *Chronicles* are at pains to establish that the royal line of Devānaṃpiya Tissa and Muṭasiva was different from the Siṃhapura dynasty of which Vijaya was the founder. They must anyhow make it appear as a Śākya or Īkṣvāku family. The Siṃhapura line became deflected, they say, and was continued only through a prince who happened to be the nephew of the kings of the Siṃhapura family after its second king Paṇḍu Vāsudeva. To make a history out of myths and legends, they have brought in by fluke an accomplished Śākya princess called Bhaddakaccānā from a country beyond the Ganges to be the queen consort of Vijaya's brother and successor Paṇḍu Vāsudeva[1]. The legend of princess Bhaddakaccānā and the appearance of the Okkāka (Īkṣvāku) princes as *Gāmaṇis* or Headmen of certain important villages may be taken to presuppose the immigration and settlement of the Īkṣvākus from the banks of the Kṛṣṇā in South India.

If we ask ourselves the question why the reign of Muṭasiva was not found favourable to the Buddhist mission, it is not enough, I think, to say 'because of his old age' (*vuḍḍho Muṭasivo rājā*). The explanation indeed is

1 *Mahāvaṁsa*, viii. 20.

that the aged king was no longer open to new conviction, who was, therefore, in the eye of the Buddhist propagandist but a *muṭa* (Pali *muṭṭa)* or 'bewildered' Siva. But the real fact behind the prudence of Mahinda seems to be deeper than this.

Muṭasiva was evidently, like Aśoka's father Bindusāra, a votary of the Brāhmans and supporter of other religious sects. The *Chronicles* rightly lead us to think that the hermits and wandering ascetics had penetrated into the island much earlier. Side by side with the dreaded Yakkhas who continued to receive periodical offerings, the higher Hindu gods, Viṣṇu and Śiva, stood as the objects of profound veneration. The god Uppalavaṇṇa or Viṣṇu was being looked upon as the divine protector of the universe, as also of the island, while Śiva as the grantor of salvation was the highest deity to the *Paribbājakas* or Brahmanical wandering ascetics. So we are told in connection with the arrival of Paṇḍu Vāsudeva that when his thirty-two companions appeared in the garb of *paribbājakas,* the local people extended at once proper homage to them.

The memorable work done by Paṇḍukābhaya immediately after his victory in the war against his uncles was the conversion of Anurādhagāma into Anurādhapura. Here he was anointed as Paṇḍukābhaya. It is noteworthy that in founding this great city, which thenceforward became the capital of Lankā, he, precisely like an Indian monarch, consulted the astrologers and foretellers as well as persons well-versed in the art of town-planning and the general science of architecture.

Four suburbs were made around the city. The Yakkha shrines were built on its four sides, and one inside the palace area, the tree-shrine of Vessavaṇa Kubera being assigned to the west side along with that of the demi-god of disease (*Vyādhideva*)[1]. Four tanks were excavated at the four gates, each named after him. The *Caṇḍālas* were employed to do the work of city-scavengers, night men, carriers of corpses and guards of the cemetery on the north-east of which he founded a village for these municipal workers, while to the north of it, and between it and the Rocky mountain (Pāsāṇapabbata) the dwellings of the hunters were caused to be made,—the *vyādhas* who should better be connected with the Veddās.

On the north of this Rocky mountain and as far as the Gāmanī Tank, he caused many hermitages to be built for the hermits, to the east of this as well as of the cemetery, the abodes for two Jainas and others for the recluses of various orders. In this very quarter he caused an abode to be made for a Jaina called Kumbhaṇḍa. On the west of this and to the east of the hunters' dwellings were lodged five hundred families of alien faiths (*micchādiṭṭhika-kulā*), while beyond the abode of the Jaina named Jotiya but below the Gāmani Tank were built the retreats for the *Paribbājakas* along with the abodes for the Ājīvikas and the Brāhmans. The halls for cure (sotthisālā), too, were founded here and there.

The evidence thus supplied by the *Chronicles*,

1 The earlier reading, corrected by Geiger, was *Vyādhadeva*, the 'Hunter-god'.

especially regarding the Aryanisation of your great island, is entirely in agreement with what Aśoka says in his R. E. XIII concerning the previous aryanisation of all the countries in Jambudīpa with the solitary exception of the Yona territory by the various orders of Śramaṇas and Brāhmaṇas. He tells us that when he was promulgating this edict of his in the 13th or 14th year of *abhiṣeka,* there was not a single country but the Yona territory where these preachers of the Indo-Aryan faiths were not, or where the inhabitants were not believers in the religion of one or another of them. Thus as much as in Ceylon as elsewhere, these exponents of the Indo-Aryan culture were the forerunners of the Buddhist missionaries. The Demon or Devil was there from earlier times, never to be eliminated ; afterwards came in Viṣṇu and Śiva, but the ultimate victory waited for the Buddha and Buddhas.

The ground for Buddhism was prepared also through the political alliance and the exchange of envoys, presents and greetings between Devānampiya Tissa and Devānampiya Asoka. In Aśoka the Buddhist kings of Ceylon found a great living embodiment of the Cakkavattī ideal of the Buddha. The personal example and tradition of Aśoka served to awaken in your kings a new consciousness of obligations to all the citizens and denizens of the country under them, a new sense of responsibility of using the government only as a means of bringing happiness to the subjects in manifold ways, educating them to moral excellences of character, strengthening the cause of general piety, giving strength and support to the religious teachers of various schools of thought for the promotion of the cause of learning and culture, and maintaining the unity and purity of the Buddhist Church. A great impetus also came to public and humanitarian works, such as the foundation of hospitals for men and animals, the excavation of tanks and canals for the abundant supply of water for drinking, irrigation and other purposes, going in circuit for supervision and inspection of administrative duties entrusted to various officials, religious foundations, the development of art and architecture, the periodical royal proclamations, the utilisation of writing for the purpose of recording the royal messages and benefactions, the use of the spoken dialect as official language, and the like. The subsequent history of Ceylon is just to see how many of your enlightened kings emulated the fame of Aśoka and how far they succeeded in this very matter.

The Buddhist mission under Mahinda brought with it the Words of Buddha in Three Baskets, the lives, experiences and utterances of the Wayfarers, the notable examples of the life of piety lived by the laity, men and women, the *Jātakas* and *Apadānas*, and the traditions of the early Buddhist monastic and educational institutions in India. It also brought with it the commentatorial tradition and the doctrines and views of the early Buddhist sects and schools of thought, the inspiring memory of the places and objects associated with the life of the Master. The Three Baskets were filled with the lofty teachings of the Enlightened One, the rules of discipline and decorum carefully laid down by him, as well as the priceless treasure of the Buddhist psycho-ethical concepts and methodology. The great Bo-tree Assattha stood as a living symbol of Buddhism, and a living branch of it was brought over for planting on the virgin soil of Ceylon. It served to give an impetus to the erection all over the island of the *vihāras, pariveṇas, cetiyas, dāgobas, dānasālās, vejjasālās, as well as* the representation of the *Jātakas* in sculptures and frescoes *(lepacitta).* It enabled the Theras of your island to develop an historic sense unsurpassed by any other nation in the ancient world. Nothing of it was in vain.

The successful propagation of Buddhism meant the transplantation of the *Saddharma* in a productive soil, genial climatic temperament and sea-girt environment, where it was destined to remain ever green. The tradition of Buddhism was continued with unabated zeal. The Councils were held during the reign of Devānampiya Tissa, Duṭṭhagāmaṇi and Vaṭṭagāmaṇi for the rehearsal and fresh canonisation of Buddhavacana. The Sinhalese dialect was ere long developed under the influence of Pali into a rich literary language, and with the single exception, perhaps, of Tamil, there is hardly any other spoken dialect in Jambudvīpa in which an extensive literature was produced at so early a date. What particularly distinguishes Sinhalese is the enormous amount of a technical literature, which was produced in the shape of various original commentaries on different Pali texts, and that before the arrival of Buddhaghosa from India in the 4th or 5th century A.D.

As you know better than others, I need not expatiate on the great affection in which your kings and clergy and people have held the Bo-tree since its first arrival or the many benefactions of your rulers in its name.[1] But if the planting of the Bo-graft from Mahābodhi during the reign of Devānampiya Tissa (247-207 B.C.) had made the first landmark of the history of Buddhism in the island, the arrival and enshrinement of the Tooth-relic during the reign of Kitti-Siri-Meghavaṇṇa (A.D. 362-389.) and the arrival and enshrinement of the Hair-relic, probably during the reign of Meggallāna I (A.D. 552-572) went to make two later landmarks of the same. There was yet another object,—a Pali text, namely, the first book of the Abhidhamma Piṭaka called Dhammasangaṇi, the enshrinement and worship of which during the reign of Kassapa II (A.D. 634-703) and Vijayabāhu I[2] created the fourth landmark.

The affixing of the Indian honorific *Devānaṁpiya* to the name of Tissa is traceable to the influence of the peronal example of Aśoka. According to Megasthenes, this honorific *(pūjāvacana)* was particularly applicable to the philosophers, *i.e.,* the Śramaṇa and Brāhmaṇa teachers, who were popularly believed to have been

1 The hold of the Bo-tree on the affections of the royal families of Ceylon is evident also from the personal names of several kings ending in the word *bodhi.*

2 The barefooted standing figure on the front face of the boulder at the entrance to the Potthagala vihāra may be identified better with Vijayabāhu I holding reverentially in his hands a palm-leaf MS. of the Dhammasangaṇi.

'most dear to the gods', a fact, which is equally borne out by the Etadagga Section of the Anguttara Nikāya. But its significance as an affix to the name of a cakkavatti was defined in the Pāli book of *Apadāna,* and that was precisely the sense in which it came to adorn the name of Aśoka, as also those of Tissa, Gamaṇi Tisa (Saddhā Tissa) and Tisa Abaya (Vaṭṭagāmaṇi Abhaya)[1] :

Imasmiṁ Bhaddake Kappe eko āsi janādhipo |
mahānubhāvo rājā'si cakkavatti mahābalo ||
So 'haṃ pañcasu silesu ṭhapetvā janataṁ bahuṁ |
pāpetvā sugatiṁ yeva Devatānampiyo ahuṁ ||[2]

"In this Good Era", said Thera Pilinuavaccha, "there was a lord of men, of great personality was he, a mighty king overlord. In his identity I became 'dear unto the gods' by establishing the multitude in the moral precepts of conduct and enabling them to get a happy destiny (in heaven, after death)".

The strong foundation of the Buddhistic history and civilization of Ceylon was laid by Devānampiya Tissa under the guidance of Thera Mahinda. The only task left by him to his long line of successors to accomplish was either its preservation, or expansion, or resuscitation, additions and alterations, or further development and embellishment. But what were the works actually done by him ?

The memorable works executed by Devānampiya Tissa are carefully enumerated in a chronological order in the twentieth chapter of the *Mahāvaṁsa* .

---

1 *E. Z.,* Vol. I, p. 142 foll.
2 *Apadāna,* i, p. 60.

"In the first place, he erected the Mahāvihāra; Secondly, the Cetiyavihāra; thirdly, the Thūpārāma after completing the Mahāthūpa; fourthly, the living shrine of the Bo; fifthly, a stone-pillar at the Mahācetiya (with an inscription recording the prophecy of Mahinda about the erection of *thupas* by others in future)[1], as well as the Collour-bone shrine (at Mahiyangaṇa); sixthly, the Issarasamaṇaka (better, Isi-ramaṇaka) vihāra (at the place where Mahinda converted 500 votaries of Issara or Siva); seventhly, the Tissa Tank; eighthly, the Paṭhamathūpa; ninthly, the Vessagiri-vihāra (at the place where Mahinda initiated 500 men of the Vessa caste); and lastly, the delightful Upāsikāvihāra, the Hatthāḷhaka-vihāra, and two nunneries. He was also the founder of the Jambukoḷa-vihāra at the port of Jambukoḷa in Nāgadipa, and likewise of the Tissa-mahāvihāra and the Pacina-vihāra (both at Anurādhapura)"[2]

No inscription of Devānaṃpiya Tissa has yet been discovered. But the tradition is emphatic in saying that he had caused a stone-piller to be set up bearing an inscription. Without such a beginning in earlier reigns, it is difficult to account for the use of the honorific *Devānaṃpiya* as an affix to the name of Gamaṇi Abaya and his father, which fell out of use in India after Aśoka's successor called Daśaratha.

Besides the two nunneries, the most important monastic institution founded by him was the Mahāvihāra

---

1 Cf. *Mahāvaṁsa*, XV. 173:
Iccāha thero, therassa vacanen' idha bhūpati |
ussāpesi silatthambhaṁ taṁ pavattiṁ likhāpiya ||

2 *Ibid*, XX. 17-25. Cf. Wijesinha's Translation.

or Great Minster which was destined to play a very important part in the Buddhist religious and literary history. It remained unrivalled until the foundation of the Abhayagirivihāra or North Minster by Vaṭṭagāmaṇi Abhaya (44, 29-17 B.C.).

The hard national struggle for existence began in the ancient history of the island with the advent of some Tamil horse-dealers and usurpers in c. 177 B.C., and subsequently of a powerful Tamil horde under the command of Eḷāra from the kingdom of Coḷa. The tragedy of the serious situation created by them, precisely as afterwards, from time to time, by the invaders from the opposite shore, frequently from Coḷa and rarely from Pāṇḍya, was due to the fact that they were no respecters of the national feelings and institutions, and appeared with the sinister design of a ruthless destruction of life and property, which followed in the train of plunder and loot and the desecration of Buddhist sshrines.

The most valiant prince who succeeded, like Candagutta Moriya, grandfather of Asoka, "in shaking off from the neck of the country the yoke of slavery', and thereby became entitled to the proud position of a national hero was Duṭṭhagāmaṇi (101-77 B. C.). The national feeling of the entire island ran so high against the Tamil intruders that when the king lost his peace of mind to think that he had secured his exalted royal state at the cost of countless lives, even the eight saintly Buddhist Theras consoled him, saying, "Thou hast, O Lord of men, committed no such act as to stand in the way to heaven. Thou hast killed just one man and a half, one a full believer and the other a half. The rest being heretics and wicked, are like unto beasts. Thine is now the task to cause the religion of Buddha to shine forth in its full splendour. Subdue thou this mental affliction."[1]

The trouble was not, however, over with the fall of Eḷāra at the hands of Duṭṭhagāmaṇi who raised aloft to seven storeys the Lohapāsāda (Brazen Palace) built by Devānaṃpiya Tissa, founded the famous Marīcavaṭṭi-vihāra and the great *dāgoba* called *Mahāthūpa* on the model, more or less, of the Indian *stūpas* at Sāñcī and Bharhut, and, above all, brought the Buddhist Fraternity of Ceylon into contact with the leading Theras of India.

Nearer his time, Vaṭṭagāmaṇi Abhaya, or Devanapiya Tisa Abaya of the inscriptions, had to be in the rôle of a victor of the same description. In connection with his final victory, the *Chronicles* lead us to understand that the Jainas and other religionists had their privileges left intact through 21 reigns since Paṇḍukābhaya. When a remark made inadvertently by a Nigaṇṭha named Giri went to show that he was mentally in sympathy with the Tamil invader, Vaṭṭagāmaṇi seized his abode and converted it into a Buddhist site. But this is a solitary instance of forfeiture of a privilege enjoyed by a religious head by way of punishment for his tendency to treason, and it must not be construed as an instance of religious persecution.

1 *Mahāvaṃsa,* XXV. 109 111. The translation is abridged and free.

I must not omit also to mention that apart from founding the Abhayagiri-vihāra which with its later offshoots made distinct contributions to Buddhism, Vaṭṭagāmaṇi played well in respect of the Theravāda Canon the same part as was played some time later by the Kuṣāṇa king Kaniṣka in respect of the Sarvāstivāda texts by committing it for the first time to writing.

Among the successors of Vaṭṭagāmaṇi, his own son Coranāga was decidedly a black sheep in the fold as a reckless destroyer of twelve *vihāras,* by whom we should not judge the almost unbroken tradition of piety of the kings of Ceylon and their services to the Buddhist Churches. But the case of king Mahāsena with whom the Chronicle of the Great Dynasty from the time of Vijaya, was taken as closed needs some comment. His antagonism to the Mahāvihāra teachers is said to have been instigated by a Ceylon monk who was a partisan of the *Vetullavāda (Vaitulyavāda)* which made its way into the island and was entertained by the rival school of Abhayagiri. In the eyes of the Mahāvihāra school the Vaitulyakas were preaching heresy and so they deserved to be driven out.

It would seem that the action of the Mahāvihārins was a little hasty, but the king's acts of vengeance were out of proportions. That Vetullavāda represented some form of Mahāyāna is undoubted. Hwen Thsang informs us that the Mahāvihārins were opposed to the Great Vehicle *(i.e.,* Mahāyāna) and adhered to the teaching of the Little Vehicle *(i.e.,* Hīnayāna), while the Abhayagirivāsins studied both the Vehicles and

The next king, Kitti-Siri-Meghavaṇṇa, the son and successor of Mahāsena, who made ample amends for the wrongs done by his father to the Mahāvihāra, was really the transitional link between the Ancient period and the Mediæval. In his wise rule, clear foresight, breadth of vision and impartial attitude towards all we see the lost rhythm of the national life of the island fully restored. As we proceed downwards from him to the Augustan period of the Vijayabāhus and Parākramabāhus, we cannot fail to observe that your island lay more and more open to the Sanskrit culture of India, or that your outlook was broadened, or that Ceylon was out to establish its cultural relations with India, China, Siam and Burma, as also to carry its own literature and civilization far beyond its confines.

Here I am to close this lecture, heartily thanking you for your courtesy and patient hearing. The space of time at my disposal has not permitted me a comprehensive survey even of the ancient history and civilization of your island. Much of what I intended to place before you for your consideration remains unsaid. I may be excused for that. But I hope and trust that whether you agree with me or not on all the points raised in the two lectures, you will not misunderstand my intention. Lastly, none of the views and suggestions offered is meant to be the last word on the subject, there being no finality in the search for truth.

---

1 *Mahāvaṁsa,* XXX. 100.

LECTURE III

CEYLON'S CONTRIBUTIONS TO BUDDHISM

As a fitting sequel to the two lectures delivered in the History series, presenting my views on the manifold relations between India and Ceylon and the problems of the ancient history of the island, I was expected to deliver this lecture on the subject in which the rising generation of students here cannot but be keenly interested. And I am much grateful indeed to the authorities of the Ceylon University for their courtesy in asking me to acquaint you with my views concerning Ceylon's contributions to Buddhism before I leave the island.

The weighty reason which has impelled me to address you on this subject is that neither you in Ceylon nor we in India have yet a clear idea of the nature and extent of Ceylon's contributions to the development of the cultural tradition of the religion which has guided and moulded the life and civilization of the island as a whole. The general opinion which has gained ground in India about Ceylon's contributions to Buddhism is that Ceylon is the country where the Theravāda or Pali Canon was carefully preserved, but for which this price-

---

* This third lecture of History series was delivered at the University of Ceylon on March 23, '44.

less literary treasure meaning the oldest known and most authentic version of Buddha's Words and early Buddhist tradition would have been completely lost to the world. If it be argued that the Pali Canon has also been preserved in Siam and Burma, the fact is undeniable that it was possible only because of a legacy from Ceylon. For it is from Ceylon that both Siam and Burma obtained at least one authentic version of the Pali Canon and Commentaries. If it were further argued that the eastern coast of South India between the Kṛṣṇā and the Kāverī was equally a stronghold of the Theravāda form of Buddhism, and, for the matter of that, there was a distinctly South Indian version of the same, the reply should be that, historically speaking, the eastern coast of South India, particularly the country of Andhra and Coḷa, and the island of Ceylon belonged to one and the same domain of Theravāda Buddhism.

We are indebted, no doubt, to Ceylon for this. But does this fact alone entitle the island to our admiration? The preservation of the original Buddhist texts in the island may have been just a matter of accident, We can say in the same breath that we are equally indebted to Tibet, the Himalayan country of Bhoṭa, for the preservation in the original and mostly in literal and mechanical translations of the later Buddhist works that were otherwise lost in the land of their origin—a praise which is almost in the same measure due to the ancient civilized land of China, particularly for the preservation of the Canonical texts belonging to different Buddhist sects and schools of thought other than the Theriya, and that mainly through freer and more intelligently done translations. Similarly the kingdom of Nepāl and the State of Kāshmīr and Jammu are entitled to our gratitude together with Eastern Turkestan for the preservation of a fairly large number of later Buddhist works, mostly in Sanskrit and rarely in Prakrit. Is this in itself, I ask, much of a contribution, which can speak well of the genius and intellectual capacity of a great and ancient race such as yours? I would say, No. To properly adjudicate on the nature and extent of Ceylon's contributions to Buddhism, to form a correct estimate of their cultural value and historical importance, one has got to show that instead of being merely a passive recipient and a Yakṣa-like zealous custodian of the priceless treasure brought over from India, the enlightened rulers and erudite Theras as well as the main people of Ceylon combined to actively react upon it and enriched it with new additions by way of intelligent interpretations of its contents and elaborations of the system of thought, producing distinctive forms and styles of Buddhist art and architecture, and helping forward in various ways the cause of expansion and better appreciation of Buddhism beyond its confines.

It is a matter of common knowledge that through the first Buddhist mission led by Mahāmahinda Ceylon obtained a version of Buddha's Words in Three Baskets as orally handed down from teacher to teacher, and that this was followed by the compilation of the Commentaries called *Aṭṭhakathās*. The *Chronicles* of Ceylon and other available traditions indicate that if the history of Pali Canonical texts had started from the days of the First Buddhist Council held at Rājagaha under the presidentship of Thera Mahākassapa, that of the compilation of their *Commentaries* in Sinhalese began from the time of arrival of the Buddhist mission in this island under the headship of Thera Mahinda. This is not, however, to say that there were not earlier literary processes facilitating the work of both Mahākassapa and Mahāmahinda. There are among the Canonical texts themselves many that represent the books of exegesis, I mean the *Niddesas* and *Vibhangas*. But they differ in their method, style and technique from the *Aṭṭhakathās* that take us down to a stage of literary and scholastic development not only beyond the corpus of authoritative texts which goes by the name of Buddhavacana Pāli but beyond the stage represented by the two treatises on textual and exegetical methodology called *Nettipakaraṇa* and *Peṭakopadesa,* and no less by the interesting and instructive Pali work of high literary merit called *Milindapañha*. These are for a certainty the earlier foundation on which the grand edifice of the *Aṭṭhakathās* was built up.

Here one may legitimately inquire as to whether or not the corpus of Buddhavacana received from India was allowed to remain intact as a closed book. And if any additions or alterations were subsequently made in Ceylon, what was their precise nature and extent?

I believe that there is much truth in the tradition which is particularly recorded in the *Saddhammasangaha* that just as there were held three orthodox Councils in

Northern India for the rehearsal and affiliation of the Canonical texts, so there were held three similar councils in Ceylon, one during the reign of Devānampiya Tissa, one during the reign of Duṭṭhagāmaṇi, and the third during the reign of Vaṭṭagāmaṇi. Even if we ignore the first two, at least for the paucity of information about the procedures adopted and the results obtained, the third of them is highly important as it led to the first commitment of the then known texts of Pali Canon to writing. The Three *Piṭakas* and their commentaries, if any, were all transmitted until that time by an oral tradition.[1]

The date of compilation of the commentaries in Sinhalese must be assigned to a time after Vaṭṭagāmaṇi, although the exegetical process leading to it was earlier. We are not also to think that no book was included in the Canon since its commitment to writing towards the close of the 1st century B.C.

The *Parivāra* was, among others, the most noteworthy addition to the *Vinaya Piṭaka* which, as recited and fixed at the First Council in India, comprised no more than what is called *Ubhatovinaya, i.e.,* the two books of the *Suttavibhanga* distinguished as Bhikkhu and Bhikkhuṇī. The century following it saw the compilation of the Vinaya *Mahāvagga* and *Cullavagga.* As for the compilation of the *Parivārapāṭha,* it is clearly stated in its *nigamana* (epilogue) that it was caused to be written as a Vinaya treatise by an erudite Thera named Dīpa

---

1 *Mahāvaṁsa,* XXX. 100.

for the benefit of his pupils in course of lecturing to them. The profoundness of learning and method to which the treatise bears a clear testimony was admittedly a ripe fruit of careful research and long pondering:

Pubbācariyamaggañ ca pucchitvā'va tahiṃ tahiṃ |
Dīpanāmo mahāpañño sutadharo vicakkhaṇo ||
Imaṃ vitthāra-sankhepaṃ sajjhāmaggena majjhime |
cintayitvā likhāpesi sissakānaṃ sukhāvahaṃ[1] ||

It is impossible in the face of the statement in the *Cullavagga*, Ch. XI, that only two Vinaya books were rehearsed at the First Council to believe in the tradition recorded by Buddhaghosa in the introduction to his *Dīghanikāya Commentary* that all the five books of the extant *Vinaya Piṭaka* were rehearsed there, to the exclusion of the two *Pātimokkhas* as separate texts. The *Cullavagga* account of the Second Council held in 100 B.E. presupposes the existence of some of the *Khandhakas* or *Saṃyuttas* now met with in the *Mahāvagga*. The citations from the *Bhikkhu Suttavibhanga* clearly prove its existence as an authoritative Vinaya text. The epilogue to the *Parivāra* expressly represents it as a treatise which was 'caused to be written',—a state of things which is inconceivable before the reign of Vaṭṭagāmaṇi. There is every reason to think that Dīpa, the author of this masterly digest of the contents of the *Vinaya Piṭaka,* was a Thera of Ceylon.

We need not attach much importance to the compilation of the two *Pātimokkhas* as two separate texts

---

1 Vinaya, Oldenberg's ed., V, p. 226.

with an appropriate introduction to each, which, too, appears to have been accomplished in Ceylon, this being, after all, a mechanical work within the ability of all scholars acquainted with the texts of the *Suttavibhaga*. The *Khuddakapāṭha* is a short Sutta manual for the beginners which was not universally recognized as a Canonical text must also have been a compilation made in Ceylon. The Theras of Ceylon may also be credited with the composition and compilation of the *Buddhavaṃsa, Cariyāpiṭaka* and *Apadāna* in their present forms, —the three legendary chronicles that, together with the *Khuddakapāṭha*, were not canonized by the Dīghabhāṇaka school. The mention of Sīhala in some of the MSS. of the *Buddhavaṃsa* is not accidental ; it may be treated as a positive evidence of its being a handiwork of Ceylon. The *Buddhavaṃsa* embodying the legends of twenty-four Buddhas was the composition and compilation of a time when Buddhism was spread as far north-west of India as Vajirā from which the name of the Vājiriya sect was derived, as far south-east as Kalinga, and as far south as the island of Ceylon.[1] As the citations in the *Jātaka Commentary* and Dhammapāla's commentary go to indicate, the present text of the *Cariyā Piṭaka* is only a reduced form of a larger anthology.[2] Though the legends in some form or other were of an Indian origin, the forms in which they are presented in the three companion works seem to show the literary skill

1 *Mahāvaṁsa*, V. 13.
2 Introduction to D. L. Barua's edition of the *Cariyā Piṭaka Comy*. (P.T.S.).

of Ceylon, though it is not of a high order. The contemporaneity of the legends embodied in the *Buddhavaṃsa* and *Apadāna* with the *Arthaśāstra* ascribed to Kauṭilya-Viṣṇugupta may be seen from the following comparison of certain common references in them:

Arthaśāstra, II. 11:

Māgadhikā Pauṇḍrikā Sauvarṇakuḍyakā ca patrorṇāḥ Tāsāṃ Sauvarṇakuḍyakā śreṣṭhā. Tathā Kauśeyaṃ Cīnapaṭṭāś ca Cīnabhūmijā vyākhyātāḥ.

Buddhavaṃsa, XXIV, 11:

Paṭṭuṇṇaṃ Cīnapaṭṭañ ca koseyyaṃ kambalam pi ca |
Sovaṇṇapādukañ[1] *c'eva adāsiṃ satthusāvake*[2] ||

The most important and, in many respects, the most original contribution of Ceylon consists in the priceless wealth of the Sinhalese Commentaries forming the authoritative literary basis, besides the Pali Canonical texts, the *Netipakaraṇa*, the *Peṭakopadesa* and the *Milinda*, for all the Pali commentaries, sub-commentaries glosses, the later Pali manuals and their various commentaries, sub-commentaries and glosses. These older commentaries, produced in Ceylon in the Sinhalese language, are clearly presupposed by all the extant Pali commentaries to the Canonical texts. With the single exception of the *Andhaka-Aṭṭhakathā*, utilised by Buddhaghosa in one of his Commentaries, there is no other

1 The *Arthaśāstra* list enables us to correct the Pali *sovaṇṇapādukaṁ to Sovaṇṇakuḍḍakaṁ.*
2 Cf. *Apadāna*, ii, p. 359.

work of this class in any part of India to vie with the three sets of Sinhalese Commentaries called the *Mahā-aṭṭhakathā*, the *Mahākurundiya* and the *Mahāpaccari*.

The first of them, as its name implies, was produced in the school of the Mahāvihāra or Great Minster. As Dr. Malalasekera points out[1], the *Mahā-aṭṭhakathā* is the oldest and most important of the commentaries on the three *Piṭakas*, 'brought, according to tradition, to Ceylon by Mahinda, who translated it into Sinhalese', from which circumstance it became known as *Sīhala-aṭṭha-kathā*. On the historical materials contained in it were based the two earlier Pali Chronicles, *viz.*, the *Dīpa-vaṃsa and Mahāvaṃsa*. It is often referred to simply as *Aṭṭhakathā*. The second, also called *Kurundi-aṭṭha-kathā* and *Kurundigandha*, derived its name from the Kurundaveḷu-vihāra in Ceylon where it was compiled. This *vihāra* must certainly have been different from the Kurundavihāra built by Aggabodhi I (A.D. 564-597) and repaired by Vijayabāhu I (A.D. 1058-1115). Dr. Malalasekera would seem right in suggesting that it was probably "chiefly concerned with Vinaya rules, for we find frequent references to it, particularly in the *Samantapāsādikā*". The third, *viz.*, the *Mahāpaccari* derived its name, according to tradition, from the circumstance of its having been compiled on a raft, somewhere in Ceylon. Like the *Mahākurundiya*, this commentary also seems to have been chiefly concerned with the *Vinaya Piṭaka*, its comments being quoted and discussed by

1 Malalasekera. *A Dictionary of Pali Proper names*, under *Mahā-aṭṭhakathā*.

Buddhaghosa only in his Vinaya Commentary.[1]

Besides these three Sinhalese Commentaries and the *Andha-aṭṭhakathā* produced and prevalent in South India, we have mention of such older commentaries as the *Saṃkhepa-aṭṭhakathā*, the *Āgama-aṭṭhakathā* and the *Porāṇa-aṭṭhakathā*. Mrs. Rhys Davids introduces the six earlier commentaries as follows :

"(1) The commentary of the dwellers in the North-Minster'—the Uttara Vihāra—at Anurādhapura.

(2) The *Mūla*, or *Mahā-aṭṭhakathā*, or simply ,the *Aṭṭhakathā*' of the dwellers in the 'Great Minster'—the Mahāvihāra—also at Anurādhapura.

(3) The *Andha-aṭṭhakathā*, handed down at Kāñcīpura (Conjeeveram) in South India.

(4) *Mahāpaccari* or Great Raft, said to be so called from its having been composed on a raft somewhere in Ceylon.

(5) The *Kurunda-aṭṭhakathā* so-called because it was composed at the Kuhundaveḷu Vihāra in Ceylon.

(6) The *Saṃkhepa-aṭṭhakathā* or short commentary, which, as being mentioned together with

---

1 *Samantapāsādikā*. Siamese Ed., i, p. 3 :
Tassa Mahā-aṭṭhakathaṁ sarīraṁ
katvā mahā-paccariyaṁ tath'eva,
Kurundināmādi-suvissutāsu
vinicchayo aṭṭhakathāsu vutto.
yo yuttamatthaṁ apariccajanto
tato pi antogadha-theravādaṁ.
saṁvaṇṇanaṁ sammāsamārabhissaṁ.

the Andha Commentary, may possibly be also South Indian."[1]

Most probably the *Āgamaṭṭhakathā* on which Buddhaghosa's Commentaries on the first Four *Nikāyas* were based, the *Vinayaṭṭhakathā* forming the basis of the *Samantapāsādikā*, and the *Porāṇaṭṭhakathā* containing the foundation of the rest of the commentaries as well as of the earlier Pali Chronicles[2] were broadly the three main divisions of the *Mahā-aṭṭhakathā* belonging to the Mahāvihāra school. There were also some traditions or traditional views in verses that passed as sayings of the *Porāṇas* or ancient teachers.[3]

When Buddhaghosa began to write commentaries he had before him four things to guide him in the matter, *viz.*, *Suttaṃ* (Canonical texts), *Suttānulomaṃ* (Pro-canonical works)[4], *Ācariyavādaṃ* (Commentaries of different schools), and *Attano mati* (Individual opinions). In the general order of preference the Canonical texts stood first, the individual opinions last, and the middle two in between them. But as wisely opined by Buddhaghosa in his *Samantapāsādikā*, none of the four was to be given precedence over the rest without proper scrutiny, careful testing and verification, and due consideration.

1 Mrs. Rhys Davids, *A Buddhist Manual of Psychological Ethics*, p. xxii.

2 Cf. *Atthasālinī*, p. 80, where a reference is made to the legends of king Duṭṭhagāmaṇi and others as embodied in the *Mahāaṭṭhakathā*.

3 B. C. Law, *The Life and Works of Buddhaghosa*, p. 65 ff.

4 Such as the *Netti-pakaraṇa*, *Peṭakopadesa* and *Milinda*. Buddhaghosa takes the word to mean the four *mahāpadesas*.

Thus within the bounds of loyalty and fairness there was room left for the development of the schools of interpretation representing the opinions of collective bodies of teachers and the free play of reason and progressive spirit. Buddha himself is said to have carefully laid down the fourfold method (*cattāro mahāpadesā*) of testing the validity and acceptability of an interpretation of his Doctrine and Discipline.[1]

There is no wonder then that in the Pali commentaries attributed to Buddhaghosa the views of different Sinhalese Commentaries and those of individual Theras of Ceylon have been quoted and discussed. As attested by them, the Dīghabhāṇakas, Majjhimabhāṇakas, Dhammapadabhāṇakas, and the like, who were originally but different schools of reciters of the Canonical texts[2], developed in Ceylon also into different schools of interpretation and opinion.[3]

The schisms which occurred in Ceylon dividing the Sangha at first into two rival sects and schools of Mahāvihāra and Abhayagiri, and subsequently the latter into two subsects called Dhammaruci and Sāgaliya proved to be contributory factors to the development of Buddhist literature, thought, art and architecture in the island. As for the occurrence of these schisms and the rise of the sects in Ceylon, there is no unanimity as yet in the evidence of the *Dīpavaṃsa* and the *Mahāvaṃsa*, the first of

1 *Samantapāsādikā*, i, p. ff.
2 Barua & Sinha, *Barhut Inscriptions*, note on *Bhānaka*.
3 B. C. Law, *op. cit.*, p. 62 ; Malalasekera, *Dict. of Pali Proper Names*, *sub voce Dīghabhānaka* and *Majjhimabhānaka*. Also *Atthasālinī*, p. 18.

which is quoted by name in such works of Buddhaghosa as the *Samantapāsādikā, Atthasālinī* and *Kathāvatthu-aṭṭhakathā.* The earlier Pali Chronicle does not speak of any feeling of animosity which existed between the Mahāvihāra and the Abhayagiri. As was then expected, there was just one Buddhist Church, the members whereof recited together the sacred texts and caused then to be reduced to writing.[1] The earlier Chronicle is unaware of the existence of any sects by the name of Dhammaruci and Sāgaliya, and the same remark hōlds true of Buddhaghosa whose account of the early Buddhist sects and schools is wholly based on its authority.[2] Even with reference to Mahāsena, the utmost that the *Dīpavaṁsa* has got to say is that the king came to extend his royal support and patronage to two persons, Mitta and Soṇa, and others who were of their opinion. Mitta and Soṇa were castigated by the orthodox as Dummitta and Pāpasoṇa for their wickedness in allowing persons under the age of twenty to be ordained as monks and holding the use of ivory fans as legal on the part of the monks.[3]

The later Chronicle, on the other hand, supplements the list of six Buddhist sects which arose in India after the earlier eighteen with a list of two sects called Dhammaruci and Sāgaliya, which arose in Ceylon.[4] It seems at first sight that the *Great Chronicle* traces the history of the first separation of the Abhayagiri monks

1 *Dīpavaṁsa,* Ch. XX: Oldenberg's Ed., p. 103.
2 *Ibid,* V. 54; *Kathāvatthu-A.,* p. 3.
3 *Ibid,* xxii, 65-75.
4 *Mahāvaṁsa,* V. 13.

from those of the Mahāvihāra to the latter part of Vaṭṭagāmaṇi, as also that of the secession of the Dakkhiṇavihārikas from those belonging to the monastery of Abhayagiri.[1] The *Mahāvaṃsa* proper does not clear up the historical connexion of the Abhayagiri sect with the Dhammarucis and Sāgaliyas. It is, moreover, silent on the heretical views of Mitta and Soṇa.

The partial reconciliation of the *Mahāvaṃsa* account with that in the earlier Chronicle is possible only on the hypothesis that the first separation between the two Vihāras took place not during the reign of Vaṭṭagāmaṇi but some time after that. According to the *Mahāvaṃsa,* the leader of the Abhayagiri schismatics was a Thera, Tissa of versatile learning, castigated as Bahalam-assuti Tissa, who led the schism to avenge the humility of excommunication meted out to his teacher Mahātissa. The secession of the Theras of the South Vihāra from those of Abhayagiri took place even some time later.

As the *Mahāvaṃsa Ṭīkā* would have us believe, the Theras of Abhayagiri were given the name of Dhammarucika when they seceded from the Mahāvihāra,[2]—a fact which is nowhere suggested in the *Mahāvaṃsa* proper. The same authority mentions also the points concerning certain minor rules of the *Vinaya*[3] on which the Abhayagiri seceders differed from the Mahāvihāra adherents of Theravāda, thereby justifying the connection which is

1 *Ibid,* xxxiii, 95-98.
2 *Mahāvaṃsa Ṭīkā,* p. 176.
3 *Ibid,* p. 676f.

sought to be established in the comparatively modern Sinhalese Chronicle, *Nikāya Sangraha*, between the Abhayagiri schismatics and the Vajjiputtakas of Vesāli. The *Nikāya Sangraha* simply supplements the *Mahāvaṃsa* story by adding that the Abhayagiri monks after the first separation from the Mahāvihāra "were strengthened by the arrival of some monks from Pallarārāma in South India" who were descendants of the Vijjiputtakas. The Abhayagiri leader, Mahā-Tissa, assumed himself the name of Dhammaruci who happened to be the teacher of those capricious monks from South India, and his followers became known as Dhammarucikas.[1]

In the *Mahāvaṃsa*, the Abhayagiri monks who started their mischievous activity during the reign of Goṭhābhaya *alias* Meghavannābhaya are given the appellation of Vetullavādins instead of that of Dhammarucikas. A Coḷa monk, called Sanghamitta, is brought into the scene to enact a tragic drama. We are told that after Goṭhābhaya banished sixty inmates of Abhayagiri who were found on enquiry to be the advocates of Vetullavāda, to avenge their cause, Sanghamitta, their Colian league, who was an adept in occultism and black arts, came across to Anurādhapura and managed to win the favour of Gothābhaya. The Abhayagiri monks became very powerful in their new establishment known as the Jetavana vihāra and figured as the Sāgaliyas. The course of things did not stop there. Some three hundred and fifty years after that and during the reign of Dāṭhopatissa, two Theras of the same name of Dāṭhavedhaka,

1 Malalasekera, *Dictionary*, i, p. 1148.

one belonging to the lesser Kurunda Pariveṇa and the other to the Kolambahālaka Pariveṇa, seceded from the Mahāvihāra by adopting into the *Vinaya Piṭaka* the Sāgalika version[1] of the two *Vibhangas* and the Dhammarucika version[2] of the *Khandhaka* and the *Parivāra*[3].

According to the comparatively modern Sinhalese tradition in the *Nikāya-Sangraha,* "A monk called Mahā-Tissa, incumbent of Abhayagiri, was convicted of living in domestic intercourse and expelled by the Mahāvihāra fraternity. They were strengthened by the arrival of some monks from Pallarārāma in South India, descendants of the Vajjiputtakas. Their teacher was Dhammaruci, and when they joined the Abhayagiri monks, Mahā-Tissa himself took the name of Dhammaruci and his followers became known as Dhammarucikas."[4] And as to the Sāgalikas or Sāgaliyas, they "took their name from their leader, Sāgala Thera, and their separation (from the Dhammarucikas) took place in the reign of king Goṭhābhaya."[5]

The information supplied in the *Nikāya Sangraha* regarding the Sāgaliyas is ingenious but not in conformity with the account in the *Mahāvaṃsa* which does not associate the Sāgaliyas with the reign of Goṭhābhaya. We are told, on the other hand, that king Goṭhābhaya sent

---

1,2 Note that the names of Sāgalika and Dhammarucika, are misplaced in Malalasekera's edition of the *Mahā vaṁsa Ṭīkā,* p. 176.

3 *Mahāvaṁsa Ṭīkā,* pp. 175-6; also *ibid,* p. 676.

4 Malalasekera, *Dictionary,* i, p. 1148.

5 *Ibid,* ii, p. 1000

into exile some sixty inmates of Abhayagiri who were found on examination to be Vetullavādins, to avenge whose cause a Colian monk called Sanghamitta, an adept in *bhūtavijjā* and such other occultic practices and black arts, came to Anurādhapura from the Indian shore and began to work inimically to the interests of Mahāvihāra.[1] He succeeded in his sinister plans in the reign of Mahāsena with the aid of his wicked counsellor Soṇa. The disaster was, however, averted through the intervention of the king's good friend and counsellor known as Meghavaṇṇābhaya.[2] Thereafter king Mahāsena, coming under the influence of the Thera of the Dakkhiṇavihāra called Tissa, built for him the Jetavana vihāra in the garden of Joti adjoining on the boundary of the Mahāvihāra.[3]

The *Mahāvaṃsa Ṭīkā* throws no light on the nature or character of *Vetullavāda* or its upholders who became active at Abhayagiri during the reign of Goṭhābhaya, nor is the name of *Vetullavāda* met with in any Indian inscriptions or texts. The name was evidently a Sinhalese invention. Buddhaghosa had the knowledge of the *Vetulla Piṭaka*[4] which he has condemned as *a-Buddhavacana* or unauthentic Word of Buddha. In his commentary to the *Kathāvatthu*, Buddhaghosa has characterised *Vetullavāda* as *Mahasuññatāvāda*[5] or the Mahāyāna doctrine of the Great Void and attributed certain

1 *Mahāvaṁsa,* xxxvi. 110-113.
2 *Ibid,* xxxvii. 2-28.
3 *Ibid,*xxxvii. 32-33.
4 Malalasekera, *Dictionary,* ii, p. 918.
5 *Kathāvatthu-A.,* xvii. 6.

extraordinary views to the Vetullavādins, all relating to the non-utility of making gifts to the Sangha and offerings in the name of Buddha. If these attributions are correctly made, there is little doubt that the *Vetullavāda* took Sangha to be a *Paramattha Sangha,*—an Order according to its ideal definition, and not a *Laukika Sangha* encouraging the merit-making business through gifts made to it, and also took Buddha to be a transcendental being beyond the reach of all offerings.[1] Thus it sought to bring into clear relief the ideals of Buddhism by throwing into shade the degeneracy of the religion of Buddha into a cheap merit-producing artifice. But the views in the *Kathāvatthu* which are ascribed to Vetullavāda are not strictly to be identified with the Mahāyāna doctrine of *mahāśūnyatā.*[2]

The earlier Chinese pilgrim, Fa Hian, who arrived at Ceylon evidently during the reign of king Kitti-Siri-Meghavaṇṇa, found it more congenial to reside for two years at Abhayagiri when it was at the height of its power. He witnessed a ceremonial procession led by the reigning king in honour of the Tooth-relic of Buddha enshrined in the Abhayagiri Hall, as well as a representation of 500 *Jātakas,* meaning that the Abhayagiri version contained just 500 birth-stories, which was according to the *Culla Niddesa* (p. 80), the Canonical total of the *Jātakas.* The Abhayagiri monks numbered 5,000, while the Mahāvihāra was tenanted by 3,000

1 *Kathāvatthu Aṭṭhakathā,* xvii. 6-10.

2 variant, *mahāpuññatā,* Siamese ed.

monks, among whom one was a very eminent *śrāmaṇa* revered as an *Arhat*. He returned to China with a copy (obtained from Abhayagiri) of the Mahīśāsaka version of the *Vinaya Piṭaka,* a copy of the *Dirghāgama,* a copy of the *Saṃyuktāgama* (?), and also a collection of *Prakaraṇa (Abhidhamma) Piṭaka* (?).[1] None of these was a Mahāyāna work. He nowhere specifically mentions, as Hwen Thsang does,[2] that the Abhayagirikas studied both Vehicles (Hīnayāna and Mahāyāna), while the Mahāvihārins adhered exclusively to the teaching of the of the Little Vehicle, opposing that of the Great.[3]

I place before you all the available materials for a history of the early Buddhist sects in Ceylon just to enable you to form your own opinion about it. Although Hwen Thsang was aware of the tradition according to which the separation between Mahāvihāra and Abhayagiri took place two hundred years after the establishment of Buddhism by Mahinda, it lends no weight to the tradition itself which was of a later origin and has found no mention in the *Dīpavaṃsa.* If we have rightly followed the course of events, the secession of one sect from another rested on differences in certain unimportant Vinaya rules. It is evident from Fa Hian's testimony that the Abhayagirikas held the Mahīśāsaka version of the *Vinaya Piṭaka* as authoritative. The legality of ordaining under the age of twenty, conferring ordina-

1 Beal, *op. cit.*, i, p. lxxixf.
2 Beal, *op. cit.*, ii, p. 247.
3 Beal, *op. cit.*, i, pp. lxxii-lxxx.

tion through messengers, and of using ivory fans[1] is the Vinaya heresy which the *Dīpavaṃsa* attributes to Mitta and Soṇa of Mahāsena's time is mentioned in the *Mahāvaṃsa Ṭīkā* as the cause of the separation between Abhayagiri and Mahāvihāra as early as Vaṭṭagāmaṇi's time. The *Nikāya Sangraha* brings in the influence of Vajjiputtaka monks from the Pallarārāma in South India with Dhammaruci as their teacher to account for the transformation of the Abhayagirikas into a Sinhalese sect of the Dhammarucikas. The information supplied in the *Mahāvaṃsa Ṭīkā* is important as indicating the historical process behind the development of the Paccari and Kurunda Commentaries in Sinhalese on the *Vinaya Piṭaka*. It is not improbable that the *Kurunda* or *Kurundaveḷu aṭṭhakathā* was just another name of the Jetavanika, and the *Paccari aṭṭhakathā* was the Sinhalese or Pali name for the Pallari *alias* Abhayagiri. Though the differences for this reason or that were going on between the monks of the Mahāvihāra and the Abhayagiri from an earlier time, these came really to a head during Goṭhābhaya's reign. The terms *Vetullavāda* and *Vetullapiṭaka* or *Vedaḷhapiṭaka* invented at the Mahāvihāra were meant only to signify a doctrine or scripture which was irregular to or irreconcilable with Theravāda tradition, but which was not necessarily Mahāyāna at first. The Abhayagiri school, whatever else it might be, stood obviously for a comparative study of the texts of different Buddhist sects, though Theravāda was its main

1 *Mahāvaṁsa Ṭīkā*, p. 676.

stand. In other words, the rivalry between the two schools was a sign of health, and to it we owe the enrichment of Buddhist ideas and the growth of the profoundly learned *Vinaya Vinicchayas* (Legal Decisions) that have been quoted *in extenso* in the *Samantapāsādikā*, and formed the bases of the metrical manuals of Buddhadatta and the groundwork of the *Pālimuttaka Vinaya-vinicchaya-sangaha*, which is a masterly Vinaya treatise compiled in Ceylon by Sāriputta, a Thera of the Jetavana Vihāra, in the time of king Parakkamabāhu I and at his instance. Although the data available are yet meagre, it seems probable that there were two slightly different versions of the earlier Island Chronicle, *Dīpavaṃsa*, some variations in readings being noticeable in the text quoted by Buddhaghosa and the other edited by Oldenberg[1]. The two schools produced two different commentaries on the *Mahāvaṃsa*, the Cambodian version retaining probably the Commentary written at Abhayagiri and bearing the evidence of a greater Indian contact. If the Mahāvihāra made a great hero of Buddhaghosa as the author of the *Visuddhimagga*, the Abhayagiri vihāra had all the more reason to be proud of its celebrity, Thera Upatissa, who forestalled Buddhaghosa in his *Vimuttimagga*.[2]

The Pali scholiasts headed by Buddhaghosa have

---

1 Cf. the *gāthā* describing Suvaṇṇabhūmi in connection with the Buddhist mission sent to it.

2 For the connection of Upatissa with the Abhayagiri school, see Dr. P. V. Bapat's *Vimuttimagga and Visuddhimagga*, introd., pp. xxxix, xli, lviii.

enjoyed all the credit at the cost of the Theras of Ceylon, and their writings regarded as masterpieces have not only eclipsed the glory of the Sinhalese *Commentaries* but driven them out of existence. The *Buddhaghosuppatti* cheerfully records the fact that when Buddhaghosa admirably rendered the Sinhalese *Commentaries* into Pali, these great works standing to the credit of Thera Mahinda were heaped up into a mound and burnt up. The contemporary king of Ceylon remarked, saying, "I have never seen before a *samaṇa* like him who is religious, of quick intellect and really meditative."[1] The voice of Buddhaghosa was considered as deep as that of the Buddha himself. The Theras of Mahāvihāra proclaimed him to be veritably a Metteyya, the Future Buddha.

In fairness to Buddhaghosa and other Pali scholiasts who were Indians it may be said that they frankly acknowledged their indebtedness to the Sinhalese *Commentaries*. Although they wrote out the *Aṭṭhakathās* with meticulous care and almost as independent works, they humbly stated that all that they did was to replace in them the Sinhalese language *(apanetvā Sīhalabhāsaṃ)* with the language of the Canon which latter in their belief was, 'a lovely and faultless diction' *(āropetvā manoramaṃ bhāsaṃ Tantinayānucchavikaṃ vigatadosaṃ)*[2]. Thus indirectly the Sinhalese language was underestimated. What pains me especially is that their Sinhalese

1. *Buddhaghosuppatti*, ed. by James Gray, p. 53 f,

2. *Sumangala-vilāsinī*, i, p. 1.

brethren could be so easily persuaded to acquiesce in this, forgetting that in condemning their own language they themselves would stand self-condemned. The loss of the old *Commentaries* in Sinhalese is irretrievable. Sinhalese, as may be seen from the numerous early inscriptions of Ceylon, was an Aryan speech, in which was produced an extensive exegetical literature, and that at so early an age. It is, however, a fair statement when it is said in the introductory stanzas of the *Samantapāsādikā* that the presentation of the work in Pali was intended to render it widely accessible even to the *Bhikkhus* outside Ceylon whose language was not Sinhalese.[1]

As to Buddhaghosa, the master commentator, to whom the tradition has indiscriminately ascribed several commentaries it may, perhaps, be established now beyond doubt that Buddhaghosa, the author of the Vinaya Commentary, *Samantapāsādikā* with its sequel—the *Kankhāvitaraṇī* is not the same individual as Buddhaghosa whose great fame rests on the *Visuddhimagga*. The latter, too, is a different individual from the putative Buddhaghosa who passes as the author of the *Dhammapada-aṭṭhakathā* and the extant *Jātaka Commentary*. It may be taken for granted from internal references

---

1 *Samantapāsādikā*, Siamese Ed., i, p. 2:
Saṁvaṇṇanā Sīhaladīpakena
vākyena esā pana saṁkhatattā
na kiñci attham abhisambhūnāti
Dīpantare bhikkhujanassa yasmā
tasmā imaṁ Pālinayānurūpaṁ
saṁvaṇṇanaṁ dāni samārabhissaṁ.

that the author of the *Visuddhimagga* was also the author of the *Commentaries* to the first Four *Nikāyas* and the seven books of the *Abhidhamma Piṭaka*.[1] The Cūlavaṃsa describes him as a Brāhman youth from Bodhimaṇḍa (Bodhgayā) and refers his literary activities in Ceylon to the reign of Mahānāma. He is said to have travelled to Ceylon at the instance of his teacher, Thera Revata. But this Revata finds no mention in any work of Buddhaghosa. The *Cūlavaṃsa* mentions Sanghapāla as the leading Thera of Mahāvihāra with whom Buddhaghosa learnt all about the *Commentaries* and Theravāda, a fact which is corroborated by the compliment paid to the great Thera by Buddhaghosa himself in the *nigamana* to his *Visuddhimagga*[2].

Buddhaghosa, the author of the *Visuddhimagga*, resided sometimes at Kāñcīpura (Conjeeveram) and other places (in South India) and sometimes at the Mahāvihāra in Anurādhapura. Among other places in South India, in the *nigamana* to the *Papañcasūdanī* we

---

1 Rev. A. P. Buddhadatta in his article on Buddhaghosa in the recent issue of the Journal of the University of Ceylon seeks to maintain that Buddhaghosa who was the author of the *Visuddhimagga, Samantapāsādikā* and commentaries to the first four *Nikāyas* was not the author of the commentaries to the seven books of the *Abhidhamma Piṭaka*. It may be pointed out that the *Abhidhamma Commentaries* refer to the *Visuddhimagga* as the work in which certain topics were more elaborately treated evidently by the same author, while the *Vinaya Commentary* makes no such reference either in its Prologue or in its Epilogue.

2 *Mahāvihāravāsinām vaṁsajassa vibhāvino vuttino |*
ajjhesanam gahetvā va karontena imam mayā ||

have mention of an important town and emporium of trade of which the name varies as Mayūrarūpapaṭṭana and Mayūrasuttapaṭṭana (in Siamese edition), which may have been just a mistake for Madhurasuttapaṭṭana, meaning the city of Madoura noted as a mart for cotton fabrics. The *Saddhammasangaha* connects Buddhaghosa also with Nāgapaṭṭana (modern Nāgapaṭam)[1]. The great contemporaries at whose request or in response to whose wishes he compiled the *Visuddhimagga* and eleven other works were Bhadanta Sanghapāla of the Mahāvihāra, Bhadanta Dāṭhanāga of the Sumangala vihāra, Bhadanta Buddhamitta of Mayūra (Madhura?) suttapaṭṭana, Bhadanta Jotipāla, Bhikkhu Buddhaghosa[2] described also as Yati Buddhaghosa[3]. In none of these works there is reference to the contemporary king of Ceylon. The earlier kings of the island who find mention are Duṭṭhagāmaṇi Abhaya, Mahānāga *alias* Coranāga (3 B.C.–1 A.D.). Among the Indian kings, we have mention of Sātavāhana (variant Setavāhana) who is mythical more or less. The length of reign given to king Mahānāma (A.D. 409-31) in the Geiger's edition of the *Cūlavaṃsa* is 22 years; it is just 12 years according to the text cited by Dhammatilaka in the Siamese edition of the *Visuddhimagga*, iii, p. 385.[4] Rev. Dhammatilaka bases his account of this Buddhaghosa on the legends in the *Saddhammasangaha*, the *Mahāvaṃsa* (*i.e.*,

1 *Saddhammasangaha*, J.P.T.S., 1890, p. 53.

2 *Nigamana* to *Atthasālinī*.

3 *Nigamana* to *Sammohavinodanī*.

4 *bhūtvā dvādasavassāni Mahānāmo mahāmati,*

Geiger's *Cūlavaṃsa)*, the *Buddhaghosanidāna (i.e., Buddhaghosuppatti)* and the *Vaṃsamālinī (i.e., Mahāvaṃsa Ṭīkā)*, and refers us especially to *Ñāṇodyaya*,[1] an earlier work ascribed to Buddhaghosa in the *Cūlavaṃsa.*

As for Buddhaghosa, the author of the *Samantapāsādikā* translated into Chinese by Sanghabhadra in A.D. 489, the case is altogether different. In the *nigamana* to this great work its author expressly refers to the contemporary ruler of Ceylon as king Siri-kuḍḍa Siripāla Siri-nivāsa or simply as king Siri-nivāsa and states that he began to compile it in the 20th year and completed it at the commencement of the 21st year of the reign of this king.[2] He undertook to write this Commentary when peace prevailed after a troublesome time. His words in the *nigamana* betray a fearful feeling of uncertainty about the political condition of the country,[3] which is conspicuous by its absence in the writings of Buddhaghosa, the author of the *Visuddhimagga.* And it is not quite correct to say with Dr. B. C. Law that the author of the *Samantapāsādikā* "apoligises for undertaking to write, *first of all,* a commentary on the *Vinaya Piṭaka,* contrary to the usual order of Dhamma and

---

1 *Visuddhimagga,* Siamese ed., iii, p. 386:
Visesaṁ ñātukāmena tattha tattha yathārahaṁ |
Buddhaghasanidāne pi Vaṁsamāliniyam pi va
Ñaṇodaye visese pi viññātabbā va viññunā ||

2 *Palāyantassa sakalaṁ Lankādīpaṁ nirabbudaṁ |*
rañño Siri-nivāsassa siripāla-yasassino |
āraddhā ekavīsamhi sampatte pariniṭṭhitā ||

3 *Upaddavā kule loke.....*

Vinaya."[1] There is no such apology offered by him. All that he says is that he began to write a commentary to the *Vinaya* on the existence of which depended the existence of Buddha's Order.[2]

Elsewhere the additional epithet of *Sirikuḍḍa* is given to the same contemporary ruler. It is not historically sound to identify this ruler with Mahānāma simply on the ground that Mahānāma has been honoured with the epithet of Siri-nivāsa in a Sinhalese work of later date.[3] The *Dhammapada Commentary*, which too is ascribed to Buddhaghosa, is said to have been compiled in a monastery erected for him at Anurādhapura near about the Mahāvihāra and Mahābodhi shrine by king Sirikūṭa whose identity is yet to be established. There are two important internal data of chronology afforded by the *Samantapāsādikā*, the first of whcih is the allusion to the Rudradāmaka and other coins (Ruddadāmakādi), rather in their debased forms, and the second consists in certain quotations from the *Dīpavaṃsa* mentioned by name. The first datum compels us to place the date of compilation of the *Samantapāsā-*

---

1 *The Life and Work of Buddhaghosa*, p. 77.

2 *Samantapāsādikā*, i, p. 2.

3 Malalasekera, *The Pali Lit., of Ceylon*, pp. 84, 96. The employment of the epithet of *Siri-nivāsa* is not decisive in an orgument of identity on account of the the fact that in the epilogue to *Cūla-Niddesavaṇṇanā*, the same epithet adorns the name of king Siri-Sanghabodhi:

rañño Siri-nivāsassa Sirisanghassa Bodhino.

dikā at least in the latter half of the third century A.D.[1]; and as regards the second, if the *Dīpavaṃsa* was then extant as closed with the reign of Mahāsena, the date of the *Vinaya Commentary* must be placed after Mahāsena's rule. To these must also be added the fact that the growth of the Kurundiya or Kurundaveḷu Commentary which is presupposed by the *Samantapāsādikā* was not possible before the erection of the Jetavana vihāra by king Mahāsena. Seeing that the writing of the *Samantapāsādikā* is definitely referred to the twentieth year of the reign of the contemporary ruler, our choice must lie between Kitti-Siri-Meghavaṇṇa who is known as a great contemporary of Samudragupta with a long reign of 47 years and Mahānāma with a reign of 22 years. The length of the reign of the latter being given also as 12 years in a Siamese text of the *Chronicle,* we may preferably rivet our attention on Meghavaṇṇa, the greatest king of Ceylon after Devānampiya Tissa and Duṭṭhagāmaṇi who rightly deserved all the three epithets of *Siri-kuḍḍa, Siri-pāla,* and *Siri-nivāsa.* Among the earlier kings, one might single out the name of Sirināga I (A.D. 249-68), the immediate successor of Kuḍḍanāga (variant Kuñcanāga), but unfortunately the length of his reign is given as 19 years. One may easily rule out the name of Mahānāma also for these two reasons that he could not, after all, be a good royal patron of the Mahāvihāra and that his reign was not so eventful politically as to fit

1 C. D. Chatterji, *Numismatic Data from Pali Literature* in B. C. Law's *Buddhistic Studies,* i

in with the picture of the time envisaged in the epilogue to the *Samantapāsādikā* :

palāyantassa sakalaṃ Lankādīpaṃ nirabbudaṃ ;

"when all the disturbing forces having fled away, the whole of the island of Lankā was rendered unulcerated", the allusion here being evidently to the quelling of the disturbances caused by the Tamil hordes and others.

The distinctness of Buddhaghosa, the author of the *Visuddhimagga,* from his namesake who was the author of the *Samantapāsādikā*[1] may also be established on another important ground. At the time of the stay of the former the head of the Mahāvihāra was Bhadanta Sanghapāla in accordance with whose behest *(ajjhesanaṃ gahetvāna)* the *Visuddhimagga* was written, whereas at the time of the arrival of the latter Thera Buddhasiri was the head who was evidently succeeded in his office by Bhadanta Buddhamitta with whom the latter studied the *Vinaya Commentaries.*[1] Buddhasiri must have died shortly after his arrival at Mahāvihāra, otherwise he would not have said, "perfectly remembering whose behest I would begin to write the Commentary :

saṃvaṇṇanaṃ dāni samārabhissaṃ
ajjhesanaṃ Buddhasirivhayassa
Therassa sammāsamanussaranto.[2]

During the sojourn of Fa Hian for two years in Ceylon, probably also in Meghavaṇṇa's time, a very eminent *śramaṇa* of the Mahāvihāra who was revered as

1 *Epilogue* to the *Samantapāsādikā.*
2 *Prologue* to *ibid.*

an Arhat died, and he was an eye-witness to the grand funeral rites with which the king and people of Ceylon disposed of his dead body. The contemporary eminent *Śramaṇa* of Abhayagiri was known as Dhammakitti (*Ta-mo-kui-ti*) It would seem most probable that the earlier Chinese pilgrim has recorded here the demise of Thera Buddhasiri of the Mahāvihāra. If so, Buddhaghosa, the author of the *Samantapāsādikā*, must have been at Anurādhapura at the time of Fa Hian's visit.

When the Chinese pilgrim was residing in Ceylon, he heard an eloquent Buddhist religious preacher from India whose discourse was evidently based on a legendary work, which, if not actually the *Anāgatavaṃsa* ascribed to a Colian monk called Kassapa, was at least a prototype of it. The main theme of this work was the advent of the Future Buddha, Maitreya, in connection with which it contained a prophecy regarding wanderings of the almsbowl (*pātra*) of Buddha originally preserved at the time in the borders of Gandhāra. The places where the alms-bowl would be taken thereafter until Maitreya's advent were the western Yüe-chï country, Khotān, Kouche, Siṃhala (Ceylon), Mid-India, and lastly, the heaven of Tuṣita. A similar prophecy is recorded by Buddhaghosa, the author of the *Visuddhimagga*, in his commentary to the *Bahudhātuka Sutta, Majjhima Nikāya*.[1] It is very likely that Kassapa, the Colian monk and putative author to whom the *Anāgatavaṃsa* is

---

1 *Papañca-sūdanī*, Siamese ed., III, p. 523 f.

ascribed, was no other than Kumāra Kassapa at whose request the *Dhammapada-aṭṭhakathā* was undertaken to be written[1], as well as that this Kumāra Kassapa was probably the eloquent Indian preacher who was at Anurādhapura in Fa Hian's time. He must have been, as an individual, different from Guṇabhadra, a *Śramaṇa* of Mid-India, who on his way to China in A.D. 435 passed through Ceylon and translated thereafter into Chinese two books of the Little Vehicle called *Saṃyuktāgama* and *Abhidharmaprakaraṇapāda*[2] of which the copies were obtained, as we saw, by Fa Hian, from Abhayagiri. This Indian monk may have been the agent to carry with him the texts of Upatissa's *Vimuttimagga*[3] and Buddhaghosa's *Samantapāsādikā*[5] from Ceylon to China.

If the credit for the writing of the Pali Commentaries to the *Vinaya Piṭaka,* the first Four *Nikāyas,* the whole of the *Abhidhamma Piṭaka,* and the eight or nine[4] out of the sixteen books[5] of the *Khuddaka Nikāya* belongs to two Buddhaghosas, Buddhadatta and Dhammapāla, all of whom were Indians, the credit of authorship of the remaining eight or seven books is due certainly to the Theras of Ceylon, and it is to be divided

1 *Dhp. A.*, iv, p. 236.

2 Nanjio, *Catalogue*, p. 415 f.

3 Bapat, *op. cit.*, introd., p. xvii.

4 Eight excluding and nine including the commentary on the Apadāna.

5 Counting the *Culla-Niddesa* and the *Mahā-Niddesa* as two books.

among Culla Buddhaghosa,[1] Mahānāma[2] and Upasena[3].

On such grounds as the difference in language and style between the *Dhammapada Commentary* and the *Aṭṭhakathās* 'which undoubtedly belong to Buddhaghosa', the author of the *Visuddhimagga,* the authenticity of the tradition ascribing the former to Buddhaghosa has been doubted by Spence Hardy, Burlingame and others. Dr. B. C. Law has sought to defend the tradition on the grounds stated in his work on Buddhaghosa. None of them has so far been interested to inquire and ascertain if there was a Ceylonese Buddhaghosa who has been confounded with Buddhaghosa of either the fame of the *Visuddhimagga* or that of the *Samantapāsādikā.* Buddhaghosa of the *Visuddhimagga* fame himself states that he undertook to write his commentaries to the first two *Abhidhamma* books at the instance of one Bhikkhu or Yati Buddhaghosa who was obviously a younger colleague of his in the Mahāvihāra.

The distinctness of Buddhaghosa, the author of the serial commentary, *Paramatthajotikā,* from Buddhaghosa, the author of the *Samantapāsādikā,* and Buddhaghosa, the author of the *Visuddhimagga,* may be established on the internal evidence of the four commentaries included in the *Paramatthajotikā series.* Let us examine, first of

1 Known as the author of the *Paramatthajotikā,* a serial commentary to the *Khuddakapāṭha, the Dhammapada,* the *Sutta-nipāta* and the *Jātaka-nikāya.*

2 Known as the author of the commentary to the *Paṭisambhidāmagga.*

3 Known as the author of the commentaries to the two *Niddesas.*

all, the *Khuddakapāṭha Commentary* in which each section is a masterly dissertation going ahead of the treatment of the topic or topics met with in the writings of other two Buddhaghosas.[1] The same argument holds true in the case of the *Dhammapada Commentary.*[2] The *Jātaka Commentary* which, as shown by Dr. B. C. Law, has come down to us in two slightly different recensions, Ceylonese and Cambodian-Pagan, narrates somewhat differently the birth-stories which are cited in the writings of other two Buddhaghosas. Dr. Malalasekera is inclined to identify the author of the *Jātaka Commentary* with Culla-Buddhaghosa at whose request the commentaries to the *Abhidhamma* were written.[3] The text of the *Jātaka-aṭṭhakathā* edited by Fausböll was written at the instance of Thera Buddhadeva of the Mahiṃsāsaka sect of which a representative group of monks was found by Fa Hian in the island[4], precisely as there existed a Vanavāsī fraternity in the eighth or ninth century A.D.

In the next stage of fruitful activity one is to watch how the Theras of Ceylon and those of South India, parti-

1 Compare the dissertation on the Three Refuges here with that on the same subject in the *Sumangala-vilāsinī* to the *Sāmaññaphala* Sutta, and the dissertation on the Ten Precepts with that on the same subject in the *Samantapāsādikā.*

2 Compare, for instance, the explanation of the verse, No : 4 : *pare ca na vijānanti* etc. here with that offered in the *Samantapāsādikā* to the *Mahāvagga*, Ch. X.

3 *Dictionary,* ii, p. 307.

4 *Ibid,* i, p. 270, under Ānanda who "became head of the Vanavāsī fraternity in the island."

cutarly those belonging to the country of Coḷa, vied or co-operated with each other in producing the sub-commentaries in the form of *Ṭīkās* and *Anuṭīkās,* as well as in preparing compendia and manuals. Although the credit of writing all the earlier *Abhidhamma Ṭīkās, Anuṭīkās* and manuals and compendia is due to the Colian Theras, as regards the Anuruddha's compendium, *Abhidhammatthasangaha,* forming as it does the basis of an extensive *Abhidhamma* literature in Burma, the *Porāṇa Ṭīkā* and the *Vibhāvanī* stand to the credit of Ceylon. The authoritative *Ṭīkā, Sāratthadīpanī,* to the *Vinaya Commentary* is equally a notable contribution from Ceylon.

If thus in the matter of development of the *Abhidhamma* literature the position of the South Indian Theras was supreme, in the field of *Chronicles,* in both Pali and Sinhalese, the position of the Theras of Ceylon was unique and unrivalled. With the legendary prototypes in the *Buddhavaṃsa, Cariyāpiṭaka* and *Apadāna* and the traditional sayings in verse in the background, the Theras of Ceylon composed, first of all, the *Dīpavaṃsa,* and next, the *Mahāvaṃsa* with its continuation up till Parakkama's time.[1] Such chronicles in Sinhalese as the

1 The *Mahāvaṁsa* proper with Duṭṭhagāmaṇi as its hero was composed by Mahānāma; the *Cūḷavaṁsa* with Parakkamabāhu the Great as its hero composed by Dhammakitti: the second portion of the *Cūḷavaṁsa* with Kitti-Siri as its hero by Tibboṭuvāvē Siddhattha and concluded with a chapter added by Hikkāḍuvē Siri Sumangala. A laudable attempt has been made by the Venerable Yagirala Paññānanda to bring it down to modern time.

Pūjāvaliya, the *Rājāvaliya* and the *Nikāyasangraha* deserve here respectful mention. The *Mañjuśrī Mūlakalpa* and Kalhaṇa's *Rājataranginī* are the two later Indian legendary chronicles of the *Dīpavaṃsa* type with much less historical accuracy. The *Purāṇas* contain dynastic lists of kings, but it has been found that the chronology of the rulers of Magadha as found in the two Pali *Chronicles* of Ceylon is more authentic and reliable. The *Mahāvaṃsa* proper which is not unduly judged as the national epic of Ceylon with Duṭṭhagāmaṇi as its hero stands as a literary masterpiece from the pen of Thera Mahānāma. It may not be an epic of as high literary merit as Vālmīki's *Rāmāyaṇa*, Sautī's *Mahābhārata* or Firdausi's *Shah-nama*,— an epic it is throughout with a keen sense of history, the simplicity of diction, the purity of style, and the sobriety of judgement. Its central idea or moral looms large at the end of each chapter bringing out the evanescent character of kingly career and dynastic rule and emphasizing the importance of the meritorious deeds that alone are left behind to be gratefully remembered. I would call and always judge it as the great and only national epic of Ceylon chiefly for the reason that through it the national mind, self-consciousness and character have found a permanent expression.

Although inspired by Sanskrit models from India, the Theras of Ceylon acted as pioneers in the matter of Pali lexicography, as well as in the field of Pali grammar. Two powerful schools of grammar developed in Ceylon, one, the Kaccāyana, and the other, the Moggallāna, the first in the line of Kalāpa Kātantra, and the second in the line of Pāṇini, Candra and Kātyāyana, each having to its credit a large number of learned treatises.

The *Jinacarita* written by Thera Vanaratana Medhankara of the Vijayahāhupariveṇa may not be a poem on the life of Buddha of as high poetic merit as Aśvaghoṣa's *Buddhacarita,* but it is undoubtedly the best work of its kind in Pali.

In the field of folk literature produced in Ceylon the name of the *Rasavāhinī* figures foremost as a collection of stories in Pali by Vedeha, a monk of the Vanavāsī fraternity in Ceylon. But even this work with its better grouping of the stories broadly under two heads, as those relating to India and as those to Ceylon, was, as pointed out by Geiger and Dr. Malalasekera, based on an earlier work called *Sahassavatthuppakaraṇa,* which finds mention in the *Mahāvaṃsa Ṭīkā* as being one of its sources.

Although there are traces of some later Buddhist works in Sanskrit which pass indiscriminately under the name of Mahāyāna, there is none known to have been written in Ceylon by a Ceylonese author. But Ceylon can certainly boast of her great son, Āryadeva of the Śūnyavāda school, who is known as the author of the *Śatavaipulya Śāstra* (*Śatasāhasrikā Prajñpāramitā?*) and who figured as one of the four Mahāyāna Dikpālas placed in charge of the southern quarter, *i.e.,* South India.[1] If Buddhaghosa's identification of *Vetullavāda* (better *Vaipulyavāda*) with *Mahāsuññatāvāda* (the great Doc-

1 Beal, *Buddhist Records,* i, pp. 188 f., 231; pp. 97-99, 210, 227, 302.

trine of the Void)[1] be correct, Āryadeva must have flourished in the country of Coḷa and Ceylon in at least the fourth century A.D.

Literature with the collective experience and thought of the country embodied in it is just one of the phases—may be the most important phase—of culture. There are other phases to consider, notably the art and architecture in and through which the national mind and heart of Ceylon found a tangible expression. As to that, I may observe at the outset that there may not be any contribution which is either wholly original in conception or superfine in execution but the remnants that still linger are not without their distinctness and artistic merit. The *leṇas* or so-called caves to be seen here and there, especially those of old, are all invariably natural rock slopes and projections or grottoes which are rudely touched by human hand. The rock slopes (*pabbhāras*) are slightly chiselled, leaving the edges untouched so as to prevent rain-water from streaming down over their inner surfaces serving as ceilings or roofs. The earlier monastic buildings in Anurādhapura and Pulatthipura have nothing very remarkable about them save and except their excellent ground plans, groupings, early use of cement and engineering skill in combining brick-work with stone in the art of masonry, even utilising intervening rock elevations above the ground. The semi-circular piece of moonstone forming the door-sill to the central building and finely carved with the four animal figures and lotus plant and geese device of Aśoka's

1 *Kathāvatthu Commentary,* P.T.S. ed., XVII. 6.

monoliths is certainly a striking feature, to which might be added the urinal plate of stone with the Vaijayanta palace carved on it, which is eloquently expressive of the Buddhist clerical contempt for worldly or heavenly prosperity. Crowning all is what is popularly known as the *makara torana* which is delicately executed and neatly decorated. The *dvibhanga* pose of the standing figure of the two Nāgas on the guard-stones is really beautiful. There is nowhere to be noticed much of ornamentation and gorgeousness. The high-walled Lankātilaka vihāra stands as the acme of perfection reached in the whole of Ceylon in respect of monastic architecture. The brick-built parapet with its fine, polished and weather-proof plaster-coating on the fresco-side of the Sigiriya rock cannot but remind us at first sight of the mirror-like polished surface of Aśoka's monoliths.

The Mahāthūpa with its lofty height and imposing but graceful mound stands as the architectural landmark of the island. Other *Dāgobas* around it conform all to its ground plan, general appearance, technique and style of art, even including the Kaṇṭaka cetiya on the Cetiyapabbata (Mihintāle). An exception to the general rule is offered by the Thūpārāma which is *ghaṇṭākāra* (bell-shaped) and enclosed by a colonnade formed of rough-hewn and palmyra-palm-shaped pillars of stone, which obviously supported a roof. Another exception is afforded by far the later paddy-shaped *(dhaññākāra)* shrine, such as the Dāgoba at Kelāniya. The art tradition of the Thūpārāma colonnade continued up till the twelfth century and may be seen maintained at Mādirigiriya and Vāṭadāge (Polunnāruva). The Mahāthūpa class of Buddhist *stūpas* in Ceylon came subsequently to be provided with four *vahalkaḍas* or entrance-points, containing each an image inside it, a feature which is so prominent at the Shwe Dagon Pagoda of Burma. Though for the general form, technique and purpose the island was indebted to the art tradition of the *stūpas* at Bharhut and Sāñcī, the Mahāthūpa represents even without its *vahalkaḍas,* a purely Ceylon architecture as regards its inner inspiration, main conception and method of execution. In it the Indian *harmikā* or *hti* with the parasol or parasols supported upon it is replaced by the *chatrāvalī* forming a pinnacle tapering gradually to a vanishing point,—an architectural device more delicately worked out in the Shwe Dagon.

The Sīhagiri (Sigiriya) stands as "a mighty rock", which only the stony heart of a parricide like Kassapa I could have the courage to bring under the control of human will and to direct his artist or band of artists to use the inner face of its hood-like projection as the suitable ground for the finest and most delicate of the Ceylon frescoes. The Sigiriya ladies who are typically the court beauties of the island are all to be seen in various dancing gaits and poses. But they are not to be taken as going to pay their worship at the nearest shrine because they are carrying flowers in their hands. It seems to me that what is intended to be displayed is the wily art of the court ladies or expert courtezans of the royal harem to please their only beloved person—the king. As the graffiti on the parapet go to indicate, the impressions produced by these ladies on the visitors with poetic temperament were far from being religious and the feelings evoked were other than devotional. The themes of later paintings are almost invariably taken from the Pali versions of Buddha legends, and their colour effects are generally very sober and fine.

I need not dwell at length on the bronzes of Ceylon which are all later and belong mostly to northern districts of the island. These are legacies of Mahāyāna influence from South India and represent nothing but a provincial development of the South Indian art. Attention is drawn by Dr. A. K. Coomaraswamy to the figurines of Avalokiteśvara and Jambhala or Kubera, one glowing in its spirituality and distinguishing itself from the other representing the most earthy of the worldly-minded. The art and architecture testifies to the fact that the religious heart of the island knew no compromise between the way to the Victoria of Indra's heaven and that to the bliss of *Nirvāṇa.*

Almost all the images of Buddha installed for worship at Anurādhapura and other places in Ceylon are in *dhyānamudrā* or meditation-posture, and they represent as such the state of enlightenment of Buddha. They are lacking, as pointed out to me by Dr. Paranavitana, in the fine æsthetic grace and spirituality of the Gupta art but excel in their masculine vigour, stateliness and general expression suggestive of deep insight. I might here perhaps add that the Anurādhapura images of the early period conform stylistically to the late Kuṣāṇa type, and if any definite historical connexion is to be established, it must be with the oldest known Bodhgayā image of Trikamala's time, the Ceylon type being an improvement on it. The great predilection of the Buddhists of the island for all symbols of Mahābodhi, living or artistic, is too well-known to need comment.

All lovers of Buddhist art in Ceylon cannot but be interested in the two figures, one, a bare-footed and standing sage-like figure carved on the face of a boulder at the entrance to the Pothgal vihāra erected by Vijayabāhu I holding up gracefully in its hands in a grave and subdued manner a palm-leaf manuscript without its wooden covers, and the other, a standing figure of Buddha with the two hands put on the breast, popularly known as the "Weeping Ānanda", just to the left of the lying-in figure of Buddha, both on the right side and in front of the small rock-cut cave temple at Polunnāruva erected by Parakkamabāhu I. The first figure may be correctly taken, I think, as a representation of either Kassapa V explaining the text of the *Dhammasangaṇi* or Vijayabāhu I making the *daṇḍissara* offering of a manuscript of the *Dhammasangaṇi*, preferably the latter. The standing figure of Buddha in above attitude may confidently be taken to represent Buddha on his arrival at Kusīnārā, giving out that he felt tired and asked Ānanda to prepare a bed for him. Thus the two figures, one standing and the other in a lying-in posture, stand for two consecutive links in the narrative of Buddha's demise.

Ceylon's contribution to Chinese Buddhism is little as compared with that made to Buddhism in Siam and Burma. So far as Siam is concerned, it appears, on the whole, to represent only a Cambodian extension of the Theravāda Buddhism of South India and Ceylon. With regard to Burma, one may observe that from the time of Vijayabāhu I of Ceylon and Anwaratha of Burma the history of Buddhism is mainly a narrative of intellectual and ecclesiastical co-operation between the two countries.

Parakkamabāhu I is known as the king of Ceylon who "succeeded in reconciling the three sects of monks —the Mahāvihāra, the Abhayagiri and the Jetavana and held a convocation under a Thera called Mahākassapa"[1]. This is said to have resulted in the final disappearance of the Vaitulya heresy (*i.e.*, Mahāyānism) from the island.[1] During the long period of decadence of the Buddhist faith which followed, the island came to have in place of three earlier sects of monks three new ones formed—the Siyāma, the Rāmañña and the Amarapura, the first, which is the most powerful of the three, acknowledging the debt of gratitude of the Sangha of Ceylon to Siam, and the remaining two to Lower and Upper Burma.

If with the establishment of the Portuguese rule and the Portuguese Church began the period of tribulation and decay of the religion of Śākyamuni in the island, that of the regeneration of the Good Faith and Buddhist culture and civilization certainly began during the British rule. The effect of the ruthless persecution of the Buddhists by king Rājasīha I of Sitawaka was disastrous to Buddhism. The revival of the religion began with

1 Malalasekera, *Dictionary*, ii, p. 149.

Sangharāja Saraṇankara who thoroughly reformed the Sangha and revived the Buddhist learning in the island under the patronage of Kitti-Siri-Rājasīha. And in the history of this regeneration and the world-wide study of Buddhism a notable part was played by Vādībhasīha Guṇānanda[1] of Ceylon whose writings and powerful debates directed against Christianity attracted the attention of Madame Blavatsky and Col. Olcot. Under the ægis of the Buddhist Theosophical Society founded by Col. Olcot in the island a few Buddhist colleges were ushered into existence. So far as Buddhist learning is concerned, the three great foundations are the Vidyodaya Pariveṇa due to the effort of the Most Venerable Siri Sumangala, the Vidyālankāra Pariveṇa due to that of the Most Venerable Dhammārāma, and the Mahābodhi Society due to that of the Anāgārika Dhammapāla. The University of Ceylon has come to be a *fait accompli* through the joint effort of Dr. Jennings, its first Vice-Chancellor, and Dr. Kannangara, the present Minister of Education. But to be treated as a national foundation, this young seat of learning must make an adequate provision for Buddhist learning since by that alone it can aspire in a large measure to make lasting contributions to Buddhism and world culture.

During this period the island of Ceylon has found in the Anāgārika a towering Buddhist personality and leader, and in Dr. A. K. Coomaraswamy a great living authority on Buddhist art and architecture. The name of Sir Baron Jayatilaka, founder of the Y. M. B. A., and

---

1 Popularly known in Ceylon as Migeṭṭuvatte Gunānande.

a friend, guide and philosopher to the Vidyālankāra Pariveṇa, will go down to posterity as a born teacher and patriot and a cherisher of progressive ideas to whom we owe a good deal for the revival of the study of Sinhalese and Sinhalese literature.

In the field of archæology, the names of Wickramasinghe and Dr. Paranavitana loom large as worthy successors of Müller and Bell. Similarly in the field of Pali scholarship, the places of Richard Childers and Rhys Davids have been worthily occupied by Rev. A. P. Buddhadatta and Professor G. P. Malalasekara as editors. So far as Professor Malalasekara is concerned, his edition of the *Mahāvaṃsa Ṭīkā* is a standing monument to his critical scholarship, while his *Dictionary of Pali Proper Names* will not easily cease to be used as a book of reference.

I can say that the University of Ceylon has started its life and career with a small band of young scholars noted for their critical acumen and eagerness to learn. But the future of the educational progress of the island as a whole will depend to a great extent on the co-operation between Dr. Kannangara in whom one may find a patriot and educationist with vision and Dr. Jennings in whom we eagerly wait to find a Britisher who came to the East as the builder of civilization.

It is a matter of considerable importance that the Buddhist Sangha of Ceylon should be awakened to a new self-consciousness and sense of national duty. There should be just one Sangha called Sīhalasangha and that there should be founded a Buddhist University affiliating to it all the Pariveṇas that are and that be. It is rather sad that the present-day monks of Ceylon are lacking in the practice of meditation wherein lies the source of spiritual vigour and new religious and cultural inspiration. They seem to look outward at the cost of inwardness with the result that when they preach the religion, they are found to be generally unimpressive. They being still the shepherds to the masses, it is high time that they should be worthy of the rôle they are required to play.

Among the benevolent donors, I cannot help mentioning the name of the late lamented Simon Hevavitarane, younger brother of the Anāgārika, whose generous bequest has been fruitful in the publication of a fairly large number of Pali commentaries and works in Sinhalese characters, precisely as one should mention also the name of the benevolent donors from the royal House of Siam to whose munificence we owe the publication and free distribution of the Pali Canon and Commentaries in Siamese characters. And among the various Buddhist journals and magazines, the Mahabodhi founded by the Anāgārika is still the most well-known and powerful.

APPENDIX TO LECTURE III

EPOCHS OF THE ART OF CEYLON

By Mr. Nandadeva Wijesekera, M.A. (Cantab.)

It may be safe to assume that Sinhalese art commenced its career from the time of Devānampiya Tissa, although the inheritance of earlier elements from the time of Paṇḍukābhaya cannot be discounted. With the introduction of Buddhism there ensued a period of great artistic activity in which sculpture, architecture and painting played a worthy part, combining to facilitate the propagation of the new religion. Much of this art was Buddhist in spirit but Indian in appearence. It was also in part secular.

Though from time to time classes of artists and craftsmen arrived in the island from India, the Sinhalese example may be said to embody the genius of the Sinhalese even if the Indians helped in their production. What we have therefore are Sinhalese reactions to Indian cultural and religious impacts. The earliest source of this inspiration emanated from North India and the Kistna region with Amarāvatī as the focus.

During the sixth century Sinhalese art blossomed out in all its beauty. It was again the Indian Gupta tradition that inspired the Sinhalese as well. In technique and expression these examples show in a remarkable manner the close affinity—almost amounting to copying to Indian models. A unique feature of the art of the period is the paintings at Sīgiriya. This is a coeval phase of the maturity of the Gupta tradition that stands unrivalled at Ajaṇṭa and Bāgh. Sīgiriya is a court art and not religious in its aim. It had little appeal to the ordinary people. But on the other hand we have at Anurādhapura and Tissamahārāma a religious art of sculpture and architecture well worthy of the national genius. Paintings both for embellishment and religious persuasion existed. But unfortunately these have vanished due to various causes.

The Buddha figures of the sixth century Anurādhapura stand out as masterpieces of technical perfection and religious expression. The stupendous edifices such as palaces and dāgobas, monasteries and secular buildings built of stone or brick still bear eloquent testimony to the ancient Sinhalese skill and constructive foresight both in art and architecure which at that time composed one whole.

Then follows an obscure period of less activity from which very little is known and survives. There is as it were a break in the continuity of the national heritage. But we have the fine stone carvings at Isurumuniya in Pallava style. The paintings at Hindagala and Dimbulāgala, few pieces of sculpture at Anurādhapura, and dāgobas constitute the remains. Perhaps at this time a new spirit of Buddhism dominates. This may have been due to the influence of Mahāyāna. It at least helped to popularise the worship of the Buddha and Bodhisattvas. Some art remains that may be called Mahāyāna have also been found.

In the XIIth century art was revived at Polonnaruva and Dimbulāgala. It is at Polonnaruva that we have the best expression of the times. In sculpture and painting as well as in architecture, the South Indian—Pallava and Cola—style influenced the Sinhalese considerably. But these are worthy examples that compel admiration from not only the Buddhists for whose cause they were produced but from all Ceylonese whose heritage it is today.

Great movements of art flourished and faded away. The people had a voice in shaping them but the patronage and the money came from the richer society and noble classes. But after XIIth century art passes into the hands of the popular classes. It got neither patronage nor due respect. It raises its head once more during the time of Kīrti Srī but lapses gradually into oblivion from which state it may be said to be struggling to find expression to-day.

LECTURE IV

BUDDHA'S GREATNESS AND ROLE

Buddhaguṇā or the attributes determining Buddha's[1] greatness are, according to an ancient declaration, inestimable, and, therefore, unthinkable *(acinteyyā)*. And yet I ventured to choose it as my subject for this lecture when it occurred to me that the contemplation of it is no bar to any person, however humble. There was even a deeper reason, which weighed on my decision, namely, that there could not be a better subject to give our anxious thoughts to now, when we are in the grip of a terrible world war and when the entire civilization of man is in a melting pot.

And I am much grateful indeed to the Buddhist Brotherhood of the University of Ceylon for kindly inviting me to come to this Island and say how I contemplate the great subject proposed. I am particularly grateful to Professors G. P. Malalasekera and H. C. Ray and Rev. Rahula who wrote to me on behalf of this Brotherhood, and I was very pleased indeed to know that the Brotherhood which is purely an organisation of the

---

* This is the first lecture of the Religion series delivered at Colombo on March 15, '44 under the auspices of the Buddhist Brotherhood of the University of Ceylon.

1 The *Buddha-visaya* which is counted among the four unthinkables is explained by Buddhaghosa as meaning *sabbaññutādi Buddhaguṇānaṁ pavatti ca anuvhāvo ca.*

Buddhist students was composed of such serious-minded learners and youths as to be interested in a subject like this. I can say that Mr. W. J. Fernando, its President, and the other members of the Brotherhood have not been found wanting in attention and courtesy to me and that they have done all that is possible for them to make my stay here both comfortable and profitable.

To contemplate Buddha's greatness and rôle is to contemplate man's potential or actual greatness and function in the universe. Can there be, I ask, a greater subject of study for mankind than man himself, either potentially or actually that he is? You and I may not be interested in any other problem of the universe or any other riddle of existence, but can we help, so long as we are thinking beings, considering our place and position as well as mission in the whole of life? The island of Ceylon, as once known to us Indians, was separated from the mainland just by a river, and yet how great is the difference which this has made to the history and civilization of Ceylon. Similarly man is separated from the rest of creation just by a few ounces of the brain matter, and yet has not this fact created a wide gulf of difference to his position and career! In course of this lecture I am to ask you to consider, in all seriousness, the problem of man's place and duty in terms of Buddha's greatness and rôle.

It is the common aim of the divines and philosophers to establish man's supreme position in the world and to make him fully conscious of his potentialities and possibilities. Whether we say with the Jewish Prophets that 'God created man in His own image, after His likeness', or say with the early Greek philosophers that 'man is the measure of everything', the two statements are the same as regards their import as to man's supreme place and function. In the Rāmāyaṇa (vi. 119. 11), when the deifying agents, the Lokapālas, Indra, Varuṇa, Śiva and Brahmā, tried to flatter Rāma by reminding him of his divinity and divine mission on earth, the poet Vālmīki made him say at once, silencing them, *ātmānaṃ manuṣyaṃ manye Rāmaṃ Daśarathātmajam,* "I consider myself simply a man, son of Daśaratha." This was for a certainty the bold utterance of an age when man was sufficiently self-conscious of his own position as man apart from all the attribution of divinity to him. But this self-consciousness was not gained in a day. It took man millenniums to evolve into this paramountcy in self-consciousness and self-assertion.

The problem of man's place and duty may be shown indeed to have presented itself to the thinking men of all Ages and of all climes. The Brāhmans faced through their *Epics* and *Purāṇas* the problem of the successive advent of the Manus or Patriarchs as divine regulators of individual, domestic as well as social life through law and justice, side by side with the problem of the successive advent of the Avatāras or Re-incarnations of Viṣṇu or Śiva, particularly of the former. The problem of the successive advent of the Tīrthankaras or Makers of the New Schools of religious thought engaged the Jaina thinkers. The Buddhist thinkers endeavoured through their *Jātakas* and *Avadānas* to offer a solution for the problem of the successive advent of the Buddhas or Enlightened Ones, Tathagatas or Truthfinders and Pathfinders, with their eminent Disciples. The Jewish thinkers sought through their *Testaments* and *Talmuds* to solve the problem of the successive advent of the Holy Prophets. Among the Western thinkers, after the great Plato, one may single out the name of Pringle Pattison as one whose mind has been wholly occupied with the problem of God and man's place in the cosmos.

It may be said to the credit of our own thinkers that they, instead of setting up any arbitrary belief for our acceptance, wanted us to examine and consider the grounds on which their conclusions were based. Whether we accept or discard their findings, we are forced to admit that they arrived at certain definite conclusions after a careful and wide survey of all conceivable universes of existence, experience and action. Without leading you into the by-ways of myths and legends, poetic allegories and fancies, which often shroud serious thinking in popular literature, I would just place before you for your consideration the genuinely philosophical or scientific lines of thought followed in finding out a correct solution of the great problem before us.

The oldest known Book of Indo-Aryan Wisdom is undoubtedly and admittedly the *Ṛgveda,* the hymns of which, even apart from all other considerations, may be judged as the full flowering of human speech (*puṣpitā-vācā).* No other Book of the ancient world, hitherto, known, has surpassed it in its brilliance and excellence.

The Sumerian *Psalms* or the Egyptian *Book of the Dead* may have preceded it, but they are rather crude as regards their expressions and moral consciousness and man's philosophical and spiritual outlook. The inspired set of hymns in this *Veda of Vedas* came to represent a great upheaval of human mind with its vision spread over the whole of the visible universe. The brother-and-sister-marriage, for instance, was a time-honoured custom with the long succession of the Egyptian Dynasties, even down to the time of the last Pharaoh. The same may indeed have been once a universal custom among the ruling races and families. The *Ṛgveda* contains a famous dialogue, the *Yama-Yamī-Saṃvāda,* in which Yamī, the sister, on reaching her years of discretion, approached Yama, her brother, with the proposal to take her hand, and that on this twofold ground : (1) that they were born as man and wife in the very womb, and (2) that it was a time-immemorial practice. The brother, declining her offer then and there, said, "That may be so, but henceforth thou must seek some other suitor." Thus through the emphatic "No" of Yama, the Vedic seer meant an open departure from an age-old custom, and therein lay as much his moral courage as the social and moral advance of humanity at large. This is what I mean by the great upheaval of human thought and moral consciousness in the *Ṛgveda.*

Though the *Ṛgveda* reveals thus a higher religious consciousness of the Indo-Aryan people and marks a real advancement of humanity, its hymns go, upon the whole, to indicate that man remained overawed by the luminaries in the heaven above and the mighty and irresistible physical forces below, preponderating over man's happiness and destiny. The sages and seers tried by all means to secure their favour through eulogies and offerings, to approach them, or to rank and unite with them. Undeniably the idea of harmony and beauty in the universe flashed sometimes across their minds, and the most philosophic mind of the age became eager to discover the relation of the existing reality with its primordial ground through searching within the heart (*sato bandhūn asati niravindan hṛdi pratīṣya*).[1] And yet it looked outward to be amazed and not inward to be enlightened. With the child-like inquisitiveness and in the freshness of experiences and the vigour of life the ancient sages and seers wanted to penetrate into the mysteries suggested by the natural phenomena of daily occurrence, especially to know who or what was behind them all and whither was their course or direction. All is still so vague and uncertain.

The *Āraṇyakas* and early *Upaniṣads* enable us to watch with interest the birth of a new religious and ethical consciousness and certainly represent the second stage of Indian thought when it became preoccupied with the question of man himself, though still in relation to the world as a whole. The thought tended to be gradually ego-centric, if I am permitted the expression. The awe generated by the rulers of the external world was gone. The thinking man, *i.e.*, the thinking

1 *Ṛgveda, Nāsadīya Sūkta*, X. 129.

mind, was thenceforth interested in the question of man's true self, *Ātman* and the first axiom which came to be established as a defiinite result of earnest inquiries was : 'I am He' *(So 'ham),* or 'Thou art He or That' *(Tat tvam asi).*

This was with the progress of time followed by an age, which was characterised by a vigorous sophistic movement. Many of the old gods were dethroned from their once elevated seats, and if many of them still remained in the growing Pantheon on their high pedestals, they acquired in the meantime new attributes and new significances. The religious consciousness that emerged out of those speculative ferments with which Northern India was then seething tended to place the greatest of saints as the highest in the universe. This found in Buddha an oracular voice for the new-born assertive spirit of man which went to reverse the relative positions of men and the gods. The result of it was that in the changed situation, the gods and demi-gods, the *Rūpabrahmas* and *Arūpabrahmas* who continued to receive homage and offerings from the ignorant and weak-minded, came to be placed in the rôle of humble and devout worshippers of the most enlightened of men. And this change in the old order of things suggests indeed a complete change in man's ideology.

The truth behind the great axiom, "I am He", or "Thou art He or That", underrated by Caird, Pringle Pattison and other Christian thinkers as pantheistic, was sought to be established by showing, on the one hand, a complete analogy or parallelism between man as microcosm and the world as macrocosm, and by proving, on the other, that the highest of men is on a par, in respect of the purity of his nature, with the highest in the universe ; in other words, by placing man on the same level with the entire world of existence, life, experience and action.

As I maintain, according to the early Upaniṣad philosophy, the advancement of individual beings as belonging to different classes is to be measured by the degree of soul-life each of them develops or manifests. Evidently on the assumption that the perfect man is the measure of every form and degree of spiritual life, nourished on the hearty enjoyment of the depth of existence or true being, it is claimed in the *Taittirīya Upaniṣad* that the perfect man alone is capable of going through the whole gamut of religious experience, each scale of which has its parallel in the enjoyment of a particular individual in the hierarchy of the gods, the highest among men standing in this respect on the same level with the highest among the gods. The highest in the cosmos is Brahman[1] and the highest among men is one who is free from desires (*akāmahata śrotriya*), the *Parama-ṛṣi* in the language of the *Praśna Upaniṣad*.

In assigning the superior place to man in the scale of beings the *Aitareya Āraṇyaka* holds that man distinguishes himself at once from the rest of creation by virtue of these three great possessions : (1) the gift of speech or power of self-expression, (2) the power of

1 *Taittrīya Up.*, II. 8. Cf. Praśna Up. vi. 7, *etat paraṁ Brahma Veda, nātaḥ param astīti.*

thinking, discrimination and anticipation, and (3) the capacity to aspire for the immortal state despite his being a mortal (*martyena amṛtam īpsā*)[1].

This *Āraṇyaka* idea of man's superiority which underwent further developmene in the older *Upaniṣads* was considerably deepened by Maskarin Kauśalya who is known in Pali by the name of Makkhali Gosāla. At about the time of the rise of Buddhism, he figured as the third great leader of the Ājīvikas and was counted, therefore, among the elder contemporaries of Buddha. He appears to have been the first great biological thinker of the world. He conceived time as a cyclical order of vast geological periods called *mahākalpas.* He classified the living beings, either, according to their modes of generation, into the viviparous (womb-born), the oviparous (egg-born), the moisture-born, and the chance-born or *sui generis;* or, according to their comparative capacity for movement into immobile (*sthāvara*) and mobile (*jangama*); or, according to the number of senses possessed, into those endowed with one sense, those with two, those with three, those with four, those with five, and those with six. The plants were divided, according to their modes of propagation, into those propagated from seeds, those from roots, those from joints, those from cuttings, and those from graftings. The material things were divided, according

† *Aitareya Ār.* II. 3. 2. 1-5 Cf. Milinda, p. 32, where a distinction is made between *manasikāra* (rudimentary mind) and *paññā* (reason, wisdom), and it is held that sheep and goats, oxen and buffaloes, camels and asses possess rudimentary mind, but reasoned knoweldge they have not.

to their different formations, into solids (earth-lives), liquids (water-lives), calorics (fire-lives), and winds (air lives). Man's life was broadly divided into eight stages or periods called the semi-conscious, the playful, the trial, the erect, the learning, the mature, the master, and the self-assertive.[1] The souls were distinguished, according to their different moral colourings, into six types called the dark, the blue, the red, the yellow, the white, and the supremely white. He most emphatically maintained that in order to evolve into a perfect type of man, an individual has to go through a process of evolution through innumerable species (*yonis*) during 84,00,000 *mahākalpas*. As widely accepted throughout India, Maskarin's doctrine was taken to mean that to be born as man, a being has to undergo the process of birth in 84,00,000 species.

The biological side of Maskarin's system was received *in toto* into the structure of the Jaina religious thought, and there it was further devleoped, elaborated, elucidated, richly supplemented, and fully utilised. This may be shown also to have been in the immediate background of the biological foundation of Buddhism. Maskarin's division of souls into the six colour types, for instance, exactly corresponded with Mahāvīra's division of the same into six colour affections (*lesiyas*), agreed substantially with Buddha's characterisation of minds by five colours,[1] and was, to all intents and purposes, the

1 The meaning of the eighth stage called *paṇṇaka-bhūmi* is still open to dispute.

2 Vatthūpama Sutta, Majjhima, i., p. 26.

same, as pointed out in the Mahābhārata, as the Sāṃkhya division of the reflections of character on the soul into three colour types called the white, the red and the dark.[1]

The biological data thus supplied by Maskarin must have formed the basis of the following four pronouncements of Buddha in the *Dhammapada*:

"Difficult it is to be born as man.
Difficult it is for the mortals to live.
Difficult it is to have a chance of hearing the good doctrine.
Difficult it is to witness the advent of Buddhas."

The *Taittiriya Upaniṣad* proposed to consider man's place and duty in five *adhikaraṇas* or contexts, which is to say, in respect of the five universes of existence, experience and action, to wit, (1) physical *(adhilokam)*, (2) astronomical *(adhijyautiṣam)*, (3) socio-biological *(adhiprajam)*, (4) cultural *(adhividyam)*, and (5) personal *(adhyātmam)*. Literally, *adhilokam* refers to the physical structure of the world, *adhijyautiṣam* to the world of lights, *adhiprajam* to the world of procreation, *adhividyam* to that of learning, and *adhyātmam* to that of individuality.[2]

The process of cosmic development as a whole was carefully considered and outlined and its successive

1 See how in the *Mahābhārata*, XV. 279. 33-68 and Nīlakaṇtha's Commentary the significance of Maskarin's six colour divisions *ṣaḍjīvavarṇāḥ)* is explained in terms of the three *guṇas-sattvas, rajas* and *tamas* of Sāṁkhya. Even the term *śuklābhijātīyaḥ* is met with in *ibid*, XV. 279. 66.

2 *Taittirīya Up*. I. 3.

stages set out in the *Aitareya Āraṇyaka*. It is held that the entire cosmic process starts from Prajāpati who is the repository of the will-to-be, the will-to-create, and reaches its culmination through various intermediate stages in Brahmā representing the most intelligent cosmic agent of *karma*—thoughtful or self-willed action.[1]

As for personal development, the *Taittirīya Upaniṣad* opines that the process starts from the *annamaya* or physical plane of existence with material food as means of nourishment of the self, culminates in the *ānandamaya* or spiritual plane with bliss or beautitude as means of nourishment, and passes through the three intervening stages represented by the *prāṇamaya* or psycho-physical plane with the sensory experience and enjoyment as means of nourishment, the *manomaya* or mental plane with percepts or ideas as means of nourishment, and thirdly, the *vijñānamaya* or rational plane with conceptual understanding as means of nourishment.

This Upaniṣadic view of the personal development of man by means of five kinds of sustenance was accepted by Buddha when he, too, spoke of the five kinds of food, and premised in a general way that all forms of life depend on food for their nourishment. The five kinds of food, according to Buddha, are the food for the stomach, the food for the senses, the food for the mind, the food for the intellect, and the spiritual food for emancipated consciousness. The last kind of food

1 *Aitareya Ār.*, II. 1. 3. 1.

which is but an emotional enjoyment of the free state of consciousness goes by the name of *pīti*[1] or *nibbuti*.[2]

In accordance with the Ājīvika and Jaina scheme of existence, the lowest in the scale of evolution are the elemental lives or forms of matter. The possession of the sense of touch is the minimum requirement of individuality. The different formations of earth, water, fire and air are to be treated as individual beings in so far as they satisfy this minimum test. Like other beings, they, too, are subject to the laws of birth, growth, decay and death. The four elements feed on one another, live by co-operation, and perish by the fury of the action of one on another. In short, they integrate as well as disintegrate. So long as they persist, they show an internal cohesion, which breaks down at their death. They are all contained in space and act in time. The plant or animal organism results from a finer physical combination of them.

Though the plants stand higher in the scale than the elemental beings, they, too, are just endowed with the sense of touch. They remain fixed to the ground and are incapable of free locomotion, for which reason they are termed immobiles. The *Mahābhārata* sharply criticises the Ājīvika and Jaina opinion which endows the plants only with the sense of touch, and argues in favour of their being endowed with all the six senses[3]. Had they not possessed the organ of sight, it argues, how

1. cf. *Dhammapada, pītibhakkhā bhavissāma.*
2 cf. *Ratana Sutta : nibbutiṁ bhuñjamānā.*
3 *Mahābhārata, Śāntiparva, Mokṣadharma,* 184. 10-18.

is it that they find their way to the place where light is, and had they not possessed the organ of hearing, why should their growth be stunted by terrific sounds? So on and so forth. According to Manu's finding, the plants are possessed at least of an internal sentience *(antaḥsaṃjñā)*. On the cogency of this opinion and its argument I need not make any comment here.

The animals are to be distinguished from the plants as beings capable in varying degrees of locomotion or free bodily movement. They, too, admit of gradations among themselves according as they possess two or more senses. Whether they are womb-born or egg-born, in matters of eating, behaviour, sleeping and procreation, their position is virtually the same as that of human beings. They are all liable, in common with men, to these six vicissitudes, contigencies or limitations of mortal existence: gain and loss, pleasure and pain, life and death. Many of them are endowed, like man, with the six senses including the mind or *sensus communis*.[1] And human beings, too, are to be placed on six grades in accordance with moral colourings of their souls, and in the three, according to Sāṃkhya.

Buddha's world is primarily the world of man which he characterised by eight vicissitudes *(aṭṭha lokadhammā)*, while Maskarin characterised the larger world of life by six. The total of eight vicissitudes was made up of the six mentioned by Maskarin and the two added

1 These ideas of nature and development are all anticipated in the *Aitareya Āraṇyaka*, *Cf.* Barua, *A History of Pre-Buddhistic Indian Philosophy*, p. 56 ff.

by Buddha, the two additional items in connotation being praise and blame, which are absent where social life is not developed.[1] The six vicissitudes of gain and loss, pleasure and pain, life and death are the common lot of all animals. Besides this difference, one may observe that Maskarin's eight stages are the eight natural stages of human life, while Buddha's eight stages are the stages of the saint's moral, intellectual and spiritual advance. The course of training prescribed by Buddha is meant as a post-graduate course, while that of others is differentiated from it as under-graduate.

We have from Buddha various classifications of human types based on moral, intellectual and spiritual grounds. In the gradation of hierarchy suggested, the Perfect Buddhas are placed above the *Pratyeka,* the Pratyeka Buddhas above the Disciples occupying the eight advanced ranks, they above the *Gotrabhūs* (Graduates), they above the four ranks of the *Arūpa Brahmas,* they above the four or five ranks of *Rūpa Brahmas,*[2] they above the seven ranks of *Devas,* the *Devas* above the common run of men, these men above the brutes, brutes above the ghosts and spirits, while on the lowest level stand the various grades of infernal beings.

---

1 The eight *lokadhammas* are generally wrongly enumerated as *lābha* and *alābha, yasa* and *ayasa, nindā* and *pasaṁsā, sukha* and *dukkha,* the middle two pairs being overlapping. The correct enumeration is suggested in the *Theragāthā,* vv. 663-670.

2 The four or five ranks according to the four or five *rūpāvacarajhānas,* as in the *Dhammasangaṇi.*

The infra-human beings are only objects of pity and mercy. From the lowest level of men up to the highest level of the gods, the beings find their place and move about in the non-reflective sphere of mind. They are guided by their animal-like instincts, impulses and passions, or at the most, by the love of worldly power, prosperity and enjoyments.

The lowest reflective sphere of consciousness is represented by the four or five ranks of *Rūpabrahmas*, and the next higher by the four ranks of *Arūpabrahmas* culminating in graduation meaning the state of the *Gotrabhū*. The supramundane levels of consciousness are open to the eight ranks of advanced Disciples culminating in Arhatship. But in their case, *paññā* (knowledge) is primarily based upon the teaching of others ; it is *sutamayā*. Above them are the *Pratyeka* Buddhas or gifted seers who are self-made men with original visions. In their case, knowledge which is a first-hand one, is inadequate for convincing and guiding others ; it is just *cintāmayā*, which disappears with them. Above all stand the Perfect Buddhas who are not only the suremely gifted men with original visions and outlook, but also have the wide and the most intimate knowledge of men and things, possess the capacity for originating and introducing their own systems of thought and discipline under the weight of their stupendous personality. In their case, knowledge is *bhavanāmayā*.

In Buddha's estimation, Brahmā or Brahman of the *Upaniṣads* (*i.e.*, early Vedānta) stood for the highest religious experience and knowledge within the range of the sensuous—the world of mental forms, *i.e.,* percepts or ideas. Rising up to a higher level of consciousness, the earlier contemplatives of India are said to have gone through the four higher forms of psychical experience in which the vision or knowledge of the infinity of space, the infinity of the ideational phase of consciousness, there being left nothing but itself as object of consciousness[1], and consciousness being in its ultimate nature unpredicable in terms of perception and non-perception *(n'eva saññā nāsaññā)*[2] dawns on consciousness. It was in the last-named state of consciousness that the earlier contemplatives had their highest psychical experience and enjoyed the bliss of *Brahma Nirvāṇa.*

But Buddha wants us to understand that even after the experience and enjoyment of this form of beautitude, the human mind remains still interested in the reality and value of the world as commonly perceived or accepted. In this sense indeed, consciousness belongs to the mundane sphere. In other words, the ineffable ultimate reality of the older *Upaniṣads* did not represent, in his opinion, the highest reach of psychical experience. The *Brahma Nirvāṇa*, as realised by the Upaniṣadic and other earlier seers, is not Buddha's *Nirvāṇa,*[1] despite the fact that both are characterised negatively alike by *nêti nêti,*—as that which lies beyond the reach of thought and language.

Nirvāṇa is claimed to have been experienced by Buddha on a supramundane level of consciousness,

1 For Buddha's estimate of *Brahma Nirvāṇa,* see the first sutta in the *Majjhima Nikāya,* called Mūlapariyāya.

where it is a complete void in the sense that here it becomes emptied not only of all the content of sensory or perceptual origin but also of all determinations of thought and will under the influence of feeling. It is for the attainment of this highest conceivable state of trance and ecstasy called *saññā-vedayita-nirodha,* that Buddha deserved to be eulogised as *Yogīnāṃ cakravartin* in the *Daśāvatāra-stotra* ascribed to Śankara.[4]

While Buddha remained in this state of trance, the *abhisambodhi* or supreme inner enlightenment took place in consciousness. It dawned on the thought-free consciousness—the *bodhicitta* of Mahāyāna—as a true vision of the nature of reality. It awakened in this very state of consciousness a vivid memory of the past history of the world in so far as it was related to his conscious career. It held before it a clear view of the entire world of existence and of life where the ups and downs of beings take place according to the laws of *karma* shaping their various destinies. It aroused in it the feeling and conviction about its sinlessness or pristine purity, and called up the highest emotion of joy on the penetration into the depth of its being and the attainment or experience of its thought-free and sinless state.

The nature of reality, as realised in a flash of intuition, appeared to be not a static cosmic order but a *paṭicca-samuppāda* or *paccuppāda i.e.,* a dynamic order of becoming.

I may add that *abhisambodhi* is a great event in the life of consciousness which took place in and through a supreme *yogic* or mystical experience, and which made a world of difference in the life of Siddhārtha. Before he was but a mere *Bodhisattava,* and with and after it, he gained the status of a perfect Buddha. The inner conviction gained through this experience as to truth or nature of reality, as to his internal purity, as well as his freedom, led to self-expression and self-assertion, which meant only the declaration of his new personality :

> "Subdued have I all, all-knowing am I now.
> Unattached to all things, and abandoning all,
> Finally freed on the destruction of all craving.
> Knowing it myself, whom else should I credit ?
> There is no teacher of mine, nor is one like me ;
> There is none to rival me in the world of men and gods.
> Truly entitled to honour am I, a teacher unexcelled ;
> Alone am I a Supreme Buddha, placid and tranquil.
> To found the kingdom of righteousness, I proceed to Kāsī's capital,
> Beating the drum of immortality in the world enveloped by darkness."[1]

Buddha's *abhisambodhi* proved itself to be of far-reaching effects on man's civilization. India gained through it a dynamic view of reality in lieu of the static as in the *Upaniṣads.* The world got a religion without the belief in a personal God, but which fully functioned to create the ideals of character and conduct and to awaken and establish faith in their reality, and also a

1 *Ariyapariyesana Sutta, Majjhima,* i., p. 171.

vigorous missionary religion, which was destined to become a living force in Asiatic and world civilization. A sound system of ethics was built upon psychological foundations, defining and raising the standards of human conduct and heightening the values of human life, efforts and experiences. It gave rise to a system of philosophy, critical in its spirit, dialectical in its mode of argument, analytical in its method, synthetic in its purpose, positivistic in its conclusions, mystical in its practice but rational in its structure. The people got a new vehicle of expression, which is capable of expressing all shades of experience, forms of thought and interests of life ; an extensive literature in various languages, which is full of historical information, vivid in the description of things, technical in the employment of words and phrases, lively in human interest, inspiring in tone and dignified in expression. It has served to bring into existence a system of education encouraging originality, the spirit of enquiry, and free exchanges of thoughts and ideas ; a system of discipline, which, though thoroughgoing, is not rigid, and is intended to serve as a means to an end, and not as an end in itself. It has developed a new system of jurisprudence in which man's action is to be judged mainly from its underlying motive or intention *(cetanā)*, and the law is subsumed to be made for man, and not that man is made for the law. It has fructified itself in the foundation of a Fraternity to which admission is open to all alike, irrespective of their caste or sex, and which is democratic in its constitution and communistic in the possession, distribution and use of requisites and properties. It has advocated a grand form of imperialism, the principal aims of which are to educate the people to certain moral excellences of character, to promote the cause of piety among all nations of the earth, and, above all, to build a great nation of humanity on the basis of love, fellow-feeling, and good will, and not on that of constant strife, enmity and hostility. The last but not the least is that, it has inspired a new form of art, which is to be a tangible expression of refined human imagination, awe-inspiring and having an educative value.

If we judge Buddha simply as a human personality, he does not suffer the least by comparison ; on the contrary, he stands pre-eminent. He was born in an aristocrate *kṣatriya* family of Northern India and was of noble descent on both sides. He was born and brought up in the republican tradition of the Śākyas. His was a full stature of growth and manhood, which was tall, stout and well-proportioned ; commanding was his figure. He stood as the finest example of a healthy mind in a healthy body. His racial heritage consisted in the nobility of birth, personal dignity, manliness and social refinement. India was then the leading country of the world. The age which witnessed his advent was noted for free thinking and ardent search for truth.

As Buddha, his nature was unperturbed, placid and calm like a deep lake. His voice was clear, distinct, audible, deep and reverberating like the lion's roar. The strength of his purpose made him steady like a rock unshaken by winds. His towering personality shone forth like the great Himālaya at the foot of which he was born. Non-harming and non-hurting was his mental attitude towards all. His heart was filled with unbounded love, sympathy and compassion. His was a most balanced mind and a judicious temperament. All the immoral motives were completely destroyed within him. He preached what he practised, and practised what he preached. Pin-drop silence reigned wherever he appeared, so magnetic and powerful was his personality. His greatness was acknowledged by all alike. He is not known to have either prayed or cursed. All persons he met with good grace, and had no grievance against any. Just as his thoughts were well co-ordinated, so fully coherent were his words. He was always mindful and wakeful. A most active and well-regulated life was his. He did his duty till he breathed his last. He calmly faced death when it came, without a sigh. He spoke only of the fundamentals of thought and of man's virtue. He had the deepest insight into human and all nature.

As a thinker and teacher, the Socratic dialectics he occasionally employed to expose the incongruity and untenability of the proposition put forward by an interlocutor are both entertaining and effective. He discarded all authority but that of one's own experience, and encouraged the rational understanding of things. *Pratītya-samutpāda* formed the basic concept of his philosophy, and it was at the same time an original contribution to Indian and world thought. The fact that he appeared on many an occasion in the rôle of a critic does not stand in the way of our thinking that his real intention was to advance the cause of previous and current thoughts, as well as to heighten the value of the cherished ideals of religion and society. His was not the Kantian idea of religion insisting on the acceptance of duty as Divine command, piety or duty being for him a natural outward expression of a righteous nature within. Abandoning the practice of baptizing with the holy waters of the Jordon, Jesus Christ wanted men to be baptized with the spirit of the Holy Ghost. In India, five centuries earlier, Buddha wanted men to be baptized with an internal bathing (*sināto antarena sinānena*)[1]. His mission, in fact, was to increase the inner significance of all external practices. He repudiated indeed the idea of a personal God based upon the Zulu-like argument from father back to his father, and from all fathers back to first father to prevent an infinite regress (*apariyanta-gahaṇaṃ, anavasthā*), and replaced theodicy by cosmodicy, but did not fail at the same time to emphasize the need of developing godliness and divine attributes in man. He directed his disciples to use the entire realm of nature and society as an open school, and to gather moral qualities from all persons and all things, just as the bee collects honey from flowers without injuring them, and they were required not only to develop them within themselves but also to outgrow them.

The religious yearning in India behind the advancement of the cause of humanity found its classical expression in the prayer :

---

1 *Majjhima*, i., p. 39.

Asato māṃ sat gamaya.
Tamaso māṃ jyotir gamaya.
Mṛtur māṃ amṛtaṃ gamaya.
"Lead me from the unreal to the real.
Lead me from darkness to light.
Lead me from death to immortality."

This was variously taken in the subsequent ages to imply the course of man's advancement from ignorance to knowledge, from unconsciousness to self-consciousness, from dumbness to self-expression, from slumber to awakening, from bondage to freedom, from lethargy to activity, from hunger and thirst to abundance, from fears to the fearless state, from the mutable to the immutable, from disease to health, from strife to peace, from efforts to fruitions.

This yearning is nothing but the first religious impulse to greatness. But, as maintained in the *Jātakas* and *Avadānas*, it marks the beginning of a self-conscious career of incessant struggles for progress only when it is intensified into that form of the will which goes by the name of *praṇidhāna*, implying as it does the first strong resolution to pursue the future course of life at all costs. It presupposes these two things: (1) that the individual forming it is conscious enough that he is destined to do something great in the world, (2) that he is clear about the aims or ends to which to direct all his future efforts or endeavours.

The ends, in the case of a Bodhisattva, are stated to be these three: doing good to self, doing good to the nation, and doing good to the world at large. With the *praṇidhāna* solemnly declared and the triple aims clearly kept before the eye, the individual plunges himself into a life of struggle and faces many difficult situations in life, in overcoming which he gets the opportunity for developing certain perfectionary virtues that go to constitute the strength of his character and widen the domain of his experience and knowledge. The minor and isolated instances of such feats of heroism may be collected from the realm of life around us, as well as from the national traditions of men. The *Jātakas* and *Avadānas* hold just a number of typical cases before us, their real aim being to make a methodical survey of the entire realm of existence and of life, including the whole of human history, as far as it is known, and the anecdotes of various heroes, with a view to showing how the history of the universe can be viewed in the light of a single human life and told in terms of successive episodes of the life of an evolving individual, how, in other words, the universal history gravitates towards and ultimately merges in a continued human biography.[1]

Just think, please, for a moment what would have been the place and position of man in the universe but for the advent of the Buddha types of men, the Tīrthankara types, the Christ types, or the great Sage or Prophet types? If the world were left to the brutes, would the higher virtues have been brought to clear recognition at all? Had it been left to the vegetables, the heavenly denizens and matter and energy, would there have been the least manifestation of consciousness or mind by the

1 Barua, *Barhut*, Bk. I, p. 100f.

fullest possible development of which man is entitled to a supreme place in the universe?

The individual as well as the national advancement in the history of man's civilization is to be judged primarily by the nature of the moral principle or ideal conceived, cherished and followed in practice. When the first great Jewish Prophet, Moses, advocated 'an eye for an eye', 'a tooth for a tooth' as the sound principle for his people and when Jesus Christ enjoined on them the principle of loving the enemy, blessing them that curse, doing good to them that hate, between the two there is a long, pathetic history of the religious, moral and political struggle of the Jewish race. Similarly when in India the sages recommended 'strength for strength, mildness for mildness' as the best course of wisdom, and when Buddha spoke of and showed the way to the conquest of hatred by love, falsehood by truth and meanness by magnanimity, between the two there elapsed centuries of thought and moral evolution.

Before the introduction of Buddhism into China, the great sage Confucius was the spokesman of the highest moral wisdom of the Chinese nation. For the guidance of this ancient race, the best dictum of Confucius was: If you are going to deal with the wicked with leniency, with what are you going to deal with the virtuous?

That the Buddha's standpoint was pre-eminently psychological is undoubted. This standpoint emerged out of a biological background in India, as in the West.

The idea of evolution was always at the back of India's early religious thought. When I said this, I did not mean to say that this doctrine of evolution was Darwinian or modern, which latter is concerned with the problem of the origin of species, of a higher species out of a lower one by the law of the survival of the fittest, the adaptation to the environment, or natural selection. The Indian doctrine, whether Upaniṣadic, Ājīvika, Jaina or Buddhist, takes the species for granted, the individuals alone being liable to pass and repass through them, according to the laws of *karma*.[1]

1 Mr. D. B. Jayasinghe in his excellent criticism of the next lecture in Religion series (*The Mahabodhi*, Vol. 52, 1944, Nos. 9-10, p. 283), has pertinently raised the question whether in accordance with Buddha's idea of evolution we are 'fallen angels' or 'risen apes'. To this the only reasonable answer I might suggest is—we are both. From the psycho-ethical point of view we are 'fallen angels' in so far as our *citta* (consciousness) meaning mind in its natural or original state (*pakati-mano*) which is radiant (pure) becomes stained by the impurities meaning the influxes of sin which are foreign to its nature (*āgantukehi dosehi paduṭṭho hoti*), and we are 'risen apes' in so far as we succeed in getting rid of these parasitic corrupting factors and rendering it supremely radiant through enlightenment. From the biological point of view we are 'fallen angels' in so far as we begin to lose, as we grow up in age, the loveliness of appearance and the innocence of nature which characterize our childhood, and we are 'risen apes' in so far as we begin to develop all the brighter features of appearance and the nobler qualities of nature as we consciously advance in spirituality, knowledge and character. In both the cases the fall is from a state which is a fallible one, and the rise is from a more fallible to a less fallible or from a less stable to a more stable one. Buddha's significant description of the steadiness of our internal nature being: "Just as the one mass rock or the firmly posted city-gate pillar is not shaken by winds from the four quarters."

LECTURE V

BUDDHISM AS BUDDHA'S PERSONAL RELIGION

I stand before you rather with a mixed feeling of joy and diffidence, the diffidence as to my competence to do justice to the subject which has baffled the efforts through ages before me. I am conscious, however, of the fact that it is no mean privilege and honour to come in as successor of a living great thinker of the East of the reputation and fame of Professor Sir Sarvapalli Radhakrishnan who fills at present the responsible office of the Vice-Chancellor of the Benares Hindu University,—a rare opportunity for which I must express my grateful thanks to Mr. A. G. Ranasinha, the Public Trustee, who sent out the invitation to deliver a public lecture on Buddhism under the Dona Alpina Ratnayake Trust. I rejoiced to welcome it for a very special reason, namely, that it came, as I thought, at a very opportune moment when I could be sure of the philosophic position of Buddha, particularly as to the logical relation between *Paṭicca-samuppāda* and *Nirvāṇa* constituting the two main points of consideration in Buddha's religion. Without being clear about it, we are likely to be beating about the bush, praising the stupendous personality of Buddha but denying him the originality of thinking. It is in the light of this that you are to follow the trend of argument running through the lecture.

Today I am concerned to give you some idea of the

* This second lecture of Religion series was delivered at Colombo on March 14, '44 under the auspices of the Dona Alpina Ratnayake Trust.

nature and content of the religion which played the most important part, as I should say, in the memorable and awe-inspiring history of the attainment of Buddha's greatness and career, and which, when founded, was permeated and enlivened by the Buddha spirit. The nature and content of this religion may be generalised only in so far as it accounts for the possiblity of the attainment of similar greatness and career by others. And when I propose "Buddhism as Buddha's personal religion" as the subject of discussion, I surely intend distinguishing it somehow or other from "Buddhism as an institutional religion."

At the very outset, the question arises—what do I understand by religion, especially personal religion? As you may be well aware, we have so far various definitions or characterisations of religion. With Immanuel Kant, for instance, religion consists in the acceptance of duty as Divine command. To Hegel, religion means the knowledge of the finite mind of its nature as absolute mind. To Pringle Pattison, it implies the apprehension and full enjoyment of the depth of our being, in the absolute man being as much a complement to the world as the world is to man. To John Caird, it means the self-surrender of the human spirit to the Divine, and the function of religion consists in the elevation of man's nature above himself and the world. Radhakrishnan agrees with Caird in taking it to mean the complete transformation of man into the life of the spirit. As Waterhouse understands it, religion functions not only to create the ideals of life but also to generate and enshrine faith in their reality. To Rhys Davids, religion stands for the abiding attitude of man towards himself and the world. Max Müller, on the other hand, opines that religion implies, among others, the belief in a divine power and a hope of future life. William James, to whom we owe the distinction between personal and institutional religions, defines religion from the psychological point of view as the total reaction of the self upon life, while Matthew Arnold treats religion as morality tinged with emotion.

These modern definitions of religion have just served to bring out and emphasize the various features of religion without being able to establish a definition, which is universally acceptable. Those who truly speak with Caird and others of the business of religion as consisting in the elevation of man's state and nature above himself and the world around him have evidently at the back of their minds the etymology of the word *religion* deriving it from *re*, meaning "again", and the root *ligere*, meaning "to bind", and leading us to contemplate religion as the means of binding us again with him or them whom we believe to be the higher being or beings, or what we consider the higher state or form of existence.

Now, turning to early Indian thought in general, and to Buddhist thought in particular, we may be sure to find that from the personal point of view, religion is but a quest of Truth or the Nature of Reality, led by a noble impulse to greatness as well as to discovery, with the yearning to be firmly established in the Truth, the ultimate end of which is not only the realisation and fullest enjoyment of man's true state in the depth of his being, which is freedom or emancipation, but also the establishment of a complete harmony between the human life and the supreme religious experience. It also seeks to guide others by pointing out the way or ways of salvation.

In other words, the main foundation of this personal religion is what is called *Saddhā* in Pali, *Śraddhā* in Sanskrit, *i.e.*, faith as distinguished from *Bhakti* or devotion, which culminates in self-surrender of the human spirit to the Divine, to use Caird's phraseology. The philosophy of religion and its history, the varieties of religious experience, and the science of religion have been considered rather from the point of view of devotional religions that are all institutional in character. Religion being primarily concerned with the perfection of individuals *qua* individuals, there is also ample scope for personal religion in the institutional. And I can say that most of the weighty psychological findings of James on the varieties of religious experience are based upon the records of institutional religions, Christianity in particular.

I will, therefore, ask you not to have any misgivings on this point of distinction I desire to make between Buddhism as Buddha's personal religion and Buddhism as an institutional religion. In the present lecture, my approach to the subject is from Buddha's standpoint rather than from that of his disciples and followres whose number is legion.

In dealing with Buddhism as personal religion from Buddha's standpoint, the first thing to which I would like to draw your attention is the nature of the religious impulse to greatness and discovery, the term impulse implying the natural inclination, the natural procilivity or the natural gravitation of human mind that way,—its *tapponatā tanninnatā tappabbhāratā*.

The rise of this has been sought to be accounted for psychologically by *kusalamūlatā* or the moral heritage from one's past, and historically by such a favourable combination of circumstances as may constitute the *khaṇa* or opportune moment, *i.e.*, life in a suitable land, association with the wise, the right application of oneself, and the natural aptitudes resulting from previous good deeds[1]. Caird has carefully examined the weight of such historical explanations in the case of the phenomenal spread of Christianity as a conquering faith[2]. Here our concern is more with psychology than with history.

To enhance the importance of this impulse, the Buddhist Theras have held before us an instructive account of the long preparatory course of a gifted evolving individual. They trace back the beginning of this preparatory life to a moment when at the sight of a previous Buddha with a large retinue of his followers, his great personality, subdued looks, radiant appearance expressive of his unexcelled spiritual glow within, wonderful self-possession, gentle gait and the like, and

1 *Atthasālinī*, p. 58 ; Cf. *Maṅgala Sutta*.
2 Introduction to the Philosophy of Religion, p. 336 ff.

the great ovation with which the people gathered together to receive him, the heart of an intelligent ascetic was at once inclined to render his personal service to the Buddha and to form a strong resolve forthwith to attain to that state and to have the courage to declare it before the great man who blessed him and predicted his future greatness.

We need not go so far as that, since we have from Buddha the following psychological explanation for the rise of such an impulse to greatness :

"Here a certain person is endowed with faith, equipped with morality, replete with learning, enriched with generosity, vested with wisdom. To him the thought occurs : 'Oh ! that it were possible for me to be so reborn as to attain to the status of powerful warriors or any other higher condition of existence, on the dissolution of the body, after death'. It burns his heart, it occupies the whole of his thought, makes his mind ponder over. Such a disposition of his and constant pondering over the matter, developed and elaborated in this manner, ultimately paves the way for the attainment of his end. This is the road, this the path that leads to his goal."[1]

Please do not go away with the idea that Buddha meant to put off the fulfilment of the aim to an indefinite date beyond this life, to another existence after death. "On the dissolution of the body, after death" was a stock phrase of the time, which he made use of to convey the truth to the hearer. We have at all events a famuos discourse, in which he has dealt with the same subject at

1 *Saṁkhāruppatti Sutta, Majjhima* (No. 120.)

length with reference to here and now, to this very life. "Suppose, O great king, there were a slave, a hireling, rising up earlier, lying down later, doing the bidding, working to please, speaking to flatter,—a hanger on the face, and this were to occur to him one day. 'Wonderful it is, marvellous it is, namely, the course and maturity of virtuous deeds. Verily this king Ajātasattu of Magadha is a man as I am, and what a world of difference now exists between his royal state and my menial servitude! Suppose I, too, were to perform these virtuous deeds.' And thereafter he were to lead the life of a *bhikkhu*, renouncing the world, restrained in body, speech and mind, contented with little, satisfied, and devoted to the lonely life of meditation, and the matter were reported to you. What would you do then, would you drag him back into his old condition of servitude?" The king replied, saying, "Certainly not, Sire! I would, on the contrary, extend to him such honour and hospitality and protection as are due to him in that position."[1]

The impulses arise and vanish leading to many vagaries of thought. But here the impulse is called into play by a profound sense or feeling of awe and accompanied by a sudden throb of life felt in the entire being of the man and a life-transforming thrill of joy *(pīti)* felt in the heart. It is quickly followed by a firm resolve of the will, which, in its turn, is followed by an appropriate declaration and action. The resolution implies at once these two things: self-confidence *(sampasādana)* and aspiration or courageous step of the will *(sampakkhan-*

1 Reference is to the *Sāmaññaphala Sutta, Dīgha*, i.

dhana). It stimulates the motor energy *(viriya),* and awakens mental vision, the vivid realisation of the end or clear pre-perception of the situation which is going to arise, as well as the wisdom of following the particular course of life, setting, all doubts at rest—in short, all that is implied by the two terms, *saddhā* and *paññā.*

The firmness of the mental resolve then formed or the robust form of the will then called into being is well expressed by such words of Buddha as "whether the sky be rent asunder or the earth leaves its fixed station" *(nabhaṃ phaleyya, paṭhaviṃ caleyya),* "Let my body wither when I am on this seat, let my skin, bones and flesh be utterly destroyed, I will not move an inch from this seat until I attain the goal."[1] The same is enjoind on his followers who were to form the resolve thus : "Let my skin, nerves and bones dry up entirely, let my body of flesh and blood perish away, until my end is attained —the end which Is attainable by manly strength, manly energy, manly effort, I will not cease to strive."[2]

I have not as yet told you what made me state that the personal religion from Buddha's standpoint is primarily a Quest of Truth or the Nature of Reality. With Buddha, precisely as with the Upaniṣadic teacher Yājñavalkya, seeking *(pariyesanā, Sk. eṣaṇā),* is the essential

1 *Lalita-vistara :*
Ihāsane śuṣyatu me śarīraṁ
tvagasthi-māṁsaṁ pralayañ ca yātu
aprāpya bodhiṁ bahukalpa-durlabhāṁ
naivāsanāt kāyam etat caliṣyati.

2 *Majjhima,* i, p. 481 : *kāmaṁ taco ca nahāru ca aṭṭhi ca avasussatu, sarīre avasussatu maṁsa-lohitaṁ, yaṁ taṁ purisatthāmena purisaviriyena parakkamena pattabbaṁ na taṁ apāpuṇitvā viriyassa saṇṭhānaṁ bhavissatī ti.*

trend of life. To be in life is to seek after something. It cannot be that you will be at the same time in life and not seeking after something. You will be seeking either after progeny, wealth or fame, in short, worldly prosperity and happiness, or after something far nobler than that. The question for you and me to answer and decide is what to seek and what not to seek, to seek, in the words of Yājñavalkya, after the world or after God within us[1]; to seek, in the words of Buddha, after the world which is the ground of things contingent or after *Nirvāṇa*[2] which is eternally a free state and stands apart and other than such a world of ours.

Before a man faces this great question, his mind becomes somehow or other completely upset. This upset state of human mind is not an ordinary event. I must ask you all to realise with me the importance and seriousness of the situation which arises in human life from this upset state of mind. Take the case, for instance, first of all, of scientific discoveries. We daily see the fall of so many things from certain heights, but this passes as commonplace to us all. But Newton's mind was completely upset to notice the fall of an apple at a particular moment. How could it be that such an extraordinary phenomenon occurred in nature? And in trying to solve the mystery, he came to discover the demonstrable scientific truth which he formulated as the Law of Gravitation that stirred up the thinking minds of the world and revolutionized man's idea of the

1 *Bṛhad Āraṇyaka Up.*, iv. 4.22-25.

2 *Ariyapariyesana-Sutta, Majjhima*, i., p. 161 foll.

structure and functional order of the astronomical universe as well as man's conception of domestic, social, political and economic relations. The blueness of seawaters is a commonplace with us. But this very fact completely upset one day the mind of Raman and in solving the mystery that shrouded it, he discovered a new demonstrable scientific truth and formulated a law accounting for the structure, composition and behaviour of the molecules and atoms of matter.

The fall of an apple which upset Newton's mind led to one kind of discovery in the West. In India, as a Buddhist birth-story tells us, the fall of a withered leaf from the tree completely upset the mind of Arindama, an educated Brāhman youth, who forthwith was awakened to the fleeting nature of the world and attained to the position of a saint.[1] Vālmīki's mind was upset when the *niṣāda* shot an arrow at the male bird and killed it instantaneously when a *krauñca* pair was at play and the outcome of this was his immortal epic called *Rāmāyaṇa*. Similarly king Aśoka himself was completely upset when he pondered over the after-effects of the aggressive war he had waged against Kalinga, and its result was a momentous change in his own life along with the grand idea of *Dhammavijaya* or Conquest by Piety.

We daily come across our path innumerable sights of old age, decay, disease and death, but these pass as commonplaces. But the very first sight of them completely upset the sensitive mind of Siddhārtha, and it suggested at once to him the question : "What is all this,

1 *Sonaka Jātaka, No.* 529. Fausbôll, *Jātaka*, v. p. 248. Cf. the case of king Maghādeva of Mithilā.

why and how could it be like this ?" It set him seriously thinking—What have I been doing so long ? Being conditioned by things contingent, am I not following a course of life which leads me into things still more contingent ? Should I not, renouncing everything of the world, seek after that which is not subject to these limiting conditions of human life and of existence ? No sooner had this thought bestirred his heart than he formed the resolve to leave worldly life, and he proceeded forthwith with the quest of Truth and succeeded in making the twofold discovery of an epoch-making character.

Thus Buddha came to speak of two kinds of seeking, the two kinds of quest, the two kinds of searching : one ignoble (*anariyā*), and the other noble (*ariyā*), and said, in consonance with the earlier Indian thinkers, that the *upanisā* or way to worldly gains is one thing and that to *Nirvāṇa* quite another.

The first strong mental resolve to go out in the quest of Truth, technically called *Praṇidhāna,* presupposes these three things : (1) that the individual forming the strong mental resolve is conscious enough that he is destined to do something great in the world, (2) that he is absolutely clear about the aims or ends to which to direct all his future endeavours, and (3) that he is fully prepared to pursue the end at all costs. This act of *Praṇidhāna* is essentially an affair or operation of the concentrated human will. Behind it was the healthy belief to which the Upaniṣadic thinkers gave currency by declaring that the secret of success in life's pursuit lay in the will-power, in the right direction of the will to a rightly conceived end. The first impulsive bent of the heart towards an end must assume the form of *Sankalpa* or strong determination of the Will from which the fulfilment of the end follows. So they said: "Whatever end a person truly longs for, comes to its fulfilment from the determination of the Will; fulfilled by that, he elevates himself."[1]

Just as in the case of man's attainments, so in that of the manifestation of diverse forms of the world, there lay at the back, as they all thought and believed, the operation and direction of the creative will. Though in the *Brāhmaṇas*, this creative will *(sisṛkṣā)* came to be attributed to a personal being, called Prajāpati, representing the first idea of God or Creator in early Indian thought, it is recognized and posited in an impersonal form as *kāma* in the famous cosmological hymn of the *Ṛgveda*, known as the *Nāsadīya Sūkta*. There it is held that the process of creation did not start before *kāma*, in which lay the germ of mind or intelligence *(manaso retaḥ)*, was somehow or other stirred up in the original cosmic substance, water, full of potentialities and possibilities. The *Book of Genesis*, which represents the same stage of human thought as the ancient Brāhmaṇa texts of India, derives in the same way the whole of creation with its full structure and order from the one and the same creative will, attributed to God who alone was the moving spirit in the deep enveloped by darkness.

---

1 *Chāndogya-Up.*, viii. 2.10 *yaṁ yam antam abhikāmo bhavati, yaṁ kāmaṁ kāmayate so'sya saṅkalpād eva samuttiṣṭhati, tena sampanno mahīyate.*

As Buddha tells us in his great discourse on the Noble Quest, the quest which starts from the profound sense or feeling of dissatisfaction with the contingent character or limiting conditions of the world, implies the earnest search for something or some state of existence where these conditions are not. Thus the very search implies an innate belief in its reality and the possibility of its attainment. As he has pointed out in the *Udāna*, to ask, after once having gone forth in quest of that which is unborn, not brought into being, and undying *(ajātam abhūtam amataṃ)* if any such thing or state exists, is to beg the question. Thus the religious impulse, which is at the same time philosophical and scientific, leads the trend of life to proceed from the conditioned to the unconditioned.

In the case of Buddha, the net result of his noble quest is stated to have consisted in a twofold discovery: (1) that of the nature of reality in the form of relatedness, of which the technical name is *Paṭiccasamuppāda* or Causal Genesis. and (2) that of *Nirvāṇa* signifying the highest religious experience and the spiritual state of consciousness gone beyond all its limiting conditions, and freed from all its latent tendencies to drag it back into bondage.

The discovery of the first is aptly compared to the chance discovery of an old, buried and forgotten city, and the emotions called up by it are likened unto those awakened by the romance in the chance-discovery of the buried city. The very word "discovery" implies that the thing discovered is not created by the discoverer himself. It simply means finding it out as it had been there all the time and announcing the fact of its existence to others for their information. Thus Buddha stated the position of the Truth or Nature of Reality as found out by him, as well as his own position in relation thereto.

"In so far as *Dharma* in the sense of ancient or eternally abiding reality (*paurāṇa-dharmasthititā*) is concerned, it is a self-regulating order of cosmic life (*dharma-niyāmatā*), the suchness, realness and actuality of things (*tathatā, bhūtatā, satyatā*)[1] which exists by its own right independently of all truth-finders and path-finders, which is to say, of all thinkers and teachers, divines and philosophers ; only in so far as it signifies the *pratyātma-dharmasthititā,* its nature is accessible to an individual contemplative through intuition at a supreme moment of realisation. As thinker and teacher, he simply declared the Truth with regard to the nature of reality as realised by him *per se,* affirmed it, and pointed out the way of reaching and apprehending it, each individually by his or her own efforts. On the basis of that intuition or enlightenment was formed the basic concept of his thought which, in the sphere of religion and ethics, was interpreted, propounded and promulgated as a moral law. The path or the road which he discovered was not claimed to be new ; it was the one trodden by the Enlightened Ones of the past milleniums. The *summum bonum* of human life and the ideal of human conduct and character which he set forth was shown to be in com-

1 Cf. such terms as *ānandatā* and *sthitatā* that occur in the *Bṛhad Āraṇyaka Up.* i. 4.6-7.

plete accord with the noble experience and life of all the great contemplatives and saintly personages of the past."[1]

As for the other discovery, namely, that of *Nirvāṇa*, Buddha tells us in many places that it is the most enjoyable experience of bliss (*paramaṃ sukhaṃ*), the highest emotional state of consciousness which comes to prevail after consciousness gains or regains its free state, getting rid of all the mundane desires and pre-conceptions about the nature, reality and spiritual value of the world as such.

The free state of consciousness (*citta*) necessarily presupposes a previous state of bondage, brought about by the limiting conditions of life and of existence. Our senses, mind and intellect give us but a limited, one-sided and interested view of fact, actuality or reality. Thus often in stating the truth we either distort fact or give expression only to partial or half truths, and the result, upon the whole, is a misconstruction and misrepresentation of the fact, which is to say, the nature and order of things as it is (*yathābhūtaṃ*).

Here, you may pertinently ask whether or no, the abiding order of cosmic life which is expressed by Buddha's causal genesis is an all-inclusive reality? If so, does it or does it not include *Nirvāṇa* in it? If it precludes *Nirvāṇa* or any other element of experience,

---

1 Barua, *Asoka and His Inscriptions*, Pt. I, Ch. IV; *Laṅkāvatāra Sūtra*, ed. by Bunio Nunjio, pp. 143–4; D. T. Suzuki's *transl.*, pp. 125–6; *Saṁyutta*, ii, pp. 28, 104 ff., *Kathāvatthu*, vi. 1; Mrs. Rhys Davids, *Buddhism* (Home University Library) p. 33 ff.

material, mental, moral or spiritual, it cannot be an all-inclusive reality. Further, if it is not all-inclusive, it does not deserve the name of reality at all. To be reality it must be not only a fact but the whole of the fact, known or knowable, actual or potential.

This created a puzzle and difficulty in Buddha's personal religion, and it divided the Buddhist teachers into two sharply antagonistic schools of opinion, one maintaining that *Nirvāṇa* representing the counter-process of cessation was logically excluded from Buddha's Causal Genesis which is concerned with the process of becoming. The great Pali scholiast Buddhaghosa who has discussed this question, has sought to maintain on textual and other grounds that both the process of becoming and the counter-process of cessation are comprehended by the Law of Causal Genesis as formulated and propounded by Buddha.[1] But kindly allow me to observe that Buddhaghosa did not grasp the logical or metaphysical difficulty involved in the matter.

Buddha's Causal Genesis, as generally represented in the Buddhist texts, is an orderly sequence of the events of cosmic life. To quote the words of Buddha, "because of birth comes decay and death; whether Tathāgatas arise or not, this element stands as the establishing of things as effects." The same as to the sequence, according to law, of other recurring facts of life and of existence. If such be the order which works itself mechanically, unalterably and eternally, and if we all belong to this very reality, how can we stand out of and away from

1 *Visuddhimagga,* Ch. xvii: *Paññābhūmi-niddesa.*

it? How is the escape from the cosmic process of life and its accidents at all possible? To do justice to the two central points in Buddha's personal religion, namely, *Causal Genesis* and *Nirvāṇa,* we must be absolutely clear on the logical relation between the two.

The most welcome light on this point comes from the intellectually gifted early Buddhist sister Dhammadinnā whose views were fully approved and endorsed by the Buddha with the remark that he had nothing further to add to them. As interpreted by her, Buddha's Causal Genesis admits of two different trends of things in the whole of reality[1]. In one of them, the reaction *(paṭibhāga)* takes place in a cyclical order between two opposites *(paccanīkas),* such as pleasure and pain *(sukha-dukkha),* virtue and vice *(puñña-pāpa),* good and evil *(kusala-akusala).* This is aptly termed by Buddhaghosa as *visabhāga-paṭbhāga.* In the other, the reaction takes place in a progressive order between two counterparts or complements or between two things of the same genus, the succeeding factor augmenting the effect of the preceding one. This is what Buddhaghosa terms *sabhāga-paṭibhāga.*

---

1 From Buddha's division of human types into *onata-unnata* (degraded-elevated), *onata-onata* (degraded-degraded), *unnata-onata* (elevated-degraded) and *unnata-unnata* (elevated-elevated) in the *Aṅguttara-Nikāya* and *Puggala-paññatti* presupposes rather three trends :

(1) from degradation to degradation,

(2) from degradation to elevation and *vice versa,* and

(3) from elevation to elevation.—For Dhammadinnā's views, see Majjhima, i.p. 304 f : *Cūlavedalla Sutta.*

By the term "world", as distinguished from *Nirvāṇa,* we are to understand the first trend in the life of reality where we revolve within the cycle of reaction between the opposites. *Nirvāṇa* represents the other trend in which the course of reaction lies from strength to strength, good to further good, from that to still greater good, from pleasure to joy, from joy to gladness, from gladness to happiness, from happiness to bliss, from bliss to beatitude, from intuitional knowledge *(vijjā)* to the feeling of emancipation *(vimutti),* from that to self-mastery *(vasībhāva)* or self-consciousness as to the acquisition of the free state, and from that to the fullest enjoyment of the bliss of *Nirvāṇa.* In reply to the question as to what follows by way of reaction from *Nirvāṇa* Dhammadinnā wisely said that *Nirvāṇa* was generally regarded as the final step in the process of thought in order to avoid an infinite regress,—for the sake of *pariyantagahaṇaṃ* in her own language. But she has not failed to indicate that even if there be any further reaction, that also takes place in the line and whatever follows therefrom will also appertain to *Nirvāṇa* and, therefore, will partake of its nature.[1]

Thus Buddha's is not precisely the Heraclitean view of change, though, according to both, 'in the ceaseless transformation of all things or the process of becoming

---

1 *Majjhima,* i. p, 304: *Nibbānassa pan 'ayye kim paṭibhāgo ti? Accasārāvuso Visākha pañhaṁ, nāsakkhi pañhānaṁ pariyantaṁ gahetuṁ, Nibbānogādhaṁ hi āvuso Visākha brahmacriyaṁ, Nibbānaparāyanaṁ nibbānapariyosānaṁ.*

nothing individual persists, but only the order',—'the law of change, which constitutes the meaning and worth of the whole. It is not unwarrantable for a Buddhist who is poetically inclined sometimes to compare the process of change to the current of an everflowing river (*nadīsota-viya*) to say with a Heraclitean that a person does not step into the same river twice.

With Heraclitus the process of change means the constant transformation of everything into its opposite, the other being for him *eo ipso, i.e.*, 'the opposed', the 'flux of things being pictured as a ceaseless strife of things, which is declared to be the father of things.' 'Change and counter-change run on side by side, and the semblance of a permanent thing makes its appearance where for a time there is as much counterchange upon the one way as there is change upon the other."[1] The trend of the Heraclitean thought amounts indeed to what is conveyed by the *Great Epic* dicta stressing the fact of a cyclical rotation of pleasure and pain :

jīveṣu parivartante duḥkhāni ca sukhāni ca.[2]
sukhasyānantaraṃ duḥkhaṃ duḥkhasyānantaraṃ sukhaṃ.[3]

saṃpaśyata jagat sarvaṃ sukhaduḥkhair adhiṣṭhitam
saṃyogo viprayogaś ca paryāyeṇopalabhyate.[4]

With Buddha becoming is the causal genesis which implies the sequence, according to law, of events—

1 Windelband, *A History of Philosophy*, p. 50.
2 *Mbh.*, XV. 25, 21.
3 *Ibid*, XV. 25. 23.
4 *Ibid*, XV. 153. 9.

phenomena, appearances or experiences, that never recur in identical forms, but present themselves in such similar forms as constituting a metaphysical ground for the conception of continuity of the order (*dhamma-santati*). Each event is brought about by a conjuncture or combination of causal conditions or circumstances (*paccyasāmaggi* or *samavāya*, to use the later Buddhist phraseology).[1] In the process of causal genesis, which may be interpreted as the underlying cosmic life or moral law, it is as much possible that the reaction (*paṭi-bhāga*) of pleasure (*sukha*) is pain (*dukkha*) which is its opposite, and *vice-versa*, as that the reaction of knowledge (*vijjā*) is emancipation (*vimutti*), which is its counterpart.[2] It is equally possible that the reaction of one aspect of good is just another aspect of it, or that of the lesser degree of something is the greater degree of it. In other words, the process may be conceived either as one of a ceaseless strife of opposites, or as one in which the counterparts complete each other, or even as one of augmenting or intensifying one thing by a similar thing. If so, the true aim of combined religious, intellectual and moral efforts is so to direct thought, will and action that good may lead to greater good, that to still greater good.

Whatever else Nirvāṇa may be, psychologically viewed, it is but a perfectly free state of consciousness (*ceto-vimutti, cetaso vimokho*), a psychical condition under which consciousness feels itself to be entirely free

---

1 *Atthasālinī*, p. 58.
2 *Majjhima*, i, p. 304.

from all obsessions and preconceptions, created by the habits of thought. In so far as it implies the ultimate feeling of one's sinlessness or purity of one's internal nature, the experience is psycho-ethical in its character. And in so far as it enables consciousness to dive into its own depth of being and to fully enjoy the bliss of its true state, which is freedom, the experience is spiritual.

If there be thus at least two main trends of events in the life of reality as expressed by Buddha's Causal Genesis,[1] we get certainly a free scope for the exercise of our choice between the two.

If such be the correct interpretation of the philosophical position of Buddha's Causal Genesis, both *Saṃsāra* and *Nirvāṇa* may be consistently shown to be included in it, both as possibilities in one and the same reality. That this was the exact position may be realised from the fact that the entire mode or method of religious training which was the outcome of Buddha's personal religion was based upon the second trend, the second line of reaction implying the procession from good to greater good, from wholesome to more wholesome. The rotatory play or strife between the opposites is restricted to the *Kāma* or non-Jhanic, non-reflective spheres of consciousness. *Akusala,* the immoral or unwholesome reaction of mind, is given no place in the Jhanic or reflective spheres of consciousness and religious experience admitting of infinite gradations, though

1 Dhammapāla in his Udāna Commentary (Siamese Ed., p. 35) to the Bodhi Sutta, I. 1, rightly says: *Bhagavā Bodhirukkhamūle dhammasabhāva-paccavekkhaṇa-vasena paṭicca-samuppādaṁ manasākāsi.*

for the sake of convenience or scientific purpose these are reduced to sixteen or seventeen successive stages of progress in the life of an aspirant.

Given these two trends in the order of becoming as discovered by Buddha, and clearly held before us as such, it is up to us all to decide for ourselves which of them to seek and which not to. And here lies the scope for the freedom of the Will. Had Buddha's been simply the Heraclitean view of change, compelling us to rotate off and on with the cycle of the opposites, the grand conception of the progressive path of life as outlined by the *Aṣṭamārga*, better the *Daśamārga*,[1] which emanated out of *Buddha-jñāna*, would have been logically impossible.

Thus we are led to that stage of discussion where we may examine the nature of *Buddha-ñāṇa* or *Abhisambodhi* and its psychological bearings on the character of the inner faith awakened by it and the development of Buddha's personality.

Buddha-ñāṇa (Buddha's knowledge) is but another term for *abhiññā* or *abhisambodhi*, here the prefix *abhi* implying excelling, surpassing, superseding, transcending that which is within the access, reach, experience, apprehension, perception, vision or knowledge of the general body of mankind. Call it knowledge, call it experience, call it intuition, call it insight, even call it sensing or feeling, if you please. The advent or happen-

---

1 *Dīgha*, iii, p. 271. B. C. Law, Concepts of Buddhism, p. 36: The *Daśamārga* consists in the *Aṣṭamārga* plus *sammā-ñāṇaṁ* and *sammā-vimutti*. Cf. Dīgha, iii, 291.

ing of it takes place in a psychical sphere, on the highest conceivable supramundane level of consciousness, in the highest plane of man's experience, in the most intensified state of mental concentration, in the highest state of meditation and in the highest yogic state of trance and religious ecstasy. In so far as it gave Buddha a clear insight into the nature of truth or reality, that is to say, into the causal foundation of cosmic life and morality as well as of human thought, understanding or knowledge, it was a philosophic or scientific intuition, the content of which could be conceptualized and formulated as a definite law or laws of becoming.

But there is a purely religious or spiritual side of Buddha's *abhisambodhi.* In rising up higher and higher in the jhanic process from one level of consciousness to another, from one plane of experience to another, accompanied by introspection, he was able to go through the entire gamut of mental life, which enabled him to have an insight into the mechanism of mind, the motives or springs of action *(hetū),* the nature of consciousness and its concomitants and complexes, of which the most remarkable outcome was a system of analytical psychology forming the scientific foundation of Buddhist ethics. It enabled him also to acquire what is called the *cetopariya-ñāṇaṃ* signifying as it does the power of instantaneously or immediately entering into the mind, thought, motive or purpose of others, which is a faculty possessed, more or less, by all persons of great experience and successful men of the world. Through the yogic process all the instruments of knowing and appreciating are purified, sharpened and strengthened. The fleshy ear is sublimated into the divine, the fleshy eye into the divine, so to speak. On the purely psychical or mystical side the visions dawn on consciousness. The whole past history of the man presents itself, as it were, on the screen in a cinema show or is reflected as though in a mirror. The whole drama of life, its ups and downs, according to the destinies shaped by good or bad deeds of the individuals, is enacted as if before the eyes. The feeling arises all on a sudden that the burden of sin is gone and with the obsessions removed lightness or sense of relief is felt in consciousness as also in the whole of the being. The will is set free. The knowledge arises in a definite form as to how the ingress and egress of sin take place in man's nature. The feeling of emnacipation from the bondage created by sin, or the innate proneness to impiety and immorality arises and settles on consciousness. This is followed by the consciousness of being free, which in its turn is followed by a purely emotional state of self-enjoyment of the free state thus gained and the rejoicing over the deep conviction about the success attained.

So far as religious knowledge is concerned, we can readily say with John Caird, that it is not arrived at by a ratiocinative process of thought or gained *a priori*. It comes direct to consciousness just in a flash of intuition. If I term it a psychical or mystical experience, you may easily tolerate me provided that you have a little patience and forbearance to allow me to tell you what I precisely mean by it. You need not have any prejudice against the term "mysticism" in religion.

Here I can do no better than place before you the two handy marks by which William James characterizes it,—the marks called *ineffability* and *nöetic quality*. With regard to the first mark of ineffability, he points out that the subject of a mystical state of mind defies expression. Its quality must be directly experienced. It can neither be imparted nor transferred to others. Mystical states are more like states of feeling than like states of intellect. And with regard to the second mark of nöetic puality, he observes : "Although so similar to states of feeling, mystical states seem to those who experience them to be also states of knowledge. They are states of insight into depths of truth unplumbed by the discursive intellect. They are illuminations, revelations, full of significance and importance, all inarticluate though they remain ; and as a rule they carry with them a curious sense of authority for after-time"[1].

Buddha, too, characterises the knowledge of things that are "deep, difficult to see, difficult to understand, subtle and super-excellent", as that which lies beyond the scope of mere logic (*atakkāvacara)* and is to be reached by the wise, each by himself or herself (*paccattaṃ)*. He can speak with authority on the subject because the things he speaks of have been apprehended, experienced and seen by him. So it is said that Tathāgata the Truth-finder and Path-finder speaks of things with much authority from having apprehended and seen them (*jānato*

1 *The Varieties of Religious Experience*, p. 380 f.

passato), which is to say, from his direct knowledge of them.[1]

Wherever there is any original vision or perception of truth or of human good, the declaration is verily like this. King Aśoka, for instance, who was the most enlightened emperor with original vision, said: "Whatever I see myself as good, I desire to have it translated into action by some definite means."[2]

Thus it is claimed that in the case of Buddha the conviction, whether religious, philosophic or moral, is born of actual experience or direct knowledge. This being the case, doubt or scepticism is set at rest; it has no place in it. We may doubt everything else but not what we have actually apprehended or seen. We cannot be sceptical over our own experience. The sceptic is the common enemy of divines and philosophers. Doubt darkness counsel. It leaves human mind in a state of indecision, making it oscillate like a pendulum between two alternatives, two extremes of thought or of action, to be or not to be, to say or not to say, to do or not to do.

There is no wonder then that the entire psycho-ethical system of Abhidhamma which was a ripe fruit of the Buddha-knowledge, is designed mainly for the purpose of combating and completely overcoming doubt, perplexity or scepticism and allied mental concomitants and complexes in their various forms and degrees of intensity.

---

1 *Majjhima*, I, p. 7: *jānato ahaṁ passato āsavānaṁ khayaṁ vadāmi, no ajānato na apassato.*

2 S. R. E. I, II: *yaṁ kichi dakhāmi hakaṁ taṁ ichāmi kiṁti kaṁmanā paṭipādayehaṁ duvālate ca ālabheham.*

The two great weapons for combating this powerful enemy are faith (*saddhā*) and knowledge (*paññā*), which go together, one implying the other, the confirnation of the first lying in the second (*paññanvayā saddhā*). Man's personality or assertive, impressive and convincing element or factor in a forceful human character develops from the inner conviction or confirmed faith in certainty about one's position as to truth and purity.

At this point, we may consistently discuss how such a personality with such a mind, such a vision, such an experience and such an internal strength, inner conviction and self-confidence react upon the whole of life. Its reaction is nothing but wholesome, beneficial, non-harming, friendly, loving, sympathetic, compassionate, forbearing, helping and the like. Henceforth the things are seen in a new mental perspective. A new mental attitude results from the grand vision of life in its entirety and its underlying reality. The things are interpreted in a new way in the light of the new ideal and the course of human civilization gets altogether a new direction. Discipline, orderliness and decorum in human conduct and behaviour forming the regulating force of human society and other institutions are intended to be a thing to grow from within instead of being thrust from outside. Stress is laid upon the inwardness than the outwardness of things. Self is declared as the lord of self (*attā hi attano nātho*). The state-made law is not defied; it is just sought to be kept in abeyance. The quality of mercy is placed far above mere justice. The motive to action is required to be purified to make oneself sure of its wholesome expression and effect.

The outsiders were struck and deeply impressed by the moral rectitude and ethical perfection of Buddha, which, in his opinion, was but the least part of the praise that might be bestowed on him.[1] To appreciate the man is to appreciate the ideal he stands for. So he said : "He who sees the ideal, sees me indeed, and he who sees me, sees indeed the ideal" (*Yo dhammaṃ passati so mamaṃ va passati, yo mamaṃ passati so dhammaṃ va passati*). Here the man and the ideal become completely identified so that the system of thought or the religious faith may be presented either in doctrinal or personal terms (*dhammādhiṭṭhāna, e.g., mettā ; sattādhiṭṭhāna, e.g., mettāvihārī*).

Buddha's religion, whether in its Hīnayāna or Mahāyāna form, whether in its earlier or later phase, stands, as many thinkers say, for the doctrine of no soul, *i.e.,* the unsubstantiality or fleeting nature of mind, consciousness as well as the world as a whole, and in this respect it differs from the Upaniṣad doctrine, Jainism and other religions.

It is undeniable that the Buddhists themselves have unduly exaggerated Buddha's doctrine of *anātman.* The idea of a changeless reality is indeed inconsistent with both experience and reason : it is an *a priori* notion of being , reached in the sphere of abstract thinking. The philosophical position, that "I have both changed and not changed", or that "I have changed in appearance only, not in reality" is indefensible. To defend it is to

1 *Dīgha,* I, p. 3.

be obliged to have recourse to the doctrine of *Māyā* or illusion. According to Buddha's position, whatever is in reality or actuality is equally subject to the laws of change, of the sequence of opposites or similars[1]. The fact of change enables us to conceive and speak of continuity or procession (*santati*). It is not fair to reality to say that it behaves in one way with the world and in another way with the soul, universal or individual, allowing it to enjoy the prerogative of remaining always where it is. If we agree with Buddha and Dhammadinnā that the course of life and of things is fundamentally a course of reaction of one thing from another in two series, *Saṃsāra* and *Nirvāṇa*, the question still remains: For whose good is religion, whatever it is, really meant?

If, as some of the Buddhist thinkers overstress the point, Buddha's thought reduces the individuals and things to nothing, extinction or annihilation becomes inevitably the goal of human life, from the very suggestion of which the Buddha-mind always recoiled. From the new position made out of Buddha's Causal Genesis, it follows that going away from the world simply means the change brought about in the trend of life so that the

1 Mr. Jayasinghe acutely observes: "It does seem right that if the *paṭicca-samuppāda* contains the first two of the Noble Truths, then the second two must come in with the upward trend. Dr. Barua's suggestion has one advantage. It will remove all grounds for levelling a charge of pessimism against Buddhism. Quite incidentally in these two trends we see the foundations of two of the bright lights of modern philosophy. For the sequence of opposites is obviously the principle of contradiction and the sequence of similars the well-known principle whereby the *quantitative* changes give rise to *qualitative* ones."

course of reaction may lie from the wholesome to the wholesome.[1] The most interested part of life is *citta* or mind, which is essentially a stream of consciousness. We uproot its immoral instincts and impulses, destroy once for all its immoral motives and complexes that are coloured by them. It is not suggested that the course of reaction from the wholesome to the wholesome stops anywhere in the life of consciousness itself with the attainment of *Nirvāṇa*. The end is suggested simply for preventing an infinite regress in thought.

Thus I present for your consideration just a few salient points of the formative process of Buddhism from Buddha's personal standpoint,—a religion, which was destined to become a great force in man's civilization. Whether you agree with me or not on all the points raised, I sincerely hope that this formative aspect of Buddhism will not fail to interest you. The farther and farther we go away from Buddha, the more and more we are apt to lose sight of him from our midst. It is indeed from Buddha's point of view that Buddhism can claim to be a religion for all in all spheres of progressive life.

1 Arguing from the premises that the Buddha himself refused to attach to the upward trend the prominence which he has undoubtedly given to the *paṭicca-samuppāda,* Mr. Jayasinghe finds reasons to doubt if the *paṭicca-samuppāda* contains the Buddha's views on reality. It will be seen in the Appendix to this Lecture that this very premiss is open to dispute. It was no fault on Buddha's part that the Suttas present just one aspect of the *paṭicca-samuppāda,* namely, that in *avijjā* context only. An illustrative formula, *avijjā-paccayā sankhārā*, etc. was mistaken by the Theras for the whole of the law. It is not quite correct to say that the upward trend comes into play only when a man becomes an Arahat. The upward trend is the real trend of life which we fail to see on account of a parasitic overgrowth of a secondary nature concealing beneath it the primary one.

APPENDIX TO LECTURE V

THE BASIC CONCEPT OF BUDDHISM*

Though it may sound rather strange to say that every great thinker or true philosopher of the world is really a man of one thought, it is nevertheless a truism in history. Just as a central idea, called moral, runs through an epic narrative interweaving various episodes into a unity, so a central thought pervades a whole system of thought or of faith built upon its basic concept or creed. As regards Buddhism, its basic concept is *pratītya-samutpāda,* a term which has been variously represented in English by 'causal genesis', 'dependent origination' and 'causation'. We need not quarrel over words. Let us better try to realize its full philosophic and doctrinal significance as the basic concept of Buddhism in general and of Buddhist thought in particular.

In the *Ariya-pariyesana Sutta,* Buddha tells us that the noble quest which had impelled him to pass from home into the homeless state of a wanderer or seeker of truth happily led him to a twofold discovery, *viz.,* (1) that of *iha-pratyayatā pratītya-samutpāda,* and (2) that of *nirvāṇa.* The discovery meant the finding out of the thing or things longed for. That was in Buddha's case the non-contingent, that which is not subject to the limiting conditions of life and existence.[1]

---

* Although no lecture was delivered on this subject by me, the essay is included in the Religion series on the ground that it is an outcome of the discussions held with the teachers and students of the Vidyālankāra Pariveṇa and others of points arising out of Lecture V. See also the same in Dr. B. C. Law Volume I.

1 *Majjhima,* i, p. 161 ff.

If thus the claim made be that of a discovery only, it stands to reason to premise that the discoverer himself does not create the thing he discovers but simply finds it out as it is (*yathābhūtam*). Buddha's discovery is, therefore, aptly compared to the accidental discovery by a traveller of an old, buried and forgotten city as well as of the path leading to it.[1] Hence was his well-deserved epithet of *Tathāgata* meaning the Truth-finder and Path-finder.[2] Buddhism which was an outcome of that discovery became thus both a way of truth and a way of life. As a way of truth it became concerned with *the thing as it is or the things as they are,* and as a way of life, its concern was with *the thing as it ought to be or the things as they should be,* i.e., the ideal or ideals of life conformably to the form or forms of truth as stated as well as to the nature of reality as discovered. To be intelligible to human understanding and effective as guidance to thought and action the form or forms of truth must be either philosophical or scientific, logical or psychological. To be inspiring to life and appealing to human heart and effective in their diverse expressions, the form of the ideal or ideals must be either ethical or aesthetic, literary or artistic, social or political, religious or educational, national or international.

So far as the mental or subjective aspect of the discovery goes, it is an unprecedented experience with an

1 *Saṁyutta,* ii, p. 104 ff.; Mrs. Rhys Davids, *Buddhism* (Home University Series), p. 33 ff.; *Laṅkāvatāra-Sūtra,* ed. Bunio Nanjio, pp. 143-4; Suzuki's Transl., pp. 175-6; Barua, *Asoka and His Inscriptions,* Pt. I, Ch IV.

2 I accept above English renderings of the epithet offered by the late lamented Mrs. Rhys Davids.

objective content referring to an existing fact, an actuality or reality. This experience has to pass successively through three mental modes before it becomes a public property as a body of doctrine and discipline (*dharma-vinayam*) or a system of thought and faith, namely, intuitional or mystical, conceptual or apprehensible, and achitectonic or systèmatic. With each mode is connected a particular form of mental activity, whether it be nöetic, ideational or rational, where the prospect of success calls up the emotion of joy (*prīti*) and the attainment of success is followed by the enjoyment of self-satisfaction, happiness, bliss or beatitude (*sukha*). The experience which is presentative at the first mode becomes representative at the second and expressive or presentable at the third.

According to the Pali scholiast Dhammapāla, whilst reflecting on the nature of reality the Blessed One got hold of the causal genesis in his mind.[1] This may be taken to mean that with Dhammapāla *pratītya-samutpāda* or causal genesis represents the true nature of reality. But in the words of Buddha, the term is applicable as much to the true nature of reality as intuited as to the true nature of reality as conceived and formulated; it is applicable to the same as presented, interpreted, expounded, elaborated, elucidated and applied.

Pratītya-samutpāda as intuited in its presentative character is otherwise known as *paurāṇa-dharmasthititā*,

1 *Udāna Commentary*, Siamese Ed., to the Bodhi Sutta, I,: *Bhagavā Bodhirukkhamūle dhamma-sabhāva-paccavekkhana-vasena paṭicca-samuppādaṁ manasākāsi.*

and it stands for the ancient or eternal nature of reality which exists by its own right, independently of the advent of the Tathāgatas, independently of all modes of knowing and all forms of thought-construction and rational interpretation. The same as conceived or formulated in its representative character is otherwise known as *pratyātmadharmasthititā,*[1] and it stands for the basic concept of Buddhism and Buddhist thought as the unalterable cosmic law. The same as presented, interpreted, expounded, elaborated, elucidated and applied is known variously by the name of *pratyayākāras*[2] (causal forms), *satyas* (truths), and the like, and all of them stand for the various architectonics of thought as well as the moral law. The ideals of life and action are set out in conformity with the truths as formulated and presented, the truths are formulated on the basis of the central concept, while the central concept has behind it the nature of reality as intuited or experienced. The Buddhist creed formula, *ye dharmāḥ hetuprabhavāḥ,* etc., applies to *pratītya-samutpāda* as conceived, formulated, presented, interpreted and applied. Regarding the *paurāṇa-dharmasthititā,* the *pratyātma-dharmasthititā,* and the system of thought and faith based upon the second, Buddha's significant statement in the *Saṃyutta* is : "Because of birth, monks, decay-and-death. Whether there be an arising of *Tathāgatas,* or whether there be no such arising, in each this nature of things stands, this

1 *Laṅkāvatāra Sūtra,* pp. 143-44.
2 *Vibhaṅga,* Ch. VI, where *paccayākāra* is used as a substitute for *paṭissasamuppāda.*

that. Concerning that the *Tathāgata is fully enlightened, that he fully understands. Fully enlightened, fully understanding,* he declares it, teaches it, reveals it, sets it forth, manifests, explains, makes it plain, saying: Behold! conditioned by this, that comes to be."

In the above statement, Buddha clearly refers to and distinguishes between the three successive mental modes:

(1) becomes enlightened or awakened as to the nature of reality which exists by its own right—*abhisambujjhati;*

(2) formulates with the suggestion therefrom the fundamental law of the cosmos, which is to say, forms the basic concept of his doctrine—*abhisameti ;*

(3) states, addresses, sets forth, establishes, discloses, expounds, elucidates, in short, presents as a system—*ācikkhati, deseti,* etc.

Pratītya-samutpāda as the essential nature of reality is characterized in Pali as the elementary datum of experience, the standing order of becoming (*dhammaṭṭhitatā*), the way of the happening of things (*dhammaniyāmatā*), suchness, orderliness (*tathatā*), uncontrariness (*avitathatā*), unotherwiseness (*anaññathatā*), background of relatedness (*idappaccayatā*). It is further characterized in the *Laṅkāvatāra Sūtra* and other Mahāyāna treatises by such predicates as vacuity (*śūnyatā*), realness (*bhūtatā*) and actuality. (*satyatā*). The same set of predicates applies, *mutatis mutandis,* also to *pratityasamutpāda* as formulated, presented, interpreted and applied, though in a somewhat different sense.[1]

The positive thesis of the philosophy of Nāgārjuna, who is not without reason honoured in the *Laṅkāvatāra Sūtra* as the second Buddha, is generally missed. This is, however, clearly stated in the two opening verses of his *Kārikā*. These indicate that Nāgārjuna's primary interest was to call attention to the *pratītya-samutpāda* as the fundameital nature of reality which is not capable of verbal representations and not apprehensible by the intellect, the mode of understanding. It refuses to accept all the predicates the intellect can devise, e.g. cessation (*nirodha*), origination (*utpāda*), annihilation (*uccheda*), eternality (*śāśvata*), singleness (*ekārtha*), manifoldness (*nānārtha*), advent (*āgama*), and egress (*nirgama*). The only mental mode of witnessing or being face to face with it is intuition, immediate perception, first-hand experience or direct vision, all being means within the reach of mysticism. The powerful dialectics employed throughout his *Kārikā* are directed to expose the incapacity of all the intellectual and verbal modes of representing that nature of reality as it is, as it exists by its own right, independently of all thinkers and all ideal constructions. If the last word of Nāgārjuna's dialectics be 'be quiet', it only means the futility of the modes of understanding and the expressions of language as means of representing and stating that nature of reality, and nothing else. The incapacity of intellect and language

1 *Visuddhimagga*, ii, p. 518.

is not to be used as proof against the objective reality of that nature as intuited, witnessed or experienced,—the nature of reality to which the Buddha-mind was awakened and being awakened to which the Buddha felt with the deepest conviction that he became supremely enlightened (*abhisambuddho*). The utility of this intuition or supreme experience is not denied, for therein lies the means of stopping all aberrations of intellect and getting tranquillity which is the *summum bonum* (*prapañcopaśama śiva*).

Dr. Satkari Mookerjee characteristically observes: "The Sautrāntika may rejoin that (his) philosophy is the most perfect possible explanation of the objective world and is absolutely immune from the logical difficulties which are the besetting sins of other realistic philosophies. But the justice and validity of this claim have been disputed by Nāgārjuna and Śaṅkara, who have shown in unmistakable language that causation is the hidden rock on which the barque of realism has suffered shipwreck."[1] But reading between the lines, one cannot fail to understand that here Nāgārjuna's way of thinking is not different from the general Buddhist way. *Pratītya-samutpāda* or the essential nature of reality which exists by its own right is not the law of causation as conceived, formulated and applied. Proceeding from the experience with its elementary datum, one may come to conceive and formulate the law of causation or dependent origination, but one cannot resolve it back into the experience itself which occurred once only when it

1 *The Buddhist Philosophy of Universal Flux*, p. 57.

occurred and remains nevertheless a point of reference to *prātītya-samutpāda* conceived and formulated as the law of causation. According to the general Buddhist way of thinking, one may proceed from a chemical combination of all the ingredients used to account for the possibility of the preparation of a dish of pudding, but one cannot for that reason resolve the taste of the pudding, which is something unique, into the separate tastes of the ingredients themselves that have lost their individualities in course of the cooking.[1] The experience which is a momentary affair and never occurs twice in one and the same form accounts similarly for the possibility of the conception and formulation of a law of causation, and the law of causation or the system of thought built upon it derives its significance therefrom, but that does not mean that the experience is restorable from the law itself, far less its elementary objective datum which is not an ideal construction, and hence deserves the name of an *asaṃskṛta dhātu* or uncreated element of reality. As it is constituted, mind can just once peep into the nature of reality as it flashes through intuition or mystical experience.

Now, considered with reference to the noble quest described in the *Ariyapariyesana Sutta,* is the discovery claimed to have been made by Buddha, twofold or single? If twofold, are we not compelled to entertain the notion of there being two *asaṃskṛta dhātus* or uncreated elements of reality, namely, *pratītya-samutpāda*

---

1 *Milinda,* p. 63.

and *nirvāṇa,* which is logically absurd?[1] The uncreated elementary objective datum of experience must be single or unitary. But how is it stated to be double or twofold? Suppose we assume that *pratītyasamutpāda* alone is the element of reality, can it not be shown that *nirodha or nirvāṇa* is just a side-issue or an aspect of it?

Whether we objectively watch cosmic life, or individual life, or life of consciousness, we can have just momentary peeps or glimpses into it. At the most we can have 'point instants' or 'snapshot views' within a limited duration. In the kaleidoscopic or cinematographic view, one picture seems to pass away or to appear in quick succession or in an order or sequence, while just one picture is always present before the eyes that gaze on without reflecting or thinking. The impression left on the mind of the observer is that of the movement of pictures or appearances in the continuity of an order of change or becoming, in short, of orderliness in a continuity of which the first beginning *(pubbakoṭi, pubbanta)* and the ultimate end *(aparakoṭi, aparanta)* cannot be seen and determined. So far as the cosmic life, individual life or life of consciousness is concerned, certain experiences occur that remind us of those occurred in the past and are preserved in memory. But for the memory, the experiences that occurred previously would be lost or non-existent for ever. If the case be that of a person continuing to write a new figure on a black board with his right hand and to efface the old figure with his left, there is present always a single figure before the

1 *Kathāvatthu,* VI, 2.

observer and that which is effaced is gone for ever. But for the memory the past is past, the present is present and the future (*anāgata*) is that which is not come, that which is yet to be. With regard to the past, the correct statement is 'that it was' (*ahosi*), with regard to the present, 'that it is' (*etarahi paccuppanno*) and with regard to the future, 'that it will be' (*bhavissati*).[1]. There is no other mental mode of describing historically the event watched than representing it in terms of the three portions of time, viz., a past (*atīta*), a present (*paccuppanna*), and a future (*anāgata*), while the event itself has nothing to do with these mental modes that introduce into it the ideas of sequence, succession and duration, and thus relate it to the concepts suggestive of time and its reality. As we watch, that which strikes us is the continuity of a process of genesis at every juncture (*pratisandhi*) of which are to be noticed something ceasing-to-be and something coming-to-be, in other words, *nirodha* and *utpāda*, but the objective datum of experience is always the *utpanna* or something which has come-to-be. Something which has ceased-to-be becomes a thing of the past, non-existent for us but for memory. We proceed from the *utpanna dharma* to *utpanna dharma*, the ceasing-to-be and the coming-to-be being the mental modes of representing the junctures in the process of genesis. The observed order of sequence applies to one *utpanna dharma* ceasing-to-be and to another *utpanna-dharma* coming-to-be. One can say, therefore, that the notion of cessation is just a side-issue and a negative

1 *Poṭṭhapāda Sutta, Dīgha,* i. p. 200 ff.

aspect of the fact of sequence, either that something having ceased-to-be, something ceased-to-be, or that something having come-to-be, something came-to-be. This indeed is known as the original formulation (*ādi naya*) of *pratītya-samutpāda* conceived as the fundamental law or mode of happening in the process of genesis :

(1) *Imasmiṃ sati idaṃ hoti, imass' uppādā idaṃ uppajjati ;*

(2) *Imasmiṃ asati idaṃ na hoti, imassa nirodhā idaṃ nirujjhati.*

The first setting, called *anuloma-desanā,* is set forth in terms of advent or appearance, and the second, called *paṭiloma-desanā,* is set forth in terms of cessation or disappearance.[1] In the second Pali Abhidhamma text called *Vibhaṅga,* as well as in the Sarvāstivāda texts, the *pratiloma-deśanā* is altogether dispensed with and just the *anuloma-desanā,* is retained.[2]

In the above formulation of the general law of genesis, happining or becoming, the mental representation or verbal statement is in terms of sequence between two *utpanna-dharmas,* one ceasing-to-be and the other coming-to-be. If we cannot causally connect or interrelate them, the building up of a system of thought is impossible. When we causally inter-relate them in thought we make different causal relations out of the simple fact of sequence, and take them to subsist between

1 *Udāna,* I, 1-3 ; *Majjhima,* i, 262 ; ii, p. 32.

2 *Vibhaṅga,* Ch. VI ; P. C. Bagchi in *Epigraphia Indica,* Vol. XI, pp. 194, 199 ; B. C. Law, *Concepts of Buddhism,* p. 47 ff.

the *paccayas* (causal factors, conditions or circumstances) and the *paccayupanna-dhammas* (causally induced states, i.e., effects).[1] If the causal relation subsumed between two successive events or stages in a process of genesis involving the notions of advent and cessation, single terms are the convenient devices of thought to designate these events or stages. The notion of temporal sequence is out of place in the causal interpretation of an event, which when it takes place, takes place as a unit with regard to time and is to be viewed as a common performance of several causal factors and conditions in their momentary unification. One may think of simultaneity but not of priority or posteriority.[2] If any one speaks here of priority, it must be understood in a logical sense *(uppāda-paccayaṭṭhena)*.[3] A rational explanation of the possibility of the occurrence of an event, mental or otherwise, lies not in any single efficient cause *(eka kāraṇa)*, whether it be God or Time or Fate, but in a conjuncture of circumstances *(paccaya-sāmaggi, samavāya)*, a view, which is in different ways adopted in the Sāṃkhya, Pūrvamīmāṃsā, Nyāya and Vaiśeṣika systems of Indian thought. Though Pali scholiast Buddhaghosa pleads for the plurality of causes *(aneka-hetuto*

---

1 According to Vasubandhu, between the *samutpāda* (i.e., *hetu)* and the *samutpanna* (i.e., *phala)*. *Abhidharma-kośa*, III. 28.

2 This is Vasubandhu's definition of *samanantara pratyayaḥ*. *Abhidharma-kośa*, ii. 62 : *citta-caityā acaramā samanantarāḥ*.

3 *Dhammapada Commentary*, i. p. 23.

vutti).[1] Buddhist realism stands really for the unification (*samavāya or ekīkaraṇa*) or combination of causal factors and circumstances excluding the idea of mere juxtaposition or collocation.[2] The unification or combination must be sufficient to produce the result, which is to say, enough in itself to account for the possibility of the result produced.

The general law of happening in terms of temporal sequence (*tabbhāva-tabbhāvitā*)[3] with its causal implication was sought to be illustrated by a causal scheme of life exhibiting the twelve successive stages in the process of genesis, each denoted by a single term, *anga* or *nidāna*. The twelve terms are *avidyā*, *saṃskāra*, *vijñāna*, *nāma-rūpa*, *saḍāyatana*, *sparśa*, *vedanā*, *tṛṣṇā*, *upādāna*, *bhavā*, *jāti*, followed by *jarā-maraṇa-śoka-paridevana-upāyāśāḥ*. The convenient mode of expressing the causal nexus between any two successive stages is because of this, that: *avidyā-pratyayāt saṃskārāḥ*, *saṃskāra-pratyayāt vijñanaṃ*, etc. Unfortunately this illustrative causal scheme represented as a wheel of life (*bhava-cakra*)[4], has been mistaken for the whole of *pratītya-samutpāda* conceived

1 *Atthasālinī*, p. 59: *samavāya-saṅkhāto samayo aneka-hetuto vuttiṁ dīpeti, tena eka-kāraṇa-vādo paṭisedhito hoti. Samavāyo ca nāma sādhāraṇa-phala-nipphādane aññamaññāpekkho. Tasmā eko kattā nāma n'atthi.*

2 *Atthasālinī*, p. 60: *sādhāraṇa-phala-nipphādakattena hi ṭhitabhāvo sāmaggi na anekesaṁ samodhānamattaṁ na ca andhānaṁ dassanaṁ nāma sādhāraṇa-phalaṁ.*

3 *Abhidhammattha-saṁgaha*, Ch. VIII; *Atthasālinī*, p. 60: *assa bhāvena bhāvo.*

4 *Adhidharma-kośa*, III. 16.

and formulated as a general law of happening. The illustrative *(yadidaṃ)* causal scheme, as its twelve terms and eleven links indicate, is suited only to represent the common experience of mankind and animal world in connection with the biological development of an individual and its bearings on the feelings of others interested in his welfare. If we stop at *jarā-maraṇa (decay-and-death),* the scheme applies only to the biological career of an individual from its beginning to its end. The three terms, *śoka, paridevana and upāyāśā* (sorrow, lamentation and despair), represent the painful feelings of the kith and kin of a person on account of his death, and should, therefore, be omitted, as Vasubandhu has done, while discussing the biological career of an individual *qua* individual. The continuity of the biological career carries with it the notion of sequence or succession of *ātmabhāvas*, bodily appearances or individual *existences* within limited durations. Before we proceed further with the discussion, we should consider Vasubandhu's interpretation of *pratītya-samutpāda* in the *Abhidharma-kośa* and Yaśomitra's interpretation of the same in his *Abhidharmakośa-vyākhyā*.

Vasubandhu and Yaśomitra seem to interpret *pratītya-samutpāda,* the former tacitly and the latter explicitly, under its four aspects, viz., (1) as representing the momentary character of all forms in which the nature of reality presents itself to experience, i.e., as *kṣaṇika-pratītya-samutpāda,* (2) as representing the continuity of the order of becoming, i.e., as *prākarṣika-pratītya-samutpāda,* (3) as involving the idea of inter-relation between cause and effect, i.e., as *sāmbandhika-pratītya-samutpāda*, and (4) as differentiating the successive stages in the career of individuals, i.e., as *āvasthika-pratītya samutpāda*.[1] According to Vasubandhu, by the causal scheme of life Buddha meant the *āvasthika* aspect, and by the twelve terms outlining the same, the twelve successive stages, each exhibiting predominance of a particular feature, whether it be *avidyā*, *saṃskāra*, or the like. At each stage is to be recognized a particular organic combination or development of the five aggregates.[2]

In this architectonic of thought conceived in terms of the three portions of time, out of the twelve *nidānas* the first two, namely, *avidyā* and *saṃskāra*, are relegated to past, the last two, namely, *jāti* and *jarā-maraṇa*, to future, and the middle eight, from *vijñāna* to *bhava*, to present. The *nidānas* are classified also under three heads, viz., *kleśa*, *karma* and *vastu*. *Avidyā*, *tṛṣṇā* and *upādāna* are to be treated as *kleśas*, i.e., the mental properties or co-efficients that stain or contaminate our nature, the nature of consciousness (*citta*). *Saṃskāra* and *bhava* stand for *karmas* or the volitional phases of action shaping the destiny or determining the form of birth and rebirth. The remaining seven signify *vastus* or *loci* of *kleśa* and *karma*; these stand also for *phalas* or resultants.[3]

Viewed under the *āvasthika* aspect of *pratītya-samutpāda*, the process of genesis gives rise to the idea of an

---

1 *Ibid*, III. 25.

2 *Ibid*, III. 25: *āvasthikaḥ kileṣṭo'yaṁ, prādhānyāttvaṅga-kīrtanam*. Cf. *Atthasālinī*, p. 421.

3 *Ibid*. III. 27.

orderly sequence between successive *ātmabhāvas* or bodily appearances within limited durations of life (*addhā*). The junctures in the connected narrative of a continuous biography are called *sandhis* or *pratisandhis*. Here the past existence or episode is represented as followed by the present, and the present by the future. So far as the past existence is concerned, we are required to take cognizance of these two distinctive features, viz., *avidyā* and *saṃskāra*. Here *vidyā* and *avidyā* stand for two kinds of knowledge running counter to each other, just as two enemies who are both men are hostile to each other in their intentions and actions.[1] The term *avidyā* does not imply the absence, *abhāva* of *vidyā* or knowledge of some kind.[2] The real difference between the two lies in the fact that the animal instincts and impulses, sex-urges and lower passions are subservient to one kind of knowledge[3] and the higher instincts and impulses and nobler desires and ideas are led by the other kind. Vasubandhu defines the *avidyā* stage as the total natural disposition of the animal instincts and impulses, sex-urges and lower passions of an individual in his past life, and the *saṃskāra* stage as the sum total of the effects of past deeds of an individual as determining his destiny.[4]

As to the present life, the *vijñāna* stage is the condition of the individual just at the moment of conception

---

1 *Ibid*, III. 28 : *vidyā-vipakṣo dharmo'nyo'vidyāmitrānṛitādivat.*

2 According to Yaśomitra, *vidyāyā abhāvo 'vidye ti tu nābhipretā.*

3 According to Yaśomitra, *kleśair-anugatā hi avidyā.*

4 *Abhidharma-kośa*, III. 21 : *pūrva-kleśādaśāvidyā, saṁskārāh pūrva-karmaṇaḥ.*

and at the inception of organic development. The next stage, called *nāma-rūpa,* covers the period of organic development, the development of the fœtus in the womb, prior to the development of the six sense-organs. This is immediately followed by the *saḍāyatana* stage which is just prior to the stage of *sparśa* in which the organs of sense begin to function, bringing the individual into contact with the external world and enabling him to communicate with and feel interested in persons and things other than himself.[1] In the *sparśa* stage the individual acquires the potentiality for experiencing different feelings. The *vedanā* stage prevails when the individual begins to experience certain feelings for an object of enjoyment, and it is followed by the *tṛṣṇā* stage when he conceives the longing for the object during its enjoyment.[2] The next is the stage of *upādāna* when the individual runs after the objects of enjoyment for obtaining them. In the *bhava* stage he begins to perform such deeds as may enable him to attain to the desired future state.[3] In relation to the future life, the *tṛṣṇā* and *upādāna* stages act as the *avidyā* stage, and the *bhava* takes the place of the *saṃskāra*. In the scheme of future life the *jāti* stage is just another name for the *vijñāna* and

---

1 *Ibid,* III. 21-22 : *sandhiskandhas tu vijñānaṁ, nāmarūpaṁ ataḥparaṁ prāk ṣaḍāyatanotpādāt ; tat pūrvaṁ trika-saṁgamāt.*

2 *Ibid.,* III, 22-23 : *sparśaḥ prāk sukha-duḥkhādikaraṇa-jñāna-śaktinaḥ. Vittiḥ prāṅ maithunāt ; tṛṣṇā bhoga-maithuna-rāginaḥ.*

3 *Ibid.,* III, 23-24.

the term *jarā-maraṇa* denotes the stages from the *nāma-rūpa* to the *vedanā.*[1]

The poetical imagery depicting the *āvasthika pratītya-samutpāda* as a *bhavacakra* or wheel of life must be handled with caution. If in the order of sequence one *ātmabhāva* be followed by another and the second be neither the same as, nor quite different from, the first, there is no room for the imagery of a wheel, the series running as a, a^1, a^2, a^3, a^4 . . . . a^n .

The imagery comes in only in so far as similar stages recur in the same theoretical order of sequence in each *ātmabhāva,* and yet we are not to picture to ourselves the procession by the analogy of a single wheel in motion, it going on rather in a spiral or chain-like movement.

Vasubandhu maintains that the above formulation of the law of *āvasthika pratītya-samutpāda* was intended to set at rest all doubts as to the past, present and future existences of individuals as individuals.[2] The typical questions raised concerning the three are : Did I exist in the past or not, do I exist now or not, shall I exist in future or not, after having been what I am now what I am, what shall I become after having been what I am now ? These questions as problems are said to have been discarded by Buddha in the *Sabbāsava Sutta* on the simple ground that to admit the questions is to beg the question, i.e., to admit the answers suggested in them. Arguing therefrom one is apt to arrive at one or the other of the fol-

1 *Ibid.,* III, 24.

2 *Ibid.,* III, 25 : *pūrvāparāntamadhyeṣu sammoha-vinivṛttaye.*

lowing six conclusions : that one possesses an entity, that one does not possess an entity, that one knows self by self, that one knows not-self by self, that one knows self by not-self, that there is a soul or percipient within him, and that soul is the only entity which perdures through the whole series of bodily changes, not itself being liable to change.[1]

All that Vasubandhu means amounts to saying that by the above statement of the law the Blessed One both avoided and met the two extreme positions of self-existence and self-extinction, in other words, of eternalism and annihilationism. To subsume an entity, be it soul or spirit, which remains unaffected by organic transformations is to take up an arbitrary position in a reality where all things change but the soul or spirit alone enjoys the imperial or royal prerogative of remaining where it is, being always above the law. Nowhere in the process of genesis, in no stage of individual existence, is to be noticed such disparity between one element of reality and another, i.e., between matter and spirit, body and soul. Wherever there is any bodily appearance or individual existence, there is an inseparable combination of the five aggregates, all being equally subject to one and the same law of causal genesis. But the question still is—how far will the procession go without coming to an end for good? Does or does not *nirvāṇa* imply, in other words, the total cessation of the process of becoming meaning the *uccheda* or annihilation of individuality, of a changing individuality?

---

1 *Majjhima*, i, p. 7.

Once we assume that *nirvāṇa* means the cessation of the eschatological process of individuality, there is no escape from the charge of annihilationism which was always denied by Buddha. If, from the eschatological point of view, we say with Ajita Keśakambala, a veritable Cārvāka philosopher, that individuality ceases with death, and after death a person is not,—it is a bold case of annihilationism. Suppose the next man comes and avers that to completely get rid of individuality one must utterly exhaust the *karmic* force, which is not possible through the effort of one life. Individuality ceases entirely to be only when a perfect man dies after experiencing the first state of trance. The third man pleads for the second state and the ninth man for the eighth, and the Buddhist were to come at last to plead for the ninth state of *samāpatti*. Can we defend any of them against the above charge?[1] The *Vedānta* position is no better if it be like this that individual selves become ultimately merged in the universal self like the rivers losing themselves in the sea, abandoning their separate entities. The *Sāṃkhya* position is worse if it means that when an individual reaches the highest conceivable state of perfection, after death his soul becomes separated for ever from *prakṛti* or matter, which contains the potentiality and possibility for all organic changes, including mental. Is this precisely the ultimate eschatological position to which we are led by the logical conclusion from the trend of Buddha's *āvasthika pratītya-samutpāda*?

---

1. *Brahmajāla Sutta*, under *ucchedavāda*, *Dīgha*, i, p. 34 ff.

We can well appreciate Buddha when he took Bhikṣu Svātī to task for construing his philosophic thought as implying that *vijñāna* alone runs from existence to existence through the entire series of embodiments. By *vijñāna Svātī* obviously kept in view the Upaniṣadic *vijñānātman* or soul made up of a mass of intelligence *(vijñāna-ghana)*[1] or bare consciousness. But the criticism put into the mouth of Buddha goes to show that the word *vijñāna* was taken to mean sense-cognitions and not that because of which these mental acts and developments are possible, i.e., the *bhavāṅga citta* or *ālaya-vijñāna*,—the life-continuum, the individuated consciousness.[2] Even if Svātī's *vijñāna* were taken in this very sense, he could not be absolved from the guilt of misrepresentation. There is nowhere this suggestion that *vijñāna* or *citta* alone can exist apart from being a component factor in some form or other of the organic unity of the five aggregates.

We can similarly appreciate that in the *Khandha Saṃyutta* Bhikṣu Yamaja is severely criticised for having given out that as he construed Buddha's doctrine, it meant the cessation of the process of individuality of an Arahant with death. To put it in his own words, "on the dissolution of the body a *kṣīṇāśrava* becomes annihilated as an individual, after death he is not (i.e., does not evolve futher)." The stereotyped Buddhist arguments employed to bring the upholder of the wrong opinion to a right way of thinking are to these three

1 *Bṛhad Āraṇyaka Up.*, V, 5. 13. Note that *prajñāna* and *vijñāna* are used as variants.

2 *Majjhima*, i, p. 256 ff.

effects: (1) that none of the five aggregates as constituents of an individual existence is a permanent entity; (2) that in no stage an individuality is identifiable either with a single aggregate or with a sum total of all the five aggregates; and (3) that no individuality in any of its stages is conceivable apart *(aññatra)* from the five aggregates.[1]

By the illustrative formula, because of *avidyā, saṃskāra,* because of *saṃskāra, vijñāna,* etc. just one aspect of *āvasthika pratītya-samutpāda* is sought to be brought out. Viewing in the light of this particular formula, we are to picture to ourselves an orderly sequence of the various stages of individual life with *avidyā, saṃskāra* etc. as their distinctive features. In Theravāda Buddhism, this formula is supplemented by another, namely, because of the cessation *(nirodha)* of *avidyā,* the cessation of *saṃskāra,* because of the cessation of *saṃskāra,* the cessation of *vijñāna,* etc., to bring out another aspect of the same. Viewing in the light of this second illustrative formula, we are to picture to ourselves an orderly sequence of the various stages of individual life with *avidyā-nirodha, saṃskāra-nirodha,* etc., as their distinctive features. The *nirvāṇa* stage is to be reached when there takes place a complete cessation of *avidyā* as well as of the instincts, impulses, passions and desires led by it *(avijjāya asesa-virāga-nirodha).* Considered from this point of view, *nirvāṇa,* which is held out as the *summum bonum* of life, is negatively characterised as a

1 Read C. D. Chatterji's excellent paper, A Point of Distinction in the concept of Khandha in Buddhism, in *Bhārata-Kaumudī,* i, p. 161 ff.

state implying the exhaustion or extinction of all *āśravas*, the complete cessation of *avidyā* and of *duḥkha*. This has led many a critic of Buddhism, particularly John Caird, to think that Buddhism offers us but 'a heaven of nothingness' as the goal of life, which is to say, that in Buddhism the world has arrived only at a negative result.[1] This is undoubtedly due to the sequential setting of the stages of life in terms of *nirodha* and *kṣaya*, instead of in terms of *samudaya* and *pāripūri*.

In point of fact, whether such a setting be in terms of one or the other, behind it is the reality of causal genesis, the trend of life running through the successive stages of development. Neither the course of cosmic life, nor that of individual life, nor even that of the life of consciousness is negated thereby; it is, on the contrary, posited. By negating it, we render the significance of all such causal settings and thought-schemes of existence and of life and experience nugatory. The negation of it means the denial of the factual reality existing by its own right on which these must have their bearings in order to be significant both in thought and in the life of efforts.

To understand Buddha's real trend of thought one may do no better than to take clue from its various *mātikās* or architectonics. According to one of them, four

1 The popular prospects of an eternal and everlasting life of bliss and glory in a paradise as held out by Hīnayāna Buddhism in the Buddhakhetta *(Buddhavaṁsa)*, by Mahāyāna Buddhism in Sukhāvatī *(Sukhāvatīvyūha)*, and by other religions in the Vaikuṇṭha, the Heaven, and the like should not be brought in to bear upon the present discussion. These must be relegated to the realm of poetic fancy.

are the express or implied aims of a life of efforts, namely, the stoppage (lit. non-production) of the appearance of those sinful and unwholesome states that have not as yet arisen, getting rid of such states that have already arisen, the inducement of those wholesome states that have not as yet arisen, and the preservation, non-confusion, augmentation, increase in magnitude, development and fulness of such states that have arisen.[1] Here the first two aims relate to *nirodha* or *kṣaya* and represent its two modes, and the last two relate to *samudaya* and denote its two modes. Does it not follow from this way of stating the matter that the aim, upon the whole, is the fulfilment *(pāripūri)* of all the higher possibilities of life? The question of negation arises only when we think of getting rid of and guarding against those diseased states and future diseases that stand in the way of the healthy development of life and its progressive course.

But we must also consider here the implication of two other architectonics of Buddha's thought. Going by them, we are to adopt two different modes in classifying the living individuals, one complementary to the other, one in which the individuals are assumed to be stationary, i.e., *at rest,* and the other in which they are taken to be changing, i.e., *in motion.* According to one, they fall into these four classes: elevated *(unnata),* degraded *(avanata),* both elevated and degraded (i.e., elevated in one sense, some respects and degraded in another sense, other respects), and neither elevated nor

1 These are known as *cattāro sammappadhānā.* See *Saṅgīti Suttanta, Dīgha,* iii. p. 221.

degraded. According to the other, which is really Buddhistic, they are to be classified as degraded-elevated (*avanata-unnata*), degraded-degraded (*avanata-avanata*), elevated-degraded (*unnata-avanata*), and elevated-elevated (*unnata-unnata*).[1] Accordingly the individuals may be judged either as degraded though they appear to be at the present moment, they are tending towards elevation, or as not only degraded now but also proceeding headlong towards degradation, or as elevated though they be now, they are tending towards degradation, or fourthly, as not only elevated now but also proceeding towards further elevation. Is it not evident also from the second classifiication that the aim of Buddhism is to lead life from elevation to elevation by arresting its course from degradation to degradation?[2] Is the emphasis laid here on the negative or the positive aspect of the results of life's efforts, the passage of life from stage to stage being always the nature of reality behind all resulting efforts? To do justice to Buddha's balanced mind and comprehensive view, one can say that in his thought schemes and methods of training, the emphasis has been equally laid on both the aspects.

---

1 *Puggala-paññatti*, iv. 20.

2 This trend of Buddha's thought goes against Stcherbatsky's forceful opinion (*The conception of Buddhist Nirvāṇa*, p. 29) that "the moral law conduces through a very long process of evolution the living world into a state of final quiescence, where there is no life, but something lifeless or inanimate. In this sense the Vaibhāṣika outlook resembles the materialism of modern science." For the modern scientist's view, cf. Julian Huxley's *Essays of a Biologist*, first and last chapter (Pelican Series).

The Pāli or Theravāda illustrative formula is mostly two-armed (*anuloma-paṭiloma*) and rarely one-armed (*anuloma*); the Sarvāstivāda formula is invariably one-armed (*anuloma*), precisely as in the *Vibhaṅga*, Ch. VI. Whether one-armed or two-armed, the formula betrays the mental preoccupation about the general run of life under the sway of *avidyā* and *tṛṣṇā*. Under the aspect of cessation, too, it suggests the mental preoccupation about the stoppage of the unwholesome and the elimination of the troublesome factors, in short, negative results of life's efforts. In the *Vibhaṅga* chapter on *paṭicca-samuppāda* alone, we have specimens of different causal formulas (*paccayākāras*) including those applicable to the course of life that starts from *kusala-mūlas*. Here too the application of the law of causal genesis to the progress of higher or better life on the *lokottara* level of consciousness is barely indicated.[1] It is clearly shown that if a course of life starts from a *kusala-mūla*, the play of *avidyā*, *tṛṣṇā* and *upādāna* has no place in it, in each series *prasāda*, i.e., *śraddhā* (serene faith) is substituted for *tṛṣṇā* and *adhimokṣa* (strong bent of mind) for *upādāna*. *Prasāda* or *śraddhā* implies faith or belief in better states of existence and their realizability through right-directed efforts, etc., and *samyak dṛṣṭi*, translated by 'right view', whether *laukika* or *lokottara*,[2] is rooted in it.[3] In that case, *samyak*

1 I am greatly indebted to my esteemed cousin Mr. Birendra Lal Mutsuddi, author of the *Abhidharmārtha-saṁgraha* for drawing my attention to this.

2 See *Mahā-cattālīsa Sutta*, *Majjhima*, iii. p. 231.

3 *Saddhā-mūlikā sammādiṭṭhi*, *Sumaṅgala-vilāsinī*, i. p. 231.

saṅkalpa, translated by 'right resolve', whether *laukika* or *lokottara,* may be taken to be rooted in *adhimokṣa.* Unfortunately for Buddhism, it has nowhere been clearly shown what the illustrative formula of *āvasthika pratītya-samutpāda* should be to set forth the procession of the better stages of life that start from *vidyā.* The series from *vidyā* to *vedanā* running like that from *avidyā* to *vedanā,* its continuation may be outlined by the following terms : *samyak dṛṣṭi, samyak saṅkalpa, samyak vāk, samyak karmānta, samyak ājīva, samyak vyāyāma, samyak smṛti, samyak samādhi, samyak jñāna, samyak vimukti.*[1]

The causal concatenation from *samyak dṛṣṭi* to *samyak vimukti* will not be denied because the causal links, *sammādiṭṭhi-paccayā sammāsankappo, sammāsankappa-paccayā sammāvācā,* etc., are met with in Pali literature. The difficulty lies with the proposed causal series connecting *vijjā* with *sankhārā,* . . . *phassa* with *vedanā.* The objection may be raised that no *sankhāras* can follow from *vijjā.* This is valid only if we view the matter in the context of *avidyā* in which Buddha's doctrine of causal genesis is presented in the Pali *Nikāyas.* In this context the *saṃskāras* are rightly taken by Buddhaghoṣa as those belonging to the three lower levels of consciousness called *kāma, rūpa* and *arūpa* (*tebhūmikā sankhārā).* So when we say that no *saṃskāras* will follow from *vidyā* (higher knowledge), we mean those

1 *Dīgha,* iii. pp. 291 ; B. C. Law, *Concepts of Buddhism,* p. 36.

saṃskāras which belong to the three lower *bhūmis*. And when we say there will no longer be any rebirth, we mean that there will not again be a degradation of our nature to compel the *citta* to find itself back in the *avidyā* context. To exhaust the possibility of such degradation of our nature is the laudable aim of the progressive path taught by Buddha, and certainly not to stop the course of elevation from higher to higher forms.

In the progressive course of life which proceeds from health to health, from wholesome to wholesome, one may notice a twofold process of *nirodha*, namely, *apratisaṃkhyā* (natural, temporary) and *pratisaṃkhyā* (through knowledge).[1] When the *kuśala* states prevail, say, during the *rūpa* and *arūpa dhyānas*, the *akuśala* states cease to be present then in consciousness, but these may make their appearances after the *dhyāna* periods are over. Thus there are chances of lapses or recurrences, though not in identical forms. The prescribed course of training is intended, therefore, to exhaust these unhappy possibilities, to eliminate these chances. We reach the *nirvāṇa* stage when these possibilities are completely exhausted and these chances are entirely eliminated. Thus the fulness of life reached through the progression of wholesome stages and the thorough elimination of

1 *Abhidharma-kośa*, I, 6: *Pratisaṁkhyā-nirodho yo visaṁyogaḥ pṛthak pṛthak. Utpādātyanta-vighno'nyo nirodho 'pratisaṁkhyaya.* See for other definitions of these two *nirodhas* Satkari Mookerjee's *The Buddhist Philosophy of Universal Flux*, pp. 5, 101, 244-46, 248-49, 252.

obstacles on the way by means of two kinds of *nirodha*[1] may be taken to meet at a point, which seems to have led Nāgārjuna to hold that the ultimate reaches (*koṭis*) of *saṃsāra* and *nirvāṇa* are the same[2]. But how far will the process of life go without coming to an end?

If negatively *nirodha* and positively *pāripūri* be held out as the final goal of life's efforts, the highest conceivable state of perfection reached by Buddha or any other man, does it follow from Buddha's doctrine of *pratītya-samutpāda* that there is such a finality? Does the recorded history of men bear testimony to that? I would say, No. It is negatived by the evidence of history. Theoretically only *nirvāṇa* or fulness of life is the finality. History attests that there was a time when *nirvāṇa* or *vimokṣa* was claimed to have been realized through the first *rūpa-dhyāna* and during the first *samāpatti*. World progressed and subsequently this was found to be wrong. It came to be claimed that some one else realized it through the second *rūpadhyāna* and during the second *samāpatti*. Proceeding in this manner, and already before the rise of Buddhism, the claim was made in favour of the eighth *samāpatti*. This, too, was declared by Buddha to be inadequate, and he came to base his claim on the ninth *samāpatti*. Thus the number of *samāpattis*

1 The utility of *apratisaṁkhyā-nirodha* lies in presenting the rise of the hindrances that have not arisen, and that of *pratisaṁkhyā-nirodha* in getting rid of those which have arisen. Cf. Satkari Mookerjee, *op. cit.*

2 i.e., *yā koṭi nirvāṇasya sā koṭi saṁsaraṇasya ca.*

swelled up from one to nine as well as the number of *vimokṣas.*[1] If the number could go up from one to nine, why should it not be that like the growing number of planets, it will increase from more to more with each fresh realization or discovery? Then, again, we are not to think, when we speak of the number of planets, only of one solar system. Even assuming for argument's sake that under the present condition of human beings belonging to our planet the state of perfection reached by Buddha was not the penultimate but the very ultimate one, it does not follow from it that there are not still better conditions of beings elsewhere in the universe. The *uttaritara* slogan of Buddha, precisely like the *parātpara* slogan of the *Upaniṣads*, is inconsistent with any claim to finality, unless it be a finality *so far*, a finality hitherto known and recognized as such. Just as in a numerical series, 1, 2, 3, 4, ... *n*, the *n* remains always the theoretical finality, the same as to *nirvāṇa* which is held before us as the final goal and which is bound to recede like an ever-retreating horizon as we advance towards it.

One more question still remains to discuss. How is it possible to turn the *avidyā* series of *āvasthika pratītya-samutpāda* into a *vidyā* series, if *vidyā* and *avidyā* be diametrically opposite in fact? They are mutually contradictory as logical terms, no doubt. But, in fact, *avidyā*, as we saw, does not imply the absence of *jñāna* or knowledge of some kind. Just as two contradictory logi-

---

1 *Brahmajāla Sutta, Dīgha*, i. p. 36 ff.; *Dīgha*, iii. p. 262.

cal terms, red and not-red, comprehend together the whole universe of discourse regarding the subject of colour, so *vidyā* and *avidyā* (not-*vidyā*) may be shown to comprehend together the whole universe of discourse regarding knowledge. *Avidyā* as a kind of knowledge is based upon a certain reading of the situation of life or the nature of reality, which impels us to follow the so-called normal course of life guided by our natural instincts and impulses, sex-urges and worldly desires and passions that serve only to degrade our nature. *Vidyā* as another kind of knowledge is based upon a different reading of the situation of life or the nature of reality, which inspires us to change the direction of life and thought, to follow a different course of action which is calculated to elevate our nature.[1]

But *Vidyā* may also be regarded just as a self-conscious stage of *avidyā*, here the two terms standing respectively for that which is brought into clear recognition and that which is not. A person, for instance, is naturally good and pious but does not know that he is so and why he is so. He is then in the state of *avidyā*. Subsequently he becomes self-conscious and knows not only

1 Cf. *Muṇḍaka Up.*, i. 1-2, according to which *avidyā*=*aparāvidyā* and *vidyā*=*parāvidyā*. The former is concerned with things perishable, *i.e.*, worldly, and the latter with Brahman, the imperishable being. In the Īśa, *avidyā* meaning the normal run of life based upon the procreative institution of marriage is treated as means of preventing physical discontinuity, and *vidyā* meaning the leading of chaste life, the practice of austerities and the pursuit of higher knowledge as means of realizing the immortality of soul; *avidyayā mṛtuṁ tīrtvā, vidyayāmṛtam aśnute.*

that he is good and pious but also why and how he is so. He is then in the state of *vidyā.* Going by Buddha's discourse in the *Aggañña Suttanta,* we are to understand that the virtues that are perceivable in men when they live as children of nature become the ethical possessions of the best of men through a life of earnest effort. This is evidently the distinction Dhammadinnā sought to make between *avidyā* and *vidyā* when she premised that *vidyā* follows as a counterpart *(sabhāgā-paṭibhāga)* from *avidyā* and *avidyā* in its turn from *upekkhā.*[1]

---

1 *Cullavedalla Sutta, Majjhima,* i, p. 304. According to Buddhaghosa, *upekkhā pana andhakārābhibhūtā duddīpanā avijjā'pi tādisā vā ti ten 'ettha sabhāga-paṭibhāgo.*

LECTURE VI

BUDDHISM AS AN INSTITUTIONAL RELIGION

In the preceding lecture I tried to give you a definite and clear idea of what I understand by Buddhism as Buddha's personal religion. Buddhism from this standpoint was presented to you as a religion of which the main foundation is faith (*saddhā*) seeking and finding its confirmation in knowledge (*paññā*). The noble quest of truth, as I sought to show, is the most fruitful activity called forth by the first religious impulse to man's greatness and discovery and sustained throughout by faith. Thus in its centre is the search for truth, and not worship, in which lies the essential feature of an institutional religion based more or less on the element of *bhakti* or devotion.

As distinguished from the personal religion taken in this sense, the institutional religion insists, more or less, on the self-surrender of the human spirit to the divine. So far as the inventive or creative aspect of Buddhism as Buddha's personal religion is concerned, nothing is perhaps truer to say than that Buddha is the only Buddhist in the world. I had occasion, nevertheless, to suggest that there is in varying degrees room also for the play of personal religion in the institutional. This admitted, there is no logical difficulty in understanding the possibility of transition of the one into the other. I am concerned, therefore, to invite you

---

* This third lecture of Religion series was delivered at Colombo under the auspices of the Bauddha Sāhitya Sabhā.

in the present lecture to examine with me, however briefly, the process and nature of the transition of Buddhism as Buddha's personal religion into Buddhism as an institutional religion from the point of view of his disciples and lay followers.

I may begin by defining Buddhism from the institutional point of view as Buddha-Bhāgavatism (Deism), just as Jainism may be defined as Jina-Bhāgavatism, Vaiṣṇavism as Viṣṇu-Bhāgavatism, Śaivism as Śiva-Bhāgavatism, Śāktism as Śakti-Bhāgavatism, Christainity as Christ-Bhāgavatism and Islam as Allah-Bhāgavatism. Buddhism is that form of Bhāgavatism which derives its traits from the contemplation of the attributes of Buddha as *Bhagavān*,—a form of devotional faith of which the distinctive character is moulded by the personal religion, life and teaching of Buddha as known, understood and appreciated. Worship is in the centre of Buddhism precisely as in that of other institutional religions. Worship implies a relation between the worshipper and the worshipped.

Worship in itself is an act, an act of offering, which serves as the mode of expression of the religious sentiment of the worshipper. Through it the worshipper seeks either to approach, or to rank and unite with the worshipped. The worshipped one stands as the highest object of adoration to the worshipper. Through salutation, adoration, gifts, prayers, hymns, rituals, study, meditation and discussion, the worshipper seeks to realise and magnify the glory of the worshipped. The religious feeling of the worshipper is that there is no offering which he can make is really worthy of or sufficient for the worshipped, or that there is nothing of beauty and value which he should not give away in the name of the worshipped. Thus the worshipper is inclined to sacrifice everything he has of any value and worth, and when he has nothing else to give, he ends by offering himelf, leaving everything for the sake of the worshipped. Call it self-dedication, call it self-sacrifice, call it self-surrender, the implication is the same.

The domestic relations, such as those between teacher and pupil, father and son, brother and brother, husband and wife, lover and espouse, friend and friend, comrade and comrade, king and subject, master and servant, serves as different modes of conversation or communion between the two. These modes, taken singly, may suit the worshipper of a particular temparament, or they may be made use of successfully by one and the same worshipper.

As Ladd points out, the philosophical significance of conversations lies in the fact that the existence or reality of the person or thing spoken to is tacitly implied or taken for granted. It goes without saying that the speaker himself believes in his own existence as an individual *(ātmabhāva)*. If we, for instance, say, "O mind ! how long will you keep me in this state of woe and suffering !", we do not doubt at the moment the reality of mind; we affirm its reality. Thus in positing the reality of both, the speaker moves all along in a world of duality. This is precisely the position of Vaiṣṇavism in which the devotee is prepared to live always for the sake of his Beloved provided that he is allowed to feel a separate identity, that he is not required to merge or lose his own individuality in the Beloved.

I am aware that *śraddhā* and *bhakti* are not infrequently employed as synonyms in the daily language of man. But to understand the real distinction between the religion of *Śraddhā* and that of *Bhakti* as such it may suffice to bear in mind that in the former, *bhakti* or devotional feeling is given the lowest place; in the latter, their relative positions are reversed. In the former, faith in the sense of religious conviction born of knowledge is evaluated as the culmination of the devotional feeling, while in the latter devotion ending in complete self-surrender is regarded as the consummation of faith or accepted belief. The fact is that the same term is used in two different senses in the two systems.

In the religion founded on *śraddhā, bhakti* is regarded, *e.g.*, by Buddha, as that religious feeling which is in its essence but a domestic affection or sentiment of love *(gehasita-pemaṃ)*. In the religion founded on *bhakti, śraddhā* is treated as a selfish motive in worship for worldly gains and as such it does not come up to the devotional ideal of love for love's sake.

Without going into the merit of this conflict of ideas, I may simply point out that the difference between the two systems is really the difference between the manly spirit and manly energy on the one hand, and the womanly affection and submission on the other, which is to say, between the eternal man and the eternal woman. It is not, therefore, held without reason that a devotee is rather a woman than a man. "If thy soul is to go to heaven", says Cardinal Newman, "it must be a woman." But there are different types of institutional religions, some leaning more towards the manly faith, and some towards self-surrender. Through *bhakti* the mass religion seeks not only to vindicate itself but to establish its superior worth. Buddha characterized the mass religion of his time as consisting in *Devadhamma*, Deva-worship, which is just another word for *Devavrata* or *Devayāga*. Accordingly the Deva-worshippers are called *vatikas*, devotees, the keepers of religious vows, this religion consisting chiefly in the taking and keeping of vows to a deity, whoever or whatever the deity. This demanded a definition of *Deva or Devatā* from the cultured. As defined by Buddha, they are deities to them to whom they are objects of veneration: *ye yesaṃ dakkhiṇeyyā te tesaṃ devatā.*[1] The very same definition was offered by the great Indian grammarian, Pāṇini, in his aphorism—*sā'sya devatā*, 'the deity as his.[2] Both the definitions imply that just as a person is known by the company he keeps, so a person is known by the character of the deity he worships. It is as good to say with the Old Testament that God had created man, 'in His own image, after His likeness', as to say with Voltaire that man had created God in his own image, after his likeness, the only difference between the two being that one is theistic and the other, deistic. In popular belief every god or goddess,

1 *Culla Niddesa, sub voce devā.*

2 Pāṇīni, iv. 2. 24.

nay, every conceivable form of the Deity is a personal being, while in the interpretation of the cultured, every god or goddess means but a living form of the ideal to be approached. But whether the idea of the Godhead is theistic or deistic in its origin, when approached by the body of worshippers, its purpose is deistic.

The multiplicity of things around us, the diversity of creation, the glaring instances of social inequality and injustice give rise to a serious problem in human mind, whether or no this multiplicity or manifoldness of things may be reduced to a unity, whether or no there is any intelligent being to account for the wonderful harmony which is suggested by the diversity of creation, whether or no there is any underlying moral order accountable for a consistent explanation of happiness and misery of individuals, as well as for apparent social inequality and injustice. As a Vedic seer observed, the sun delights men with rain in season, the tempest-clouds infuse life into the earth in the form of rain, and various kinds of fire reanimate the heavens. The clouds are formed by water. From the clouds water descends in streams. The multiple principles of things are traceable in one and the same cosmic matter, and yet we are to confess—"What thing I truly am, I know not clearly : mysterious, fattered in my mind I wander." If we are all from the same primitive substance of which the sun, lightning and fire are composed, if the sun be the germ and creator of the universe', still the question remains—'What is that abiding element which, manifested in the form of the unborn sun, establishes and upholds the world-system?' The general trend of the ancient religious thought of India may be shown to have been 'towards the idea of the single, absolute and self-subsistent principle which is infinite in the sense of inexhaustible power and towards the view that all finite things and products of the self-evolution of correlated factors of one universal system and plan, and that the world therefore is a unity'. Although Ṛṣi Dīrghatamas did not know himself what that unity or single principle is, he was this much certain that it was to one and the same reality that the sages gave many a name. They called it Agni, Yama, Mātariśvan. They called it sometimes Indra, Mitra, Varuṇa, Agni, Garutman. On the fruit-bearing tree of life the Vedic seers noticed the opposite behaviour of two birds, one eating fruits, the other not eating but silently reflecting only. The religious feeling inherent in man's nature craved for a Deity on whom to wait with offerings: *kasmai devāya haviṣā vidhema?*

The eagerness to know and the eagerness to worship continued. It was held in the later Indian thought, as embodied in the older *Upaniṣads,* that we are out to seek the ground of our immortality, reality and eternality in God within us, who is at the same time the God in the universe; he is the smallest of the small and the greatest of the great. He is far beyond the reach of virtue and vice, our social justice and injustice. And it is opined: "All the books of knowledge speak of His supreme state, all penances carry the message about it, and aiming at it, indeed, man lives the holy life, the life full of virtue and chastity.'[1]

This is indeed the general Hindu view which found its most emphatic expression in the late mediæval logical treatise called *Nyāyakusumāñjali.* It tells us that the savants speak of the way to salvation,—to *svarga* (deliverance in this life) and *Apavarga* (final deliverance after death). It is in this connection that the necessity arises to ascertain the nature of the Supreme Being, the highest object of worship. It is with an eye to the underlying intelligent purpose or teleology of the world as a whole that the *Upaniṣads* speak of Him as the supreme Deity whose essential nature is absolute purity and absolute intelligence ; the Kāpilas describe Him as endowed with the eight attributes of perfection ; the Pātañjalas characterize Him as untouched by the *karmic* effects and afflictions, and as one who incarnates himself to declare the eternality of the revealed knowledge and to guide the action ; the Pāśupatas represent Him as unblemished and standing apart from all ; the Śaivas call Him Śiva who is above all modifications of matter ; the Vaiṣṇavas approach Him as Puruṣottama, the perfect Individual ; the Paurāṇikas conceive Him as the Pitāmaha or Progenitor ; the Buddhists represent Him as the Omniscient ; the Jainas claim Him as uncovered in the sense that He has no leanings to ignorance, attachment, hatred and delusion ; the Mīmāṃsakas describe Him as one given as the worshipped ; and the Cārvākas know Him as the accredited Saint. According to the

1 *Katha Up.*, I. 2. 14.

Naiyāyikas, these different schools of thought serve only to confirm in different ways their position as to the existence of a Deity.

Admitting that each institutional religion has got to place before humanity a Supreme Being or Perfect Deity for the purpose of worship, whether of human, cosmic or divine origin, whether from the theistic or deistic point of view, whether arguing from cosmology (from effect to cause, from pot to the potter), or from ontology (the changing implying the changeless as a logical necessity), or from *puruṣārtha* or teleology (from the pre-natal design, from the harmony in diversity), and also admitting that thereby they seek to satisfy different religious temperaments, one gets a chance to institute a comparison between the Godheads or Deities thus brought into being and represented, as regards their moral excellences, spiritual models, æsthetic graces and as embodiments of knowledge and truth, and as inspirers of piety and humanity. On the comparative merit of the Buddha type of the Supreme Being I may do no better than cite the well-considered opinion of Paṇḍita Rāmacandra Kavibhāratī from Bengal on whom your king conferred a distinction for his erudition and rare talent. As an apology for the acceptance of Buddha as his saviour, Kavi Rāmacandra says, expressing his judgment thus :

He who is the most perfect Deity, the most perfect personality, is acceptable to me as my lord, guide, saviour, the supreme object of adoration, be he Buddha, Śiva, Viṣṇu, Jina, Brahmā, or Indra. The criterion of judgement demands that he is all-knowing, his words are absolutely faultless and above reproach, he has not the least attachment to the world, his nature is absolutely free from three immoral motives of passion, hatred and delusion, whose heart is filled with unbounded and unselfish love and compassion. To me Śiva is not an enemy, Hari is not a foe, Jina Kevalin a rival, Brahmā Svayambhū a stranger, nor is Buddha, the Master Mind, a friend, nor is he my father, nor is he of the same family and the same caste, a Brāhman from Gauḍa that I am. But on examination I find that 'Brahmā is overpowered with *avidyā,* Viṣṇu is embraced by great illusion, which it is difficult to discriminate, Śaṅkara holds Pārvatī in his own person, owing to excessive attachment, but in this world the great *Muni,* the Lord, is without *avidyā,* without illusion, and without attachment. O, brothers, tell me, tell me, who among these is to be worshipped, for the attainment of salvation, by people possessing intelligence.'[1]

Buddhism as an institutional religion had not come into being until the formation of the Saṃgha with the laity as its supporters. The Saṃgha was from the ecclesiastical point of view a distinct religious order or institution to gain admission to which the applicants were required to possess certain qualifications or to satisfy certain requirements, and to belong to which they had to conform to, and abide by its laws, rules, regulations, formalities and conventions. From the point of view of its internal life, it was just a Brotherhood or Sisterhood of

1 *Bhaktiśataka,* Haraprasad Sastri's ed. and trans., vv. 1-3.

persons who came together to live a common life as children of the same father, as disciples of the same teacher and as followers of the same leader. From the point of view of its organization and internal cohesion, it was a corporate body or community of persons of the same piece of mind and wedded to the same ideal. From the point of view of its mission, it was a volunteer corps of persons, men and women, prepared to go through the regimental drill and discipline to combat the forces of Māra, the Evil Spirit in the world of life and of existence. The laity consisted of the kings, princes, other royal personages, the nobles, the bankers and traders, the landed aristocracy and the general folk in the rôle of worshippers (*upāsakas, upāsikās*).

Thus in the historical drama of Buddhism as an institutional religion the chief actors are Buddha, his disciples and followers and the persons who represent the laity. The prelude to this drama lies in the romantic account of the advent of Buddha, the first Act is occupied with the equally interesting story of the able ministration of Buddha and its grand success ; the second with that of the sober career of the eminent disciples and followers who survived the Master, which is to say, of the great apostles ; the third with that of the foundation of various churches and the rise of the sects and schools of thought, and their traditions ; the fourth with the activity of the missions and their successes in different parts of the world and among different peoples; and the fifth with the story of gradual decadence, exhaustion and stagnation followed by the rejuvenation of the faith.

From Buddha's point of view, the essential fact of the history thus made out lies in the manifold process of the deification of Buddha and the representation of him as *Devātideva* or the god of gods in literature, legends, art and theology. From the point of view of the doctrine, the essential fact of the same history consists in the process of its origin, first formulation, first promulgation, its subsequent additions, interpretations, canonizations, elaborations, applications, personifications and mystifications. The same carries with it the process of alphabetical, linguistic, literary, scholastic and philosophic developments.

From the point of view of the Sangha, its essential fact lies in the process of growth of the vihāras or monastic abodes, various types of educational institutions, shrines, sanctuaries and temples, in short, religious monuments of art and architecture with their endowments, the introduction and enforcement, amendments and modifications of rules, regulations, laws, formalities and various forms of convention, the rise and growth of sects and schools, the organization of churches and their missions, their rivalries and hostilities, their achievements and difficulties.

And from the point of view of the laity, its essential fact is to be read in the process of recognition of various objects of worship, development of different modes of worship, growth of piety finding its durable expressions in the erection of the vihāras and shrines of different types and artistic designs and styles, performance of various public and humanitarian works, foundation of various educational and charitable institutions and moulding of the individual, social, political, moral, intellectual and spiritual life of the community as a whole. In these respects, the remarks that hold true of Buddhism, hold true, more or less, of Brahmanism, Jainism, Śaivism, Vaiṣṇavism, Christianity and Islam. The real point of difference to be noticed between the history of one religion and that of another lies in the distinctive character each religion imparts to its various details.

The divine advent and divinity of Buddha were sought to be established by the repeated prediction put into the mouth of previous Buddhas, by the invention of legends describing his happy life in the aesthetic heaven of contentment, the supplication of the gods and angels from all the ten thousand world systems for his advent on earth for the redemption of mankind, the stories of his bodily descent, the immaculate conception of his birth, the description of the dream of queen Māyā, the divine arrangement made for the protection of the child in the womb, the walking of seven steps by the new-born heavenly babe and the declaration of his mission, the reading of the thirty-two major bodily marks by the expert Brāhman readers of the signs of a *Mahāpuruṣa*, the homage paid to the heavenly babe by all the gods, angels and archangels headed by Arahadgupta and the announcement of the beginning of the new Buddha dispensation, the jubilations in all the heavens over these events, the divine arrangement in presenting the sights of disease, decay, death and a person in the ascetic garb, the divine arrangement enabling the prince to pass out of the well-guarded city of Kapilavastu without being noticed, the supply of the sacred robes of an ascetic and bowls by the four Lokapālas, the charming story of the hairlock of the Śākya prince in the heaven of the Thirty-three gods and of the great festival held there in its honour, the highly poetical legend of the Bodhisattva's battle with and vanquishing of Māra with all his hosts, the solicitations shown and felicitations expressed by the gods and angels, the attainment of the enlightenment, the supplication by Brahmā Sohampati for the foundation of the kingdom of righteousness, the presence of the gods and angels wherever Buddha delivered his illuminating discourses, the divine aroma associated with all the woodlands and rocky caves graced by Buddha's presence, the demise of Buddha causing sadness to all the heavenly worlds and the divine arrangement in connection with the funeral on the 7th day. His divinity was also sought to be established by his unsurpassed miraculous powers displayed on many an occasion as well as by the story of his preaching Abhidhamma in the heaven of the Thirty-three gods and of his bodily descent by a staircase connecting the heaven with the earth. Special sanctity was attached to all the trees headed by the great Bo that were associated with the life of Buddha and to all the objects of Buddha's personal use, the bowl, the robes and the like, and miraculous powers were attributed to all of them. Since his demise his bodily relics were held in great veneration and duly enshrined in

Stūpas and Dāgobas with great pomp and eclat. The whole career of the Lord and Saviour of the three worlds and the greatest teacher of men and the gods was viewed as a continuous record of the overcoming of the malevolent spirits, the Yakkhas and the Nāgas, the subduing of the heretics and the unbelievers. These legends of high poetic invention supplied appropriate themes for artistic delineations through sculptures, paintings and religious poetry. Similar legends were invented in India by the devotees of Vāsudeva to magnify his glory and to invest him with divinity. With these two sets of legends in the historical background one may appreciate the legends of Jesus Christ with which his desciples, followers and devotees sought to establish his divine advent as well as divinity.

The Buddha-life, the Buddha-mind, the Buddha-wisdon,the Buddha-knowledge, the Buddha ideal and the Buddha spirit became embodied in the *Dhammakāya* or the tangible form of the doctrine,-the corpus of sacred texts which was to take the place of the Divine Master in his absence. The Saṃgha was the corporate body of holy persons who were the receivers of the great Doctrine, the most interested bearers of Buddha's words and inheritors of the *Saddharma,* privileged as custodians, embellishers and distributors of the priceless treasure.

The Buddha, the Dhamma and the Sangha were offered as three safe refuges to the afflicted humanity, and no less as three priceless jewels to be held in great affection, as three great ideals to be cherished and constantly meditated upon. The definition of them was supplied definitely bringing out the distinctive attributes of each so that the followers and devotees might not have any misgivings as to the nature of the ideals placed before them. The Buddha is defined as the prototype of the Divine Master and supreme human personality, the Adorable, the Perfect One, the living model of knowledge and virtue, the Wellgone, the Knower of the three worlds and the Unsurpassed Teacher and Trainer of tamable persons. The Dhamma is defined as the prototype of the Doctrine well-propounded by the Master, yielding the desire result here and now, in this very life and waiting for no time, the demonstrable truth with 'Come and see' as its motto, the driving force that leads to salvation and the elevation of man's nature and civilization, the essential truth of which is realisable by the wise, each by himself or herself. The Sangha is similarly defined as the prototype of the religious body of the advanced disciples of the Master, traversing the right path of progress, walking along the straight path, the path of virtue and righteousness, graceful and judicious in moral deportment, worthy of invitation and gifts and homage and forming the unsurpassed spiritual ground of virtue for the acts of piety. These three definitions of the Ideals of the presonality, the light of truth and the torch-bearers were meant to serve as the Mirror of the Dhamma *(Dhammādāsa)*. To this earlier Triad, the Mahāyāna Buddhism added the Bodhisattvas, who like the Greek gods came to represent in the East "the fair humanitics of old religion with which the religion of beauty fill the earth and the heavens" excelling in their spiritual being, mental sweep, all-embracing love and sympathy, the ideal of service, the finer religious emotions and aesthetic graces,—all that has yet been achieved and created in the sphere of abstract conception and refined imagination.

If the Triad were thus offered as the Three Refuges, or Three Jewels of the Good Faith to a Buddhist devotee either to betake to or to cherish with great affection, so far as their mutual relation is concerned, there is nothing better and more beautiful or comprehensive than what is expressed by the author of the *Kuddakapāṭha Commentary*[1]. The interest of his opinion lies also in the fact that it unfolds before us all the conceivable poetical imageries by which the devotee in any institutional religion either has expressed or may express his mental attitude towards the cherished objects.

John Caird observes by way of comparing and contrasting the religious position of Buddhism with that of Brahmanism : "So little is there in this religion any trace of positive movement that we may even represent it as saying simply that God is not-being......So far from saying 'whatever is, is right', and finding in this the sanction of our natural passions, our inhuman customs and traditions, it is true to say, 'whatever is, is wrong', and it is only in emancipation from the thraldom of sense and habit, in ceasing from the thoughts, feelings, and desires that bind us to the finite in the utter abnegation of ourselves and the world, that we rise into union with the Divine. Only in that emptiness is the Divine

1 *See Appendix.*

fulness hidden. It is in some such movement of thought that we discern that which is at first sight so inexplicable in Buddhism—its conception of God and its morality of negation and renunciation, culminating in that 'Nirvana'—the heaven of nothingness, in which the Buddhist finds the highest destiny and blessedness of man."

Caird's purpose here is clear. He makes out a negative position for Buddhism as a religion. In order to establish historically that Christianity was a complement to Buddhism in the sense that in it the religious consciousness of man found the positive ground of morality and the fulness of life. I do not blame Caird for this so much as those on whose interpretation of Buddhism his opinion was based. I can say that Buddhism was not represented in this light to the Buddhist laity, whose mind and interest were as much popular as that of any other people professing a different faith. To the laity the goal of Buddhism was held to be a paradise of bliss, far surpassing in its grandeur, beauty, serenity and ideality all the heavens or paradises conceived before. The religion was poetically presented as a large vehicle to carry all, men or women, house-holders or recluses by an imagery serving "to throw the Buddhist idea of the silent spiritual progress of man along the path of righteousness into clear relief, by contrast with the popular aspiration to attain rebirth in the heaven where Indra, king of the gods, visits the enchanting Nandana grove in a rattling chariot, surrounded by troops of nymphs making the chariot and the Paradise resonant with their music and melody and attended by a 'guard of fiendish warriors'"[1].

This was followed by the grand poetical conception of Buddhakhetta or the peaceful, blissful, sombre and serene realm of Buddha's benign influence where in the midst of the beautiful sylvan natural surroundings stands the most magnificient mansion in the spacious hall of which the Buddhas and the saintly disciples and attendants are eternally engaged in discussions to further the cause of learning and human culture. The Mahāyāna Buddhism brought at last into being the idea of Sukhāvatī or the eternal paradise of bliss forming the abode of Buddha Amitābha of infinite light to satisfy the growing spiritual need of the Buddhist.

In none of the Indian religions, the goal (*niṭṭhā*) was held to be a "heaven of nothingness". With the Brāhmans it is the 'World of *Brahmā*', with the Tāpasas the 'World of *Ābhassaras* (Lights)', with the Parivrājakas the 'World of the Good' (*Subhakiṇṇā*), and with the Ājīvakas 'the Realm of Infinite Mind' (Anantamānasa). On the other hand, in the continuous history of Indian religions we discern the successive growth of the heavens or paradises, one superseding the other. By the time of the advent of Buddha the heaven of Indra, which was once regarded as the highest conceivable abode of pleasure and joy in popular estimation, was declared to be a fool's paradise as will appear from the following verses from the Saṃyuttanikāya[2] :

"By troops of nymphs made resonant—not so !

---

2 Barua & Mitra, *Prakrit Dhammapada*, Magavaga.

2 *Saṁyutta*, i, p. 33.

Haunted by troops of fiends that paradise
Doth seem. 'Delusion' were a fitter name.
How shall there egress be?
Straight is the name that Road is called, and Free
From Fear the Quarter whither thou art bound.
Thy chariot is the Silent Runner named
With wheels of Righteous effort fitted well.
Conscience the Leaning Board; the Drapery
Is Heedfulness; the driver is the Norm
I say, and Right Views, they that run before
And be it woman, be it man for whom
Such Chariot doth wait, by that same car
Into Nibbāna's presence shall they come."

Religion, as distinguished from Metaphysics, takes and is bound to take a matter of fact or realistic view of life and things. It brings or may bring in its philosophy and idealism only to change the quality of the interpretation of its inner significance or to enhance its ethical and spiritual values. Thus we are told that Buddha presented his doctrine from two different standpoints called *Sammuti (Saṃvṛti)* or conventional and the *Paramattha (Paramārtha)* or scientific and philosophical. The *Sammuti* standpoint is one which is commonly accepted and appreciated. The *Paramattha* is the standpoint to appreciate which one needs proper training. But to be a system, Buddhism must be shown to be a complete and consistent whole coherent in all its constituent parts, the difference between the two standpoints must be more apparent than real. Nothing should be stated from any of them which is not ultimately in harmony with that which is advanced from the other. For example, from the *Sammuti* or common point of view, *dāna* (charity, liberality) which is the outcome of the mental state of *dayā* (compassion) is praised as a virtue. As an act of piety, *dāna* is a form of sacrifice *(cāga, tyāga)*. In *Nirvāṇa*, which is posited from the *Paramattha* standpoint as the goal of Buddhism, we reach the climax or fulfilment of the spirit of self-sacrifice *(cāga)*.

Well, if such be the position of Buddhism as a distinct form of devotional faith, we have got to show that nothing was more contradictory or antagonistic to its articles of faith than what is popularly called *Nāstikya* or Atheism. In fact, the dogmatic character of the Buddhist faith found its first expression in the articles of faith that went direct against the atheistic denial on the part of Ajita Keśakambala of the efficacy of the gifts, sacrifices, offering in the name of the dead, of the reward and retribution of the good or bad deeds after death, of the existence of this world and of the next, of the existence of parents after death as well as of the religious teachers who can truly instruct us about the future existence of the individuals and the destinies according to their deeds.

It is not of course possible except from the theoretical or idealistic standpoint to make out an extraordinary position for the Buddhist peoples in different parts of Eastern Asia. They, too, share the common weakness of humanity. In many matters they are no less superstitious than either the Hindus or the Jews, the Vaisnavas or the Christians, the Muslims or the Śikhs. But viewing them as a whole, one cannot fail to notice certain distinctive traits in their mental attitude towards men and things, the nature of their social relations, their acts of piety, manners and customs, thought and love of learning, aptitudes for deep thinking, creative imagination and other qualities of both head and heart.

Let us consider here just one contribution of Buddhism as a form of devotional faith to the creative art of different Buddhist peoples of Eastern Asia. It has provided each Buddhist country with a religious monument serving as its artistic landmark, e.g., British India with the great temple of Bodh Gayā, the kingdom of Nepāl with the temple of Svayambhū, the city of Pagan in Upper Burma with the Ānanda Pagoda, the Lower Burma with Shwedagon, Ceylon with Suvaṇṇamālī the Mahāthūpa, and the island of Suvarṇadvīpa (Java) with the shrine of Borobudur. I need not be surprised if you still have a good deal of prejudice against Tantricism, representing the later phases of the Mahāyāna Buddhism, the principles and ideals of which are being carefully studied and evaluated. But I may tell you that the great shrine of Borobudur, which stands as the most memorable erection of the piety and creative genius of the Mön Khmer race, is the finest outcome of this very Tantricism. This shrine, as I think, outdoes all the recognized architectural wonders of the world, if not by its size and mass, at least by the intricacy and subtlety of its structure and the spiritual meaning and appeal in all its parts as in the whole.

The part played by the disciples and followers of Buddha in the making of the long and eventful history of Buddhism is immense. They were the persons, men and women, who voluntarily renounced the world, came into direct touch with Buddha and accepted him as their teacher and guide. They were the people who were privileged to feel that they belonged to one and the same brotherhood and sisterhood under a loving father. They came from different social grades, belonged to different nationalities, spoke different dialects, and represented different religious temperaments. They were differently endowed with intellect, imagination and spiritual nature. And yet they willingly merged their individualities in the common life of a single religious order to pass as the *Sakyaputtīya Samaṇas*. The Sangha, thus formed on the principle of the unity of purpose and ideal, was compared by Buddha to an ocean into which the various rivers lose themselves to assume the common name of the ocean. As to this Sangha, Buddha never thought that he was its founder or that it waited for his guidance. In his own opinion, he was just the pioneer or forerunner (*pubbaṅgamo*) of those who came afterwards in the rôle of 'wayfarers'. The Saṃgha was a self-constituted body to be guided not by a person but by a common ideal of virtuous life. In a sense, they appeared as redoubtable knights of the Round Table of King Arthur. Though in the wake of the new faith, they came in large numbers, all were not destined to reach the goal which in their mental purview was Arhatship ; many indeed lagged behind. Even if we consider the subsequent history of Buddhism, it will be noticed that one may count on one's fingers those who made their mark and played the momentous part, and yet the importance of the work of the many who lived unnoticed and died unsung is not to be minimized. The teeming millions were the real power behind those who came into prominence and helped forward the cause of Buddhism.

Among the immediate disciples of Buddha, there were men and women of high social position, sharp intellect, clear insight and profound learning, although they mostly belonged to the three upper classes. In spite of their common heritage and common attainments as individuals, they developed certain spiritual powers and excelled others in respect of them, from which circumstance Buddha felt himself justified in dividing them into certain groups and placing foremost those who surpassed others in each group. Though for some special reasons the sisters as a body were placed below the brothers in ecclesiastical matters, theoretically in the matter of intellect, character and spirituality, women were regarded as equals of men. As Buddha expressed himself on this point, there are some women who are superior to some men in some respects, and *vice versa.* There were some among the sisters who figured equally as title-holders. The *Thera-and-Therigāthā* contain the psalms of the early Buddhist Brothers and Sisters who came to self-expression, while their inspiring past legends filled the book of Apadāna. The interest and importance of these legends lies in the fact that the pre-eminence which they had obtained was just the full fruition of their earnest *sādhanā* continued through several lives. In the case of these disciples, neither the truth in which they believed nor the path which they followed were the results of their own discovery. The religious experiences which they have given utterance to in the psalms ascribed to them are just confirmatory of those of the Master himself, and they in different words bear one and the same testimony to the greatness of Buddha. They are rightly represented, nevertheless, as the myriads of stars who surround the full-moon. They revolved like the planets round the Sun shining forth in his glory. Although they made no original discovery, they proved themselves to be of inestimable service to Buddhism as persons who put Buddha's formulations of thought in more effective forms and as those who elaborated the points suggested from time to time by the Master. Buddhist thoughts got their direction from the forms in which they expressed Buddha's ideas or the manner in which they explained and elucidated the various points of the Doctrine and the Discipline.

The famous stanza, for instance, by which Thera Assaji stated Buddha's idea of Causal Genesis became recognized as the creed formula of the Buddhists of all ages, countries and schools of opinion. The single stanza which enbodied Bhikkhunī Vajirā's opinion about men's individuality formed the scriptural authority for the subsequent Buddhist thought and discussion on the same subject. Puṇṇa Mantāṇīputta's opinion on the seven steps to purity supplied the ground plan of such later monumental works of exposition of Buddhism as Upatissa's *Vimuttimagga* (Path to Freedom) and Buddhaghosa's *Visuddhimagga* (Path to Purity). Sāriputta's authoritative opinion on the inseparability of the mental states as they occur in the unitary mental operation served as the philosophical foundation of the Abhidhamma system of Buddhist psychological ethics.

As was natural in the circumstances, Buddha's disciples and followers became interested, immediately after his demise, in collecting his words and the early tradition of the Saṃgha, thereby forming the nucleus of the primitive Buddhist Canon, as also of the entire Buddhist literature. The course of the history of Buddhism was rather dull and monotonous during the first century, and it was not quickened into a vigorous life until the Vajjiputtaka bhikkhus of Vesāli with their republican national tradition challenged the position of the Theras and formed themselves into a powerful sect and school of thought, namely, that of the Mahāsaṅghikas. This first division was quickly followed by others, seceding from both and their offshoots, each establishing a new interpretation of certain vital points of the faith and bringing about a change in the texts and language of the Canon. The traditional number of these earlier sects and schools is eighteen, including the Theriya or Theravāda which found a stronghold in Ceylon and afterwards in Siam and Burma and flourished immensely under the imperial ægis of Devānampiya Asoka. It was at the instance and with the reverential backing of Aśoka that Buddhism aspired to be a great force in the Asiatic and world civilization. Imbued with the idea of Aśoka's *Dhamma-vijaya* or Conquest by Piety and Love, it proceeded to gain the paramountcy as a universal religion of the entire human race.

I cannot but agree with Dr. N. Dutt in thinking that the rise of the eighteen sects and schools of thought was rather a sign of health than that of distemper, rather a clear proof of the increassed vitality and power of expansion and adaptability of Buddhism than that of its stagnation and death.

The subsequent tendency of these sects as separate streams, into which the main current of Buddhism bifurcated, was to converge to fewer and fewer producing these two great results :

(1) in bringing about a clear distinction between the two ideals of Saintship and Buddhahood, which is to say, between Hīnayāna and Mahāyāna on the side of religion; and

(2) in forestalling the development of the four powerful schools of Buddhist philosophy : the Mādhyamika or Śūnyatāvāda, the Yogācāra or Vijñānavāda, the Sautrāntika or Sarvāstivāda, and the Vaibhāṣika or Scholastic, the first two under the ægis of Mahāyāna and the second two under that of Hīnayāna. Their contributions to the development of the later Indian philosophy are inestimable. The growth of subtler dialectics and higher metaphysics in India was considerably due to them. They opened up the new vista of human thought and religious ideal. Aśvaghoṣa, Nāgārjuna, Vasubandhu, Asaṅga, Diṅnāga, Dharmakīrti, Kamalaśīla, and others

stand out as towering figures in the history of Indian as well as of world thought.

The later Gupta period witnessed the foundation of the world-famous University of Nālandā which flourished side by side with those of Odantapura and Vikramaśīla in South Behār, Somapura (Pāhārpur) in North Bengal, and Paṇḍita Vihāra in Chittagong Division under the Pāla kings whose long and prosperous reign formed a glorious chapter in the history of later Buddhism, not to mention many others that were founded in other parts of Bengal. Similar institutions came into existence also in other Buddhist countries, including Ceylon.

The earlier form of Mahāyāna developed in Nālandā came to be distinguished as the Bodhisattva-naya or classical from the more advanced form thereof called the Agranaya Mahāyāna with the Mantrayāna and Vajrayāna as its two branches. As a reaction against all of them arose the movement of the little understood Sahajasiddhi or Sahajiyā Cult with its continuation in the religion of the later Indian Santas—Kavīr, Dādu, Nānak, Tukārām, Caitanya and many of the Muslim Sūfīs.

During the Pāla period, Buddhism proceeded on its new career of *Trailokya-vijaya* in the supersession of its earlier career of *Dharmavijaya*. Śīlabhadra, the head of Nālandā, and Dīpaṅkara Śrījñāna from Samataṭa (East Bengal), who became the head of the Vikramaśīla University and was also connected with the Somapura Mahāvihāra are great figures in the annals of Agranaya

Buddhism, the latter specially for his mission to Tibet as real founder of the religion of Śākya-muni in the Land of Snow.

The mighty river of Buddhism flowed out of India in different channels, north, south, east and west, across the seas, across the deserts and through the mountain valleys, to irrigate and fertilise other soils, creating everywhere a glorious history for itself. As early as the time of Aśoka, Buddhism got a chance to be connected with the Greek and Semitic currents of religious thought in the Mediterranean countries.

The historians while accounting for the dwinding of Buddhism in the land of its birth lay undue stress on its hopeless internal corruption and decay. But it is so easy to flog a dead horse, to put it in the language of Professor Rhys Davids. The opinion is no longer tenable. Corruption is far from explaining the disappearance of so mighty a flow. If it were corrupt, I should rather say that greater was its right to survive along with the countless cults and creeds, rooted in grossest superistition, that pass under the bewildering general name of Hinduism. The fact is that the main mission of Buddhism in India as in other countries was cultural and as such its main citadel was not the society but its educational institutions, great and small. When these fell, one by one, at the onset of foreign invasion with the foremost idea of military conquest, Buddhism lost its foothold, and its able preachers and exponents had to flee away,—a catastrophe with its most pathetic story to be unearthed and related by competent archæologists,

The same would have been the tragedy in the life of Buddhism in your island, too, had you not been united with your kings and the Saṃgha in resisting throughout your history foreign invasions favouring other faiths and other forms of culture, no matter whether from the Indian shore or the land far across the desert.

From the drift of the discussion, it may appear to you that I have indiscriminately placed the laity in a comparatively lower position than the members of the Saṃgha. This point has been discussed in the Buddhist Canonical Texts and more elaborately in the Milinda. The householders have nowhere been denied the chances of the attainment of *Nirvāṇa,* though in the orthodox opinion, at the moment of its attainment the marks of household life vanish. But here is still a deeper consideration to make. Among the laity, the kings and the overlords held a pre-eminent position. According to the well-considered Buddhist opinion of old, all the bodily marks and minor characteristics of a *Mahāpurusha* equally distinguish a person destined to become a perfect Buddha or to figure as a righteous and enlightened emperor. In the bulk of the Pali Discourses, Buddha has spoken of the principles and ideals first from the standpoint of a righteous king emperor (*cakkavatti*) and then from the standpoint of a Buddha. In other words, there is a parallelism drawn between the two positions : one aiming at the kingdom of piety and the other at the spiritual kingdom of knowledge and virtue.[1]

1 See *Lakkhaṇa Suttanta* and *Cakkavatti-sīhanāda Sutta* in *Dīgha,* iii,

The *Cakkavatti* ideal set forth by Buddha had its fulfilment in the Dhammavijaya of Aśoka. If the members of the Saṃgha generally aspired after Arahatship, the pious kings are not rare in the history of Ceylon and other Buddhist countries who in their inscriptions have declared themselves as Bodhisattvas or aspirants for Buddhahood, which in a sense was their birthright as scions of the warrior race to which Buddha himself belonged.

Tolerance in some sense or other is a characteristic feature of the Indo-Aryan religions. So far as the general state-policy of Indian kings was concerned, they honoured and helped all sects with this difference, however, that in the case of religions other than the one in which they were personally interested, they had not taken the initiative in the founding of their institutions. The general Hindu idea of religious toleration is rather a passive one based upon the policy of non-intervention in the divine business of others. It cherished the belief that however different the paths, they lead ultimately to one and the same goal. In contrast with this Aśoka enunciated his principle of toleration emphasising its active phase. The Aśokan principle discourages the condemnation of other sects as well as the glorification of one's own sect. It insists that there should be free interchanges of thoughts and ideas, and that they should study each other's traditions so that all may be well-informed and can by helpful discussions and healthy criticisms, avoiding ill feelings and misunderstandings, co-operate for each other's growth in the essence of things (*sāravaḍhi*).

APPENDIX TO LECTURE VI

THE INTER-RELATION OF THE TRIAD AS DEFINED IN THE KHUDDAKA-PĀṬHA COMMENTARY: SARAṆATTAYA-VAṆṆANĀ

Here the Buddha is like the full moon, the Doctrine like the soothing beams, and the Order like the world whose pangs are assuaged. The Buddha is like the rising sun, the Doctrine like the radiant rays, and the Order like the world with its darkness completely dispelled. The Buddha is like the person who burns the forest of desires and complexities, the Doctrine like the fire, and the Order like the land rendered cultivable and fertile. The Buddha is like the great rain-cloud, the Doctrine like the rain-water, and the Order like the earth whose thirst is quenched by the showers. The Buddha is like the good charioteer, the Doctrine like the means of training the horses of noble breed, and the Order like the well-trained horses of noble breed. The Buddha is like the expert occulist or eye-opener, the Doctrine like the apparatus, and the Order like the persons with their eyes opened. The Buddha is like the great physician, the Doctrine like the infallible drug, and the Order like the patients radically cured. The Buddha is like the good guide, the Doctrine like the good path or the place of safety, and the Order like the body of travellers going along that path or to that place of safety. The Buddha is like the good captain, the Doctrine like the ship, and the Order like the passengers safely gone ashore. The Buddha is like the great Himalayas, the

Doctrine like the medicinal herbs, and the Order like persons healed therewith. The Buddha is like the giver of wealth (i.e., Kubera), the Doctrine like the wealth, and the Order like the person who has obtained the desired wealth. The Buddha is like the discloser of a hidden treasure, the Doctrine like the treasure itself, and the Order like the recipient thereof. The Buddha is like the assurer to say "No fear", the Doctrine like the assurance, and the Order like the assured. The Buddha is like the inspirer of confidence, the Doctrine like the confidence itself, and the Order like the body inspired with confidence. The Buddha is like the good friend, the Doctrine like the beneficial advice, and the Order like the person benefited thereby. The Buddha is like the procurer of jewel, the Doctrine like the jewel itself, and the Order like the person enriched with the jewel. The Buddha is like the good bath-attendant of a prince, the Doctrine like the good water for bathing, and the Order like the person who is well bathed (baptized). The Buddha is like the expert jeweller, the Doctrine like the good jewellery, and the Order like the princes bedecked with the jewellery. The Buddha is like the sandal tree, the Doctrine like the sandal itself, and the Order like the person whose pain is assuaged with sandal paste. The Buddha is like the source of heritage, the Doctrine like the heritage itself, and the Order like the inheritor thereof. The Buddha is like the full-blown lotus, the Doctrine like the nectar thereof, and the Order like the enjoyer of that nectar.

LECTURE VII

BUDDHISM AND EARLY VEDĀNTA

It is a rare privilege for me to have this opportunity of addressing you on such an important subject as Buddhism and Early Vedānta. I rejoice to find here by my side Swami Siddhātmānanda whom I met first in Rangoon and have the pleasure of meeting again in Colombo,—two poles asunder. I see also present in our midst Mr. M. S. Anne, the Representative of the Government of India, who has been exceptionally kind to me in many ways, and my esteemed friend Mr. Nataraja, Bar.-at-Law, who is an eminent member of the Colombo Bar and a distinguished representative of the Hindu settlers in this island. There are many others, ladies and gentlemen, whose personal acquaintance I should like to make and whose presence I surely feel. Whoever we may be, whether Indians or Indian settlers, there is no reason to think that we are aliens to this island either by land or by race and cultural heritage, the bulk of the Ceylon population being the descendants of the earlier settlers or colonisers from different parts of the mainland of India. Such being the case, the political and other aspirations of Ceylon as a whole are, after all, our own aspirations, and we have got to share the common responsibility of furthering the cause of our common culture and civilization. Although Buddhism happens to be the main religion of the island, undeniably the way for it was paved by the earlier preachers of Indo-Aryanism here as in various other parts of

* This lecture of Religion series was delivered on March 22, '44 at Colombo under the joint auspices of the Rāmakṛṣṇa Mission and Vivekānanda Society.

India. The Tāpasas, Parivrājakas, Ājīvikas and Jainas were certainly the forerunners of the Buddhists. The wave followed on the wave from the shores of India to deliver to the shores of Ceylon the lofty and eternal messages of the soul and of Buddha-mind. These are indeed the two main messages India had to cenvey to the world, one through the Upaniṣad doctrine or Early Vedānta and the other through Buddhism.

As for the Rāmkrishna Mission and Vivekānanda Society under whose joint auspices we meet here this afternoon, I am glad to observe that they seek to harmonize in their mission throughout the earth the teaching of Vedānta with the practical side of Buddhism. Ceylon is still full of inspiring memories of Swāmi Vivekānanda who was the organ voice for the serene and sweet heart of Rāmkrishna Paramahaṃsa, and the few lectures delivered by him bear happy reminiscences of this island. It was again Swāmi Vivekānanda who, besides being a living link between the two countries, boldly proclaimed in his Chicago address that Buddhism is the natural fulfilment of Hinduism.

Broadly speaking, Buddhism and Vedānta represent the two main currents of Indian religious and philosophic thought, the rest of the religions and philosophies belonging either to this or to that. If by Vedānta is meant the system of Vedānta as presented in the Sūtras of Vādarāyaṇa and developed through later interpretations, it is chronologically later than Buddhism proper and the earlier forms of Buddhist thought, nay, it is later even than the Bhagavadgītā containing, as it does, the philosophic foundation of Hinduism. If by this term is meant on the other hand the commonwealth of Vedantic doctrines as embodied in the *Upaniṣads,* its main foundation is undoubtedly pre-Buddhistic and pre-Jaina. Although the continuity of this early Vedānta can be traced through a long series of the Upaniṣad texts bringing us down to the Muslim period of Indian history and bearing clear traces of many later developments and changes in the religious and philosophic thought of India as a whole, they possess as members of the Upaniṣad family a few common traits in their general appearances, expressions and modes of presentation. The main tenets and general upshot of the earlier texts are maintained throughout. So I shall not discard them indiscriminately and leave them out of consideration simply because they appear in some respects to be later compilations. To facilitate the discussion of the subject proposed I shall confine my observations, only as far as possible, to those *Upaniṣads* which are definitely presupposed by the Pali Dialogues of the Buddha and early Buddhist literature.

To an unbiased and critical student of the *Upaniṣads* and Buddha's *Dialogues,* it cannot but appear that certain texts of the former read almost like and clearly anticipate certain texts of the latter or that certain texts of the latter are at first sight nothing but elaborations of certain texts of the former. There are certain remarkable utterances of Buddha which verbally echo those of the Upaniṣad teachers. In points of language and underlying spirit, phrases and idioms, thoughts and ideas, the Pali *Dialogues* of Buddha represent, no doubt, the next stage of cultural development. These facts, viewed superficially, have led the majority of modern Indian exponents of Hindu philosophy to deny the originality of thought and experience to Buddha. Even in the opinion of so great an exponent of Indian philosophy as Professor Sir Sarvapalli Radhakrishnan the main part played by Buddha was to democratize the philosophy of the *Upaniṣads*. Some are inclined also to the view that the real service rendered by Buddha was to confirm the truth from an *a posteriori* point of view of what was presented in the *Upaniṣads* from an *a priori*. The fact about all these opinions is that Buddhism and Jainism still pass as alien to the general thought movement of India which is sought to be grasped and interpreted under the misleading name of Hindu philosophy. The sectarian and separatist spirit is still so rampant and deep-rooted in the country that we often fail to comprehend the historical importance of the contributions of Buddhism and Jainism to the organic development of the commonwealth of Indian and world thought, and to realize how they fill in big gaps or supply many missing links in the process of that development.

It is not only the four *Vedas* with their appendices, the *Brāhmaṇas* with the *Āraṇyakas* and *Upaniṣads*, the *Śrauta* and other older *Sūtras* but also the *Bhārata* of Jaimini and the *Mahābhārata* of Vaiśampāyana are admittedly presupposed by the Pali Buddhist Canon and the earlier texts of the Jaina Canon in Ardhamāgadhī,

Even one may freely concede that the Pali *Jātakas,*–I mean, the Canonical *Jātakas,* are in many respects replicas of the anecdotes and words of popular wisdom as were embodied in the Vaiśampāyana or pre-Pāṇinian *Mahābhārata.* The prevailing religious ideals of life, the collective wisdom of the age, the notable personalities and examples of character, the accepted laws of piety and duty, the approved rules of decorum, the recognized principles of conduct, the treasured experiences and thoughts and utterances of the best of men, and the like which were the constitutive elements of Indo-Aryanism find respectful mention and are prominently held in the *Jātakas* and *Dialogues* of Buddha. These were the common property of all. What is historically important is to determine the points in respect of which Buddha struck a new note, sought to give a new direction to Indian and world thought, suggested new methods of approach to the problems of philosophy and life, defined the task of religion, broadbased the foundation of ethics and morality, tried to change the methods of education and training, and was concerned to indicate the lines on which domestic, social and national life might be developed, moulded and remoulded.

With regard to this heritage and vast wealth of all that went by the name of Indo-Aryanism and of which Buddha was a proud inheritor, his rôle was not only that of a gifted expounder and powerful preacher and disseminator, not only that of a bold critic and careful examiner, but also that of a pre-eminent leader and supplementer. These are indeed the true perspectives in which we can have a clear view of the picture of historical relationship between Buddhism and Early Vedānta.

An air of secrecy or mystery is maintained throughout the Upaniṣad tradition with the result that the *Upaniṣat* itself has come to be treated, *e.g.*, in the writings of Madame Blavatsky, as an equivalent of 'Secret Doctrine'. Even in a Sanskrit treatise like the *Arthaśāstra* of Kauṭilya or the Kāmasūtra of Vātsyāyana the word *aupaniṣadikam* which is a derivative of *upaniṣat* has been freely employed to mean a body of Ātharvaṇika (occultic) practices, not to say, of black arts. But as employed in so authoritative a text as the *Taittirīya Upaniṣad*, the word is to be treated as a synonym of 'command', 'admonition', 'instruction' to be obeyed and followed :

> *eṣa ādeśaḥ, eṣa upadeśaḥ, eṣā Vedopaniṣat,*
> *etad anuśāsanaṃ, evam upāsitavyaṃ, evāmu*
> *caitad upāsyam* (*ibid*, i. 11.4).

In a similar strain the word *upanisā* which is the Pali equivalent of *upaniṣat* occurs in Buddha's exhortation : "To this end is the discourse, the advice, the *upaniṣat*, the listening with rapt attention":

> *etadatthā kathā, etadatthā mantanā, etadatthā*
> *upanisā, etadatthā sotāvadhānaṃ.*[1]

In the *Dhammapada* verse, 76, the word *upanisā* is distinctly usad in the sense of 'path' or 'way' when Buddha declares that the way to gains is one and that to *Nirvāṇa* another :

> *aññā hi lābhūpanisā, aññā nibbāna-gāminī.*[2]

1 *Vinaya*, V, p. 164.

2 cf. Aśvaghoṣa's *Saundarananda-kāvya*, xiii. 22, 23. *mokṣasyopaniṣat vairāgyam, jñānasyopaniṣat samādhiḥ.*

The word *upaniṣat* is taken in the Sanskrit lexicon to mean a doctrine ministered in secret.[1] To explain in terms of the *Upaniṣads* themselves, the doctrine signified by *upaniṣat* is one to receive which an earnest seeker of truth and good was required to humbly approach an accredited teacher and to be respectfully seated before him, feeling his august presence.[2] Such is precisely the picture given in the prelude to each *Dialogue* of Buddha of the inquirers or learners approaching the gifted Master and sitting before him for the discussion of matters of interest and importance. The serenity and calmness of the atmosphere in which the topics of supreme interest and importance were solemnly mooted and discussed are the most striking feature of it. The Dialogues, except in rare instances where the interlocutors happened to be equals, hardly assume the form of such logical debates as are reported in the Pali Book of Controversies called *Kathāvatthu*. We have in them more of dogmatics than of dialectics, more of the experiences of master-minds through an intuitive mode of getting into direct touch with the transcendantal reality than of the ripe results of a ratiocinative or discursive process of thought.

The *upaniṣat* of the Taittirīya text which is in the form of a command, admonition or instruction is nothing but a valedictory address with which the teacher used to charge his pupil at the time of the latter's leav-

1 *Amarakoṣa*, Nānārthavarga, 293 : *dharme rdhasyupaniṣat syāt*.

2 *Muṇḍaka Up.*, i. 2. 12-13 :
tad vijñānārthaṁ sa gurum evābhigacchet samit-pāṇiḥ śrotriyaṁ brahmaniṣṭhaṁ, tasmai sa vidvān upasannāya samyak praśāntacittāya śamānvitāya.

ing the institution after finishing his Vedic course of study :

> *Satyam vada. Dharmaṃ cara. Svādhyāyān mā pramadaḥ. Ācāryāya priyaṃ dhanaṃ āhṛtya prajātantuṃ mā vyavacchetsīḥ. Satyān na pramaditavyam. Dharmān na pramaditavyam. Kuśalān na pramaditavyam. Bhūtyai na pramaditavyam. Svādhyāyapravacanābhyāṃ na pramaditavyam. Devapitṛkāryābhyāṃ na pramaditavyam. Mātṛdevo bhava. Pitṛdevo bhava. Ācāryadevo bhava. Yānyānavadyāni karmāṇi tāni sevitavyāni, no itarāṇi,* etc. (*Taitt. Up.* i. 11).

"Speak truth. Practise piety. Be not inattentive to the study of the Vedas by chanting. Do not cut off the family line after procuring for the teacher the wealth of his liking. Deviate not from truth, from piety, from good, from prosperity, from the Vedic injunctions, from duties to the gods and *pitṛs*. Attend to mother, father, teacher, guest as though to a deity. Only the works that are blameless are to be performed, not others. Etc."

The *upaniṣat* of Buddha which is in the form of a discourse, a piece of advice or an exhortation is to proclaim—

> *Vinayo saṃvaratthāya, saṃvaro avippaṭisāratthāya, avippaṭisāro pāmojjatthāya, pāmojjo pītatthāya, pīti passaddhatthāya, passaddhi sukhatthāya,. . . .yathābhūta-ñāṇadassanaṃ nibbidatthāya, nibbidā virāgatthāya, virāgo vimuttatthāya, vimutti vimuttiñāṇadassanatthāya, vimutti-ñāṇadassanaṃ anupādāparinibbānatthāya* (*Vinaya, V.* p. 164).

The discipline is for restraint, restraint is for non-repentance, non-repentance is for joyousness, joyousness for joy, joy for the subsidence of torment, that for ease, ease for concentration, concentration for knowing and seeing things as they are, that for ceasing to feel interest, that for dispassion, dispassion for emancipation, emancipation for the awareness and that for the total extinction of the thirst."

The valedictory address in the *Taittirīya Upaniṣad* may be shown to contain the main principles of Aśoka's Dhamma, particularly those inculcated through M. R. E. (Mysore version) : "Thus saith the Beloved of the gods ; respectful attention must be paid to mother and father, likewise to seniors; tender regard for living beings must be strengthened, truth must be spoken, these very attributes of piety must be propounded; likewise the teachers must be honoured by pupils with submissiveness, etc."

In the *Muktika* text (7-8), the term *Upaniṣat* stands for both the container and the contained to both of which the name of Vedānta is applied, and whether as the container (text) or as the contained (doctrine), Vedānta is extolled as the kernel or quintessence of Vedism.[1] In the *Muṇḍaka* text (iii. 2.6.), the main content of the *Upaniṣads* is appropriately represented as the well-defined knowledge of Vedānta (*Vedānta-vijñānam).* In other texts this knowledge is given the name of *Brahmavidyā* or *Brahmatattva*, which is just another word for *Ātmavidyā* or *Ātmatattva.* In the *Muṇḍaka*

1 *tileṣu tailavad Vede Vedāntaḥ supratiṣṭhitaḥ.*

text itself (ii. 2.3), the learner is advised to make use of the *Upaniṣad* as the bow, and to set on it the arrow (i.e., himself) sharpened by reverential approach *(upāsanā)*, aiming at and piercing the knowledge of the indestructible *(akṣara)*, *i.e.*, of Brahman, the absolute and transcendental being. The leading of *brahmacarya* or chaste life is insisted on throughout the *Upaniṣads* as the primary moral condition of self (individual life) for the attainment of that supreme end. Thus to be an adept in Vedānta entitled to deal with the Brahma-lore is to be the finest type of ethical man,glowing with the inner glow and outer expression of spirituality. Such is precisely the criterion of a person being an expert vedāntin suggested by Buddha in one of his very first utterances: "The Brāhman whose self has been cleansed of sins, who is nonboasting, whose nature is not stained by passions, who is self-controlled, who has thoroughly gone through Vedānta and lived the holy life is indeed the man who can expound the Doctrine of Brahman."

Yo brāhmaṇo vāhitapāpo nihuhunko nikkasāvo yattatto |
Vedantagū vusita-brahmacariyo dhammena so Brahmavādaṃ vadeyya[1] ||

Immediately after the time-honoured Vedic seers, Buddha mentions the Brāhman teachers belonging to the different Vedas, such as the Addhariyas (Adhvaryus) to be connected with the *Yajurveda* (White), say the Vājasaneyas, the Tittirīyas (Taittirīyas) to be connected

1 Udāna, I. 4.

with the Taittirīya (Black) recension of the *Yajurveda*, the Chandokas (Chāndogyas) to be connected with the *Sāmaveda*, and the Bāhvṛcas to be connected with the *Ṛgveda*, say the Aitareyas.[1] They are spoken of as the teachers who were propounders of divers paths leading to one and the same state of union with Brahmā.[2] In the *Dialogues* of Buddha we are introduced also to several contemporary religious orders of the Brāhman Parivrājakas and the schools of thought represented by them. In them we are referred moreover to the important religious orders and schools of thought founded by six Śramaṇa teachers, Brāhmans and Kṣatriyas, who were regarded as renegades to the Vedic tradition of Indo-Aryanism, including Mahāvīra, the founder of Jainism. The Brāhman Parivrājakas and Śramaṇas have been classified and named either according to their practices and habits or outward signs, or according to the doctrines upheld, or even according to the personal distinction of the founders and leaders. The *Upaniṣads*, earlier and later, contain the views and religious practices of the earlier Brāhman schools of the Śrotriyas as well as those of the various schools of the Brāhman Parivrājakas. The later texts are named also after the deities of whom the exponents of the *Upaniṣad* doctrine of Brahman and self happened to be the votaries. The *Great Epic* in its post-Buddhistic form came to embody a number of *Gītās* forming as they did a literature by themselves by way of a deflection from

1 There is a comparatively modern *Upaniṣad* called *Bāhvṛca*.

2 *Dīgha*, i, p. 237f.

the *Upaniṣads*. How much of the doctrines and practices contained in the *Upaniṣads* and these *Gītās* is really presupposed by primitive Buddhism is an all-important question to return a satisfactory answer to which we need a close co-operation of many a competent scholar.

Buddhism and Early Vedānta are concerned with the problem of the origin and development of the cosmos, the world of life, the society and the state. Both seek to determine man's supreme place in the world as a whole. Both consider man's position from the anatomical, physiological, embryological, psychological, eschatological, ethical, intellectual and spiritual points of view. The elevation of human nature by all possible means is the principal aim of both. The problem of *vidyā* and *avidyā*, their bearings on the course of human life, the Law of Karma and its bearing on the problem of freedom of the will, the problem of dream and sleep and of death and after, and the problem of memory are equally important in both. The problem of liberation or deliverance *(mukti, mokṣa, nirvāṇa)* is vital to both. The question of individuality and progress demnads a satisfactory answer from both. The need of *yoga* or *dhyāna* as means of concentration, insight, introspection, higher knowledge and the development of supernormal faculties is equally stressed in both. The cosmography with the traditional gradation of beings serves virtually the same psycho-ethical purpose as a means of measurement of the levels of consciousness, the planes of experience, and the perfection of character. Both lay the same kind of emphasis on the polite behaviour on the part of the learner according to the rules of decorum and the fulfilment of the moral conditions of the self. Both draw away the mind from things external and worldly and seek to increase its inwardness, from cares and anxieties, worry and flurry to that of tranquillity and peace. Both exhort men to grow from more to more, to go ahead (*uparyupari, uttaritaraṃ*). Both recognize the need of food or nourishment of five different kinds, stressing the great importance of spritual food to the self. The art of reading a rational meaning into rituals and popular practices is tried in both to deepen their significance.

The Bodhisattvas of the *Jātakas* are modified or unmodified heroes of the popular anecdotes with their prototypes in the pre-Pāṇinian *Mahābhārata*. They are the moralisers, instructors of wisdom, the collective wealth of which was in the immediate background of Buddhism proper.

There is yet no valid reason to change my opinion that Yājñavalkya, the founder of the Vājasaneya school, is indeed the most notable milestone in the history of Indo-Aryanism prior to the advent of Buddha. He is the historical expounder of the doctrine of *karma* referred to by Buddha.[1] Buddha's Discourse on the Noble Quest is nothing but a later elucidation of a saying of Yājñavalkya, which is met with in the *Bṛhad Āraṇyaka*.[2] It is again in contradistinction to the philosophy of Yājñavalkya that Buddha wanted his disciples to appraise

1 *Majjhima*, ii, Tevijja-Vacchagotta Sutta.
2 *Bṛhad Āraṇyaka*, iv. 4 and *Ariya-pariyesana Sutta*,

the main philosophic position of his own thought.[1] Similarly it is in contrast with the main burden of the moral of the *Great Epic* that we are required to appraise or appreciate the main trend of the Jātaka ethics.[2] The types of the old-world thought classified and defined in the *Brahmajāla Sutta* apply mainly to the teachings of the *Upaniṣads,* and partly only to those of the contemporary Śramaṇa teachers.

Buddha's vivid account of hard penances including the practice of *Haṭhayoga*[3] has its exact Sanskrit counterpart in such *Upaniṣads* as the *Yogaśikhā, Paramahaṃsa Parivrājaka, Saṃnyāsa, Turīyātīta* and *Avadhūta.* Behind Buddha's conception of *nāma-rūpa* and five aggregates is the Upaniṣadic idea of *nāma-rūpa* and five *kośas.* The same four predicates of *durangama, ekacara, asarīra* and *guhāsaya* are applied alike to *citta* and *ātmā*[4]. Buddha's description of organic functions in terms of the six *vātas* cannot but remind us of the *Upaniṣad* account of the same in terms of the five *prāṇas* (vital airs).[5]

The points of similarity, which are in some instances verbal only, go to determine the historical background of Buddhism, and these are not to be mistaken for the points of identity. It is the points of difference and distinction that are really important from the historical point of view as suggesting a new direction to Indian and world thought and as determining Buddha's origi-

1 *Bṛhad Āraṇyaka,* iv. 1 and *Mulapariyāya Sutta Majjhima Sutta,* No: 1.
2 *Jātaka,* No: 245
3 Majjhima, i, Mahāsaccaka Sutta.
4 Barua & Mitra, *Prakrit Dhammapada,* Citavaga.
5 *Ibid,* i, Mahāhatthipadopama Sutta.

nal contributions and progressive steps. The keys are supplied to the understanding of the ranges of religious experience and philosophic thought within which the points of similarity are to be noticed, as well as those within which the points of difference are to be adjudged and appreciated. The ranges within which the points of agreement are to be noticed are broadly characterised as *laukika* (mundane, popular) and spoken of as comprising the three worlds of conscious existence *(lokas)* or three levels of consciousness and planes of experience *(bhūmis)*. And the ranges within which the points of disagreement are to be noted and appreciated are broadly characterised as *lokottara* (supramundane, going beyond the popular stage, progressive) and spoken of as comprising the eight stages of conscious advance and rationality. Even within the ranges of the *consensus* of opinion there are points of difference and distinction, and in the later systems of Indian thought other than Buddhist the *lokottara* position of Buddhism is assailed with new armaments of logical thought, theology and epistemology forged in the vigorous workshop of both orthodoxy and heterodoxy.

The *Mūlapariyāya* among the *Suttas* and the *Mūlapariyāya* among the *Jātakas* are historically the most important, the first as indicating the point of departure of Buddha's thought from Early Vedānta and the second as indicating the point of departure of Buddhism from the general trend of Hinduism or popular Indian thought. In one case we are to understand the departure from the philosophy of the

Upaniṣads and in the other from the popular philosophy of the *Great Epic.* The earlier Indian philosophy outlined in the *Mūlapariyāya Sutta* is one which is embodied in the *Bṛhad Āraṇyaka Upaniṣad*, and the popular notion which is sought to be counteracted in the *Mūlapariyāya Jātaka* is one which is emphasized throughout the *Mahābhārata.*

The *Great Epic* emphasizes throughout its narrative the importance of time *(kāla)*, providence *(daiva)* and fate *(diṣṭa)* as explanations for all that happens in life to an individual, a family, a race or nation. Time destroys all beings, time recreates them, time remains awake while we are all asleep, the decree of time is inviolable :

kālaḥ pacati bhūtāni, kālaḥ saṃharate prajāḥ
kālaḥ supteṣu jāgarti, kālo hi duratikramaḥ

As against this popular notion of time, the *Mūlapariyāya Jātakā* lays down that if time be the consumer of beings, of all even including itself, it is possible for a person to consume time the all-consumer :

kālo ghasati bhūtāni sabbān'eva sahattanā/
yo ca kālaghaso bhūto sa bhūtapacaniṃ pacati ||

Although the exact Sanskrit counterpart of the *Jātaka* maxim is met with in the Śāntiparva, this new trend of thought is utterly inconsistent with the main thought which runs through the *Great Epic* narrative as also through that of Vālmīki's *Rāmāyaṇa.*

kālaḥ pacati bhūtāni sarvāṇyevātmanātmani/
yasmiṃ tu pacyate kālas taṃ vedeha na kaścana[1]||

1 Mbh., XV. 238.25.

This and similar other progressive trends of thought and ideas may be traced, even in one and the same language, in the *Śāntiparva* of the *Great Epic* and the Buddhist Canonical texts. But whereas they are introduced by the way in the former without the least regard for coherence or consistency with the main structure of the Epic thought, they form an integral part of the Buddhist thought and the very foundation of Buddhist ethics and moral discipline.

So far regarding the *Mūlapariyāya Jātaka*. Now, as to the *Mūlapariyāya Sutta* representing the first Discourse of the Buddha in the *Majjhima Nikāya*, its historical importance lies in the fact that it not only enables us to ascertain what an intimate knowledge Buddha had had of the philosophy of the *Upaniṣads* but also to understand the point of departure effected by him from its main trend of thought.

Regarding the philosophy of the *Upaniṣads* Buddha's significant statement is : "I know this well *(sañjānāmi)*, but I know also something farther than it *(abhijānāmi)*".[1] He correctly represents this philosophy when he points out that its main pre-occupation is the knowledge of the self and of the relation which subsists between the self and the not-self. The approach to all the problems of philosophy is from the point of view of self *(attā)*, wherefore one might say that the Upaniṣad philosophy is 'self-centred' or 'ego-centric.' As Buddha himself puts it, here is an attempt throughout to find out and establish one's identity with every constituent element of existence and fact of experience, to derive the self out of that, to relegate the self to the not-self, to find the self in the not-self and to establish the ownership or control of the self over the not-self, the ontological axioms being : "I am that", 'I am from that', 'I am of that', 'I am in that', 'that is mine'. A realistic attitude of mind is implied in this mode of thinking with the result that every aspect of reality which presents itself to experience or is cognized or conceived is taken and believed to be a fact or thing-in-itself. In the next *Sutta* called *Sabbāsava*, Buddha speaks of the epistemological axioms of Early Vedānta as consisting in "I possess a true self", "I do not possess a true self", "I know well the self by the self", "I know the not-self by the self", and "I know the self by the not-self."[1]

The conviction gained through the mystical or direct religious experience and the conclusion arrived at from both the lines of argument come to this that the soul within us is the true self which alone perdures unaffected in its nature through the entire series of changes which affects only the bodily or biological aspect of our individual life and existence.[2]

The dialectic movement of the early Vedāntic thought is effectively represented by Buddha in the *Mūlapariyāya Sutta*. This thought, as clearly indicated by him, started from a purely physical basis of existence, with the consideration of man's position in relation to the constituents of matter, and culminated in *Nirvāṇa*,

1 *Majjhima*, i, p. 7: *atthi me attā, n'atthi me attā, attanā va attānaṁ sañjānāmi, attanā va anattānaṁ sañjānāmi, anattanā va attānaṁ sañjānāmi.*

2 *Ibid*, i, p. 7 :

with the consideration of the state of soul, the principle of consciousness, in respect of the highest condition of its spirituality. The successive steps of thought are broadly represented as physical, biological, theological, epistemological and spiritual. At its biological step, the philosophy of the *Upaniṣads* was concerned with the consideration of the whole of life (*bhūta*)—the relative position of all living beings from plants upwards to the highest type of man, and including also all mythical personalities —the gods, angels and spirits, suprahuman or infrahuman. At its third step, it was occupied, first of all, with the consideration of the position of the *devas,* next with that of Prajāpati from whose creative energy and will-to-be the world of life comes to be and Brahmā, the deistic personal God in whom the world of mind reaches its consummation, and, last of all, with that of the higher attributes to be predicated of Prajāpati on the one hand and Brahmā on the other. At its epistemological step, it became interested, first of all, in the consideration of the modes of knowing or sources of knowledge : perception *(diṭṭhaṃ),* tradition *(sutaṃ),* inference *(mutaṃ)* and understanling *(viññātaṃ),* and next in that of the categories of thought : unity *(ekattaṃ),* diversity *(nānattaṃ),* universality *(sabbaṃ)* by which the content of knowledge may be characterised. At its last step, the Upaniṣadic thought looked beyond its logical reach and felt the need of *Nirvāṇa,* better *Brahma-nirvāṇa,* to complete the idea of the self for our spiritual satisfaction. It goes without saying that almost all the terms used and their gradation are to be found in the philosophy of Yājñavalkya.[1]

Buddhism proper as a system of thought was regarded by its propounder just as a further step from Early Vedānta. The commonwealth of Indian thought behind Buddhism is taken to suggest three different lines of reasoning : (1) that based on *dhyāna* meaning *meditation* and mysticism yielding the psychical data of experience, vision, recollection of the past and miracle; (2) that based on *tarka* meaning the formal consistency implied in a logical mode of thinking; and (3) that based on *mīmāṃsā* meaning the data of thought and principles of action derived from the authoritative texts through a methodical interpretation of them. Buddhism, distinguished in its own sphere as *lokottara* from *laukika*, or as *paramārtha* (scientific) from *sammuti (consensus* of current views) was designed by its author to develop a system of thought and moral discipline from the *anātman* or non-personal point of view, abandoning the personal standpoint of *satkāya* or *ātmavāda*.

If the main philosophic difference between Buddhism and Early Vedānta lies thus in the two standpoints of *anātman (non-self)*[2] and *ātman* (self)[3], what is precisely meant by it?

1. *Bṛhad Ār.*, iv. 4.5 : iv. 5. 6-7.
Cf. the terms *lokāh*, *bhūtāh*, *devāh*, *Brahmā*, *dṛṣṭa śruta*, *mata*, *vijñāta*, *ekāyana*, *pṛthak*, *sarva*.

2 Barua, *Prolegomena to a History of Buddhist Philosophy*.

3 Cf. *Varāha Up.*, ii. 19 :
śrutvutpannātmavijñāna-pradīpo bādhyate katham!
anātmatām parityaiva nirvikāro jagatsthitau ||
Ibid. ii. 26 : *anātmavid amukto pi siddhijātāni vāñchati!*

"None or nothing is dear if the self is not dear", says Yājñavalkya, "all is dear because the self is dear to oneself. The self, therefore, is to be seen, learnt, minded and meditated upon."[1] The true self, the abiding and unchanging element of reality within us is soul, the essence of which is bare consciousness *(citi, cinmātra)* or 'witness consciousness' *(sākṣīcaitanya)*, which is unaffected by all the changes that happen in life meaning our biological existence. This soul within us and that within the rest of things or the universe are identical in their nature and substance.

Through the *Upaniṣads* one may watch the course of an age-long philosophic contest between the warriors as kings and princes and the Brāhmans as *Śrotriyas*. It is possible that they preserve the memory of that remote age when the warriors as patriarchs were the real shepherds to the people in their double capacity of being their leaders and law-givers, rulers and educators. In the age of the *Upaniṣads* both of them figured as warm advocates of the doctrine of Brahman and earnest seekers of the true self within and without, the broad traditional distinction between them being that whereas the former professed to be *Brahmavādins*, the latter tended to be *Prāṇavādins*. The texts now extant do not enable us to make out any such clear line of cleavage between the thinkers belonging to two social orders. The difference between the two lines of thinking irrespective of their

---

1 *Bṛhad Ār.*, iv. 5. 6 : *na vā are sarvasya kāmāya sarvam priyaṁ bhavati, ātmanas tu kāmāya sarvam priyaṁ bhavati, ātmā va are draṣṭavyaḥ śrotavyo mantavyo nididhyāsitavyo.*

social equations, hinged on the question as to whether Brahman is essentially a vital principle (*prāṇa*) or a psychical one (*prajñā*). In a passage of the *Bṛihad Āraṇyaka Upaniṣad* (ii. 9. 19), 'All-gods' (*Viśvadevas*) spoken of as being three and three thousands are reduced ultimately to *prāṇa*, the vital principle, and Brahman is represented as that. In the *Aitareya Upaniṣad* (iii. 3), on the other hand, the ultimate foundation of the entire world of life is traced in *prajñā* or *prajñāna*, the psychical principle, and Brahman is represented as that. If one of these views be treated as the thesis and the other as the antithesis, the synthesis of the two is reached in the Kauṣītaki text (iii. 3) where it is declared :

> *Yo vai prāṇaḥ sā prajñā, yā vā prajñā sa prāṇaḥ*
> *saha hyetāvasmiñ charīre vasataḥ sahotkrāmataḥ.*

"That which is the vital principle is also the psychical, and *vice versa*, both residing together in a living body pass away together.

It follows from this that *prāṇa* and *prajñā* are just the two aspects or principles, *viz.*, vital and psychical, of one and the same being. Behind the notion of their inseparable association or connexion was the poetical conception of the tree of life to which cling two birds, inseparable comrades, one of them eating the sweet fruit,[1] the other looking on without eating, and on which a man sits grieving, bewildered by his own impotence (*anīśā*), and not grieving when he sees the other lord (*īśa*). With reference to a living individual, *prāṇa* stands for the life-principle with which the body as an aggregate of matter is instinct, the choleric or primal form of heat (*tejas*), the creative energy, the vitality depending on some kind of food (*anna*) and determining the duration of individual existence (*āyus*) and the animating spirit of an animated whole. And with reference to a thinking individual, *prajñā* stands for the psyche with which mind, intellect and the senses are informed, consciousness by virtue of which the awareness of one's true self becomes possible, the cognitive faculty, the power of thinking, willing and feeling, the principle of rationality, the source of intelligence, the inner light, the increaser of spirituality. The conception of *prāṇa* and *prajñā* as the principle of life and that of intelligence is valid only in the case of a *puruṣa* or soul embodied and individuated. The *puruṣas* are the sparks or particles of one and the same reality, Brahman, the ultimate ground of everything that is or that be, and they are as such the same as Brahman in their nature and essence. When the *puruṣas* are implicated in worldly relations, they form the *jīvātmans,* and when they go out of these relations and appear in their independent nature, they become *paramātmans.* The *puruṣas* become ultimately absorbed into Brahman and fresh *puruṣas* start from the same inexhaustible source of life and intelligence. The theory of absorption and fresh creation in alternation is supported by certain analogies drawn from nature which have more a sentimental appeal than a scientific value. Just as, for instance, a spider spreads out its net and draws it back into it at its sweet will, or just as the rays are radiated from and absorbed back into the solar body, so this world which is the playground of all the embodied souls is created out of and taken back into Brahman.

The Sānkhya philosophy differs from Early Vedānta mainly in this respect that it discards the absorption theory of the latter and advocates the eternal separation after perfection of the *puruṣas* from the whole of the biological side of life as represented by *prakṛti* and its modifications. The Sānkhya allocation of passivity to *puruṣa* and activity to *prakṛti* is too catachetical to be admitted as metaphysically sound. Similarly its duality between the two principles having nothing in common between them as regards their nature is most arbitrary to be defended. So far as the plurality of the souls is concerned, the Sānkhya and Jaina doctrines are in agreement, although they differ from each other in so far as in the first the soul remains untouched by all physical, sensory, mental and intellectual activities of an individual, and in the second the soul is the single element of reality which is vitally interested in all such affairs since the whole moral effect of them is to be borne by it.

The metaphysical position of Early Vedānta is sounder in so far as the plurality of the existence of *puruṣas* is derived from a single reality, Brahman. But the emanations and absorptions of the *puruṣas* from and back into that reality are represented, after all, as a mechanical affair. The transcendental character assigned to the *puruṣas* which are gone out of mundane relations is virtually the same as that which is postulated in Sānkhya.

However grand and fascinating may be such a conception of the nature of the *puruṣas,* whether in Early

Vedānta or in Sānkhya, the whole structure of thought is built on the foundation of a superstitious popular belief. In other words, its scientific foundation is weak and highly questionable. After the foetus develops in the womb from parental union and reach a certain stage of development the *puruṣa* as an entelechy enters the organism by the suture *(vidṛti)* of the head or tips of the fingers and finds its way into the heart where it lodges itself. The Russian doctors of the present age claim to have found out the weight of the souls, whereas the savants of the *Upaniṣads* managed to find out their length, *anguṣṭha-mātra,* the thumb-length which is really the length of the cavity of the heart.

The soundness of the *Upaniṣad* idea of *puruṣa* as an entelechy depends on the scientific accuracy of the embryological theory of conception and the development of the foetus in the womb. It is just a semblance of scientific truth, or at the most an approximation to it when it is premised that conception results from a parental union serving to bring the semen into contact with the blood :

śukra-śoṇita-saṃyogād āvartate garbhaḥ.[1]

This is unscientific in so far as it postulates that in the seventh month the foetus (in the case of human beings) is conjoined with the individual soul *(jīva-yuktaḥ),* that, in other words, the soul enters the organism.

Behind Buddha's enumeration of the three prerequisites of conception was another age-old popular

1 *Garbha Up.*, 2.

belief that a departed spirit destined to be reborn waits to take advantage of the parental union to enter the womb. The pre-requisites mentioned consist of the physical fitness of the parents, the sexual congress, and the readiness of a *gandharva* for ingress.[1] According to the *Amarakoṣa* (*Nānārtha.*, 409), the word *gandharva* stands for an *antarābhava-sattva*, which means either a being in the womb or a being in between the state of death and that of rebirth. The *antarābhava* idea is discarded in the Abhidhamma philosophy.[2]

Buddha has nowhere explained what he precisely meant by the expression *gandhabbo paccupaṭṭhito hoti*. Buddhaghosa understands by *gandhabba* a being bound for ingress (*tatrūpago satto*), and maintains that by the expression, *paccupaṭṭhito hoti*, is not meant that a being intending to be reborn stands near at hand watching the parental union ; here it means that driven by the machinery of his *karma* a being becomes destined to be reborn.[3]

The fact is that neither the *Upaniṣad* teachers nor the Buddhist scholiasts were aware of the fact that conception takes place only when a particular spermatazoon comes into touch with an ovum and succeeds in fertilising it. In stating the three pre-requisites of conception

1 Mahātaṇhāsaṁkhaya Sutta in *Majjhima*, i.

2 See Debate on the subject in *Kathāvatthu*, viii. 2. Acc. to the Commentary, the Pubbaseliyas and Sammitiyas among the Buddhists were believers in the interrediate state of becoming.

3 *Papañcasūdanī* to the above *Sutta* : *na mātāpitunnam sannipātam olokayamāno samīpaṭṭhito nāma hoti, kammayanta-yantito pana eko satto tasmiṁ okāse nibbattanako hoti—ayam ettha adhippāyo.*

Buddha's intention was not to endorse any superstitious belief but just to establish that a scientific explanation for the happening of an event lay not in any single cause but in a conjuncture of circumstances sufficient to account for it.

The *Upaniṣad* notion of soul gave rise to the theory of there being an internal percipient *(vedagū)*, which uses any organs of sense as a window as it pleases. Here the Buddhists propounded a more scientific view, maintaining that each sense has its own range of action with the result that it enjoys a certain degree of independence of its own in an interdependent system.[1]

The process of rectification of such fancy-born ideas may be traced, however, through the *Upaniṣads* themselves. In the *Kauṣītaki Upaniṣad* (iv. 10), for instance, when the Brāhman Bālāki affirms that he sees the *puruṣa* or personal double of himself in the mirror, the philosopher king, Ajātaśatru, points out his mistake, saying, "Do not challenge me on this. I meditate on him as the likeness *(pratirūpa iti).*"[2] In the *Bṛhad Āraṇyaka* (iii. 1. 24-25), when Śākalya foolishly enquired—"In what does the heart abide?" Yājnavalkya said, "O Ahallika, when you think the heart could be anywhere else away from us, if it were away from us, the dogs might eat it, or the birds tear it." And in the Pali *Suṃsumāra Jātaka* (No: 208), the Bodhisattva is represented as saying to the crocodile, "Even thou wert led to believe that my heart might be found hung on the branch of a tree, foolish fellow!"

1 Mlimda, pp. 54, 71.
2 Cf. *Bṛhad Ār. Up.*, ii. 1.8.

The Upaniṣad philosophers were divided in their opinion as to the relative importance of the senses and the objects, some holding because of the development of the organs of sense the objects come to be realized,[1] and some because of the need of realizing the objects the organs of sense develop. A synthetic view followed, stressing the equal importance of both the subjective factor (*prajñāmātrā*) and the objective factor (*bhūtamātrā*) without the interaction between which the sense or mental operation enabling us to have a knowledge of the external world is not possible. So we are told in the *Kauṣītaki* (iii. 8) : "If there were no objects, there would be no subjects, and if there were no subjects, there would be no objects. For on either side alone nothing could be achieved."[2] It is further opined that without *prajñā* meaning the mind consciously attending to the affair of a particular organ of sense, the organ by itself does not perceive the object.[3] "Some maintain here, that the *prāṇas* become one, for (otherwise) no one could at the same time make known a name by speech, see a form with the eye, hear a sound with the ear, think a thought with the mind. After having become one, the *prāṇas* perceive all these together, one by one. Thus it is indeed, said Indra, but nevertheless there is a pre-eminence among the *prāṇas*."[4] Thus the insistence

1 *Aitareya Ār.*, ii. 4. 1. 6.

2 *yaddhi bhūtamātrā na syur na prajñāmātrāḥ syur yad vā prajñāmātrā na syur na bhūtamātrāḥ syuḥ. Na hyanyatarato rūpaṁ kiṁcana siddhet.*

3 *Kauṣītaki, iii.* 7.

4 *Ibid,* iii. 7.

in all the *Upaniṣads* is—"Let no man try to find out what speech is, let him know the speaker. Let no man try to find out what odour is, let him know him who smells."[1]

It was on this advanced step of thought in Early Vedānta that Buddha's psychological theory of sensation was evidently formulated : "There being the eye, there being the form (within the field of vision), there being the visual cognition (conscious attending on the part of the mind to the affairs of the eye), the coming together of the three in the operation is the contact which is the *sine qua non* of sensation" : *Cakkhusmiṃ sati, rūpe sati, cakkhu-viññāṇe sati, tiṇṇaṃ sangati phdsso.*[2]

On the same advanced step of thought was built up also the Buddhist phychological conception of the unity of mental life meaning that every mental operation, when it takes place, takes place as a unit with regard to time.

On the *Upaniṣad* notion of the three states of waking, dream and sleep and the further discrimination of the state of sleep into the initial stage of *suṣupti,* the fourth stage of *turīya,* the next stage of *turīyātīta* (going beyond the *turīya),* and the final stage of *avadhūta* were built up the systems of *yogic* practice. Sleep was taken to be a periodical natural state of the self which is unperturbed by dreams. "The arteries of the heart

1 *Ibid,* iii. 8.

2 *Dīgha,* 1, p. 42, iii, pp. 228, 272, 276.

called Hitā", says Ajātaśatru, the philosopher king, "extend from the heart of the person towards the surrounding body. Small as a hair divided a thousand times, they stand full of a thin fluid of various colours, white, black, yellow, red. In these the person (*puruṣaḥ*, the personal double, the inner man) is when sleeping he sees no dream. Then be becomes one with that *prāṇa* alone. Then speech goes to him with all names, the eye with all forms, the ear with all sounds, the mind with all thoughts. And when he awakes, then, as from a burning fire, sparks proceed in all directions, thus from that self the *prāṇas* (speech, etc.) proceed, each towards its place, from the *prāṇas* the gods, from the gods the world."[1]

As Yājñavalkya explained, in the state of sound sleep the inner person (*puruṣa*) or true self within us withdraws himself from all organs of sense and all organs of action for rest in his central abode, namely, the heart which is the vital centre, and here, in this state, the vital principle (*prāṇa*) in him which is in the ethereal form of *tejas* becomes embraced, so to speak, by, or unified with the principle of intelligence (*vijñāna*, *prajñā* [2] The duality meaning the subject-object relation being thus got rid of, he becomes one, and one only, and becoming one, he neither sees nor smells, etc.[3]

It goes without saying that the *yoga* was resorted to just as a practical mode of conscious efforts to reach back

1 *Kauṣītaki*, iv. 20.

2 *Bṛhad Ār.*, iv. 4.22.

3 *Ibid.*, iv. 3. 22-34, iv. 4.2.

or attain to this tranquil psychical state of the true self within.

These semi-scientific and semi-fantastic old-world ideas were certainly behind the more intelligible account given by Buddha in the *Vedalla Suttas* of the order in which the three different functions, vocalic (*vacī-sankhāra*), other bodily and sensory (*kāya-sankhāra*) and cognitive (*citta-sankhāra*), cease and revive.[1]

The possibility of a gradual cessation and revival in a reverse order of the three functions needed an explanation, and this led to the conception of *bhavānga* or a state of life-continuum'[2] into which *citta* (consciousness) sinks or subsides as soon as a cycle or series of mental processes or activities with reference to a particular object of sense, or of thought, or of meditation is completed.[3] This Buddhist conception or scientific hypothesis of periodical subsidence of *citta* into a state of life-continuum[4] had certainly behind it the Upaniṣadic idea of the ultimate unification of *prajñā with prāṇa* in a state of sleep or a corresponding *yogic state*.[5]

In Buddhism, however, no abiding and unchanging element of reality is made out of the *bhavānga-citta* or *ālaya-vijñāna*. This is represented rather as a stream of consciousness with its normal current or flow which does not assume a representative character until it rises up to

1 *Majjhima*, i.
2 This is the expression by which Shwe Zan Aung represents *bhavanga* in English.
3 Cf. *Atthasālinī*, p. 72.
4 *Milinda*, section on *supina*.
5 Cf. *Chāndogya*, vi. 9.2 : *prāṇabandhanaṁ mana iti.*

a certain level of *manodvāra* below which it is subliminal and above which it is supraliminal.

According to the *Lankāvatāra Sūtra*, the functional cessation (*lakṣmaṇa-nirodha*) does not nesessarily imply a cessation of the normal flow of the stream of consciousness (*prabandha-nirodha*). It is with the rise of the *bodhi-citta* meaning the 'aspiration for enlightenment' that the *bhavānga-citta* or *ālaya-vijñāna* gets on into the path which makes for its intellectual, ethical and spiritual progress.

If by the term *ātmā* or *ātman* is meant a permanent being serving as the ground of immortality,—an element of reality which is eternal, immutable, invariable, not in any way liable to change, and which constitutes the true self within us and within the universe, the *anātman* philosophy of Buddha sought to establish that there is no such element of reality, no such entity to be found in any form of concrete existence (*ātmabhāva*) or in experience. If one argues on an ontological ground that the very idea of change presupposes that of a changeless being or reality, it would follow therefrom that both change and changeless are relative ideas, and that, as such, neither has its independence as a concept of reality.

From the *anātman* or impersonal way of viewing the world emerged and developed a truly scientific or philosophic method of treating and correlating the facts of experience. This thought needed certain *prajñaptis* (terms, concepts or generalised ideas) as its intellectual devices, and the business of thought was conceived as one consisting in building up the *mātṛkās* or architectonics in order to guide men in a rational understanding and interpretation of facts. The individuals as individuals, whether men or animals or things, being variables, they had to be left out of account. The scientific or philosophic thought cannot proceed on mere *nāmarūpa* or nominalistic basis; [1] it must somehow or other be conceptualistic. But to come into such a world of concepts and causality is to come away from actuality, the world of variables. When however, the concepts and causality are made too much of in the name of science or rationality and passed as correct expressions of truth or reality, a Nāgārjuna is bound to appear in the scene with his sharp dialectics to expose their hollowness and inherent logical fallacy with regard to the Abhidhamma system, and a Sādhu Śāntinātha with his critique to play a similar part with regard to Vedānta. [2] Is it not stressing the matter rather too far to affirm that none speaks to none, each individual being in fact only a temporary organic combination of the five aggregates? Just as in Buddhism the scientific or philosophic issue is not infrequently confounded with the religious or biological one, so the psychical or mystical issue is often confounded with the ontological one in Early Vedānta. The trend of the Buddhist *Paramārtha* argument, however, is that the idea of a liv-

1 *Chāndogya Up.*, vii. 1-2.

2 The reader is referred particularly to Ch. V of *The Critical Examination of the Philosophy of Religion* published in 2 vols. from the Indian Research Institute of Philosophy, Amalner.

ing individuality is identifiable neither with any single constituent nor with a sum total of all the constituents, nor is it conceivable apart from an organic combination of them all.[1]

Four different systems of *yogic* practice came to be recognized in the religion of Early Vedānta, to wit, *mantra-yoga, laya-yoga, haṭha-yoga* and *rāja-yoga*. The first of them consists in the method of developing the divine powers through the muttering of and meditation on the formulas of mystic potency for a period of twelve years. This is considered the most inferior form of the yogic practices. The second system consists in the automatic traduction of consciousness to its original state *(citta-laya)* in all postures. The third one implies the method of reaching the state of concentration and trance *(samādhi)* in which the individual soul becomes one with the universal one[2], and that through the practice of *aṣṭānga-yoga,* particularly the breathing exercise *(prāṇāyāma)* meaning perfect control of the respiratory function. And the fourth system consists in a yogic method appararently in violation of all ideas of social morality and disregard of the popular view of the sexual purity and moral continence in saintly life.[3]

With regard to the first system, it may be observed that in spite of a rational interpretation of the Vedic rituals the religion of Early Vedānta has its lapses into

---

1 *Yathā hi sanga-sambhārā hoti saddo 'ratho' iti/*
evaṁ khandhesu santesu hoti 'satto' ti sammuti ||

2 *Yogatattva Up.*, 21-27.

3 *Ibid*, 107: *samādhiḥ samatāvasthā jīvātmā-paramātmanaḥ.*

ritualism and sacerdotalism. The system of *laya-yoga* was habitual with such adepts as the *Avadhūtas* and is exemplified by the state of trance in which Mahāvīra, the founder of Jainism, was found in all bodily postures.[1] The difference, as casually suggested to me by Dr. Bapat, is one between the methods of application, one implying the practice of hard penances.[2] and the other the indulgence in the pleasures of the sense.[3]

The *mantrayoga* of Early Vedānta was at the back of the Buddhist *Mantrayāna* and *Kālacakrayāna,* just as the *vajrolī amaroli* and *sahajolī* modes of the *rājayoga* were at the back of the Buddhist *Vajrayāna and Sahaja-siddhi.*

It was on the basis of the *haṭhayoga* that Buddha built up a rational system of meditation with the practice of mental awareness *(smṛtyupasthāna)* as its grammar. There is nothing corresponding to it in the *Sāṃkhya-yoga* or *adhyātmayoga* of the *Upaniṣads* of all ages. It is difficult for this very reason to differ from Professor S. N. Dasgupta when he opines that the Yoga method of Patañjali was derived from Buddhism.

The ethical principles of life as inculcated in the *Upaniṣads,* the *Dialogues* of Buddha and the Jaina texts are for all practical purposes the same. But one must admit that their psychological foundation is nowhere so

1 *Yogatattva Up.,* 23 : *layayogaś cittalayaḥ koṭiśaḥ parikīrtitaḥ/ gacchaṁs tiṣṭhan svapan bhuñjan dhyāyen niṣkalam īśvaram.* Cf. *Culladukkhakkhandha Sutta* in *Majjhima,* i, p. 91 ff.

2 Pali *attakilamathānuyoga.*

3 Pali *kāmasukhallikānuyoga.*

clear, rational, sound and deep as in Buddhism. This is not to deny that the putting in the *Bhagavad Gītā* has a greater emotional appeal or that the Jaina presentation of the subject is more academical. But it will be admitted that in the one the insistence is on the acceptance of duty as Divine command and that in the other the cumbrousness of classifications and scholasticism make the system dull and rob it of the dynamic of conduct.

Thus the discussion may be continued. But I must not tax your patience any longer. I cannot do justice to the subject in a single lecture. And yet I hope and trust that the few lines indicated may prove useful to those of you who are disposed to consider the whole matter dispassionately and impartially.

LECTURE VIII

BUDDHISM–ITS MODERN APPEAL

I owe an apology to the Hon'ble Mr. George E. de Silva and the beloved citizens of Kandy, ladies and gentlemen, who have thronged in this Town Hall, for the delay in my arrival which was due at 6. 30 P.M. You may easily understand that one, a stranger like me, making a strenuous tour through your ancient cities abounding in antiquities full of interest and importance and keeping many engagements on the way, could not be sure of his punctuality. But, personally speaking, it is a great satisfaction to me that I find myself at last in your midst, and that in this historic city of Kandy where your kings and people made their last struggle for freedom. It is that memorable city which, as you know more than I, is full of painful reminiscences, and not far from which your valiant king Aggabodhi III, laid down his head for the national purification of your island.

No religion has any attraction for me as a religion if freedom is not its essence. Truly the Buddha declared, "Just as wherever one tastes the waters of an ocean, salt is their only taste *(ekaraso loṇaraso)*, so full emancipation is the only flavour with which the whole of the Doctrine and Discipline propounded and promulgated by me is seasoned *(vimuttiraso)*." The word *rasa* in its technical sense signifies the functional quality of a thing. When the word *rasa* is taken in this sense, Buddha's

* This lecture of Religion series was addressed to the citizens of Kandy on March 21, '44.

statement comes to this, that Buddhism as a system of faith and of thought was nobly intended to function for and to be enlivened with the functional quality of full emancipation,—no matter whether you call it freedom, deliverance or salvation. Berriedale Keith truly represented Buddha's Noble Eighfold Path as a way to freedom. If it is emancipation or deliverance, the question arises—emancipation or deliverance from what? If it is freedom, what does it really cannote?

Emancipation or deliverance, as Buddha defines it, is final release from all the conceivable states, forms and degrees of bondage. He defines freedom as a free state of consciousness, of the mind or will *(citta-vimutti, cetaso vimokho)*. The progressive path of such freedom, as described graphically by him in several Discourses, is accordingly a passage either from the greater state of bondage to the lesser or from the lesser state of freedom to the greater,—a conscious feeling of advance from stage to stage in the pilgrim's journey along the onward path.

Buddha has not concealed from us his own idea of such freedom or emancipation by way of contrast with his definition of bondage, slavery or servitude. In dwelling on the subject of servitude and emancipation and whilst sharply contrasting the painful condition of a slave or hireling with the happy state of a freeman, he painted slavery or servitude as a degraded state of woe, and brought in by way of comparison the equally trying and painful state of indebtedness, illness, imprisonment and perilous journey across a wilderness and freedom or emancipation as a state of relief and self-congratulation bringing in by way of comparison such other happy states of man as liquidation of debt, recovery from illness, coming out of prison and safe crossing of the wilderness. A slave or hireling, as he describes him, is a person who is not under his own will, who is completely under the will of his master, who is unable to exercise his free will; while the condition of a freeman is just the reverse. Having to live, move and have one's being under such conditions of one's life and existence, the spirit of man groans underneath, and the occasional flashes of thought that occur are—"When I am a man as he is, why and how is this difference between his lot and mine ! And is there no means of improving my status and bettering my condition ?" Buddha heartily accepted the Indo-Aryan maxim that all that is controlled by circumstances other than one's own will is woe and all that is under the control of one's will is weal. The Pali scholiast, Buddhaghosa, offers a person's capacity for voluntary and hearty participation in the joys of life as a test of freedom and the lot to work under compulsion and constant threat as that of bondage.

The prose text of the *Arthaśāstra* ascribed to Kauṭilya Viṣṇugupta opines that it may be no crime for the Mlecchas to sell or mortgage the life of their own progeny, but servitude shall not be condition of an Aryan. The treatise wisely prescribes the laws allowing all possible chances to the slaves to regain their freedom, intending the selling or mortgaging by kinsmen of the life of a citizen, whether he be a Śūdra, or a Vaiśya, or a Kṣatriya or Brāhman and restraining all persons who stand in the way of the manumission of slaves. Buddha enjoined in the case of the *upāsakas* that they should by all means refrain from carrying on slave-trade.[1]

Megasthenes, the Greek ambassador to the court of Chandragupta Maurya, complacently observed: 'Of several remarkable customs existing among the Indians, there is one prescribed by their ancient philosophers which one may regard as truly admirable: for the law ordains that no one among them shall, under any circumstances, be a slave, but that enjoying freedom, they shall respect the equal right to it which all possess: for those, they thought, who have learned neither to domineer over nor to cringe to others will attain the life best adapted for all vicissitudes of lot: for it is but fair and reasonable to institute laws which bind all equally, but allow property to be unevenly distributed'.

Arrian among the later Classical writers came to learn from the *Indika* of Megasthenes that all the Indians were free; and not one of them was a slave. The Lakedæmonians and the Indians were here so far in agreement. The former, however, held the Helots (aliens) as slaves, they doing servile labour, whereas the latter did not even use aliens as slaves, and much less a countryman of their own.

The modern critics of the Greek ambassador have doubted the veracity of the information supplied by him regarding the Indians among whom slavery or servitude had existed in fact in its different forms and degrees of intensity, or have at least found reason to think that he unduly exaggerated the state of things

1 Barua, *Inscriptions of Asoka*, ii, Glossary to R.E. IX.

which had then obtained in the country when he stated that all the Indians were free and not one of them was a slave. Rhys Davids thought that Megasthenes was perhaps led to make this observation for the reason that in his eye the Indian form of slavery was so mild and humane that it was nothing in comparison with either the Greek or Roman form of it. But reading between the lines, one cannot fail to see that Megasthenes was absolutely right in making the observation he had made. All that he wanted to say is that both the philosophic view of life and the spirit of the law of the land were strongly in favour of seeing all men equal in the eye of law. To say that all men are free and not one of them a slave in the eye of law is not to deny the existence of slaves in fact.

Viewing, however, the employment of slaves and hirelings in the Indo-Aryan households as a fact, Buddha became interested in commending certain essential duties on the part of both the empolyer and the employees whereby they might find their relationship mutually agreeable and helpful. In accordance with his behests, the noble-minded householder was to allot work to the slaves and hirelings according to their capacity, to pay them adequate meals and wages, to tend them in sickness, to share with them the sweets and delicacies, and to restrict their working hours and occasionally grant them leave, and the latter were to do favour to their master by rising up earlier, going to sleep later, receiving only what is given, doing the work well, and speaking in praise of him.[1]

The problem of freedom and progressive evolution cannot but lead us to consider the cosmical and biological situations of life in general, and in the case of human life in particular, the domestic, social, political, economic, educational, traditional and individual situations as well besides the cosmical and biological. In spite of our wish to the contrary, we find differences and inequalities among the individuals in respect of the genera and species to which they belong, their local and natural environs, their bodily forms, physical capacities and disabilities, spans of life and modes of living, instincts and impulses, feelings and desires, mental equipments, sexes and functions, habits and idiosyncrasies, temperaments and training.[2] The equality of beings except in respect of certain common traits and general principles is inconceivable.

The general biological relation between beings and beings as recognized in the *Aitareya Āraṇyaka* is one which exists between "the food and the eater."[3] The bigger species of whales is described in the *Jātakas* as a class of creatures which lives on the smaller species. The series of names consisting of *timi* (whale), *timingila* (whale-swallower), *timiṅgilagila* (the swallower of the whale-swallower), and *rāghava* (the swallower of the third) affords just an instance of the *mātsya-nyāya* or

1 *Dīgha*, III, p. 191.

2 *Atthasālinī*, p. 64f.

3 *Aitareya Ār.*, ii. 1.1.16. Cf. *Bṛhad Ār.*, i.4.6: *idaṁ sarvam annaṁ caivānnadaś ca.*

the fish-rule of 'might is right',—of living by devouring the weaker members of the species, which is applied in the Indian books of state-craft and popular wisdom to human affairs to characterise the general tendency of each larger and more powerful state to swallow up the smaller and less powerful ones and that of one class of men to thrive at the cost of another. The history of man's progress in culture and civilization is but a continuous record of the conflict involved in the struggle of the human spirit for the establishment of the superiority of 'the rule of right is might' over 'that of might is right' as commonly understood.

The origin of the primary struggle for existence is traceable to the biological fact that all living beings depend for their sustenance on some kind of food: *sabbe sattā āhāraṭṭhitikā, annagataḥ prāṇaḥ*. The logical axioms of thought which arose out of this biological situation of life are: To live is to eat, and to eat is to kill or to be somehow or other the cause of killing, and Not to kill is not to eat, and not to eat is not to live. Those among the Indian *religieux,* such as the Ājīvikas, the followers of Pārśva and Jinakalpika Jainas, who were led by their sincere desire to refrain from the act of killing and being directly or indirectly the cause of it had no other alternative but to end their earthly career by committing realigious suicide through starvation. Whilst in their sincere belief that their action was logically consistent with their noble creed of *ahiṃsā* or non-injury to life, they did not realise the untenability of their position until their critics, *e.* g., the Buddhists, questioned that if they had no right to kill others, what right had they to kill themselves? The criticism offered by Buddha to the Jaina position is that the cosmical situation is such that even in going and coming, inhaling and exhaling we are apt to kill or be the cause of killing of many animalculae.[1] As we are placed in life, there is no other alternative left to us than to purify our motives and practise utmost caution and self-restraint. Here the Jaina thinker may join an issue with the Buddhist and argue from fact that to judge action merely by the motive behind it would be to make the accidents or unforeseen circumstances a scape-goat for our guilt, for we may do a great wrong to others in spite of our not intending it.

From the tenour of such philosophical discussions, it becomes increasingly clear that the valley of life is so uneven, dark and treacherous in places that whatever ethical, social or legal position we take up, it remains liable to criticisms from one point of view or another. The natural cataclysms, such as great earth-quakes, cyclones, floods and volcanic eruptions occur awakening us to the fact that there is no *terra firma in* cosmical situation.[2] Similarly the serious events, such as inter-

1 Majjhima, i—Upāli Sutta. The great Persian poet and teacher Sādi says: "Walk slowly because many ants are under your feet."

2 Cf. *Maitrāyaṇa-Brāhmaṇa Up.*, i. 4: "And we see that all this is perishable, as these flies, gnats, and other insects, as herbs and trees, growing and decaying,.... other great ones, mighty weilders of bows, rulers of empires.... We see the destruction of Gandharvas, Asuras, Yakshas, Rākshasas, ... There is the drying up of the great oceans, the falling of mountains, the moving of the pole-star, the cutting of the wind-ropes."

necine and global wars, happen making us painfully alive to the fact that the existing relations between men and men, nations and nations that were erstwhile believed to be satisfactory need readjustments. All these accidents and experiences combine to force on us the admission of the hard fact or stern reality that uncertainty is the very foundation of our earthly existence. There is no form with its individuality which does not break down some day, no form which does not become obsolete and obtrusive one day or another. To put it in Buddha's words, to be formed is to be born, and to be born is to be liable ultimately to decay and death. Snap out any single moment from the life of reality, it is found to be constituted of the three phases of emergence, persistence and break down : *uppatti, ṭhiti,* and *bhanga,* which correspond with the Upaniṣad concept of *utpatti, sthiti,* and *pralaya.* As the Jainas claim, the first utterance of their last Tīrthankara, Mahāvīra, was expressive of just these three phases of life. Whilst reflecting on the fate of the dynastic history of kings Ibn Khāldūn opines that it presents the same three phenomena of childhood, manhood and decay as individual life. And your national epic, *Mahāvaṃsa,* closes each chapter of it with the pathetic reffection setting forth the evanescent character of the kingly career and dynastic rule and emphasising the value of the meritorious deeds that only perdure. This is tantamount to saying that to live best is to serve best the cause of humanity.

If eating is indispensable to living, what should be the motto of life—To eat to live or to live to eat ? If eating means living on some kind of food, what kind of food is needed for what kind of living? Is one kind of food sufficient for the fulness of life? And if several kinds are needed, which of them is needed most?

According to Buddha and other Indian and Eastern teachers, we eat to live, and to live the life in its fulness we need five kinds of food, viz., food for the stomach, food for the five organs of sense, food for the mind, food for thought, and food for consciousness or soul, the first of them being the primary and the fifth the ultimate and most essential. The motto proposed for life, on the other hand, by so great an exponent of the Bolshevic doctrine or Communistic cult of Lenin as Karl Marx is—We live at least to eat.

It is undeniable that proceeding on the above axiom of Marxism the political leaders of Soviet Russia have succeeded in reconstructing her national life on a socialistic basis. The outcome of this new scheme of life is Bolshevism or advocacy of the proletarian dictatorship by the Soviets.. It has banned religion and the idea of private property. In the new order of things each citizen combines in his person the soldier and the workman. The Bolshevic motto or axiom tends to lay stress on the need of the primary kind of food, keeping that of the aesthetic, mental, intellectual and spiritual foods in the background of thought.

I am painfully aware of the fact that present-day youths all over the world are communistically minded. But it is high time for our youths in the East to calmly consider which of the axioms is better for them—We eat to live or We live at least to eat. What pains me to observe is that whenever a new movement of thought or of life is started in the West, we in the East become inclined to welcome or imitate it without proper scrutiny. But I may tell you that to welcome a thing, which is foreign-make, without knowing its full significance and applicability to local circumstances is unmeaning, as well as that imitation is always ape. That which is in conformity with racial genius and national tradition suits the country best and is likely to be conducive to its development, maintaining its distinctive character. The question is—can we not conceive a socio-economic scheme of life on our own long-cherished axiom—we eat to live?

Religion stands banned in the Bolshevic scheme of life. The minds of youths of today are completely upset by what has been happening in the present world. Religion has ceased to have any appeal to them. They have begun to doubt its utility except in enslaving the human spirit and creating divisions between communities and communities, sects and sects. It has degenerated into trade in the name of God, holiness and salvation. Its real spirit is gone, and all that now remain of it are its dead forms. Thus our youths are looking askance at the preachers of all religions and legitimately ask—Do we need religion at all? Should we blame them for this apathy towards religion or should we boldly face the question they have pressed? The signs of the age are too prominent to mistake what they indicate, and the tendencies of the rising generation of men are too strong to resist unless we can convince them by reason and argument that by banning religion we rob the life of its zest and lose the motive spring of all higher urges that make for progress and elevation of human nature. But if religion is to guide humanity along this path, what should be its nature and form?

One thing is certain, namely, that the days of the priest-ridden and creed-infested institutional religions are numbered, if they are not dead already. Modern youth may care only for that religion which is both universal and personal, and which is compatible with science and reason. There must be no 'close-fist' *(ācariya-muṭṭhi)* or trade-secret, no monopoly of divine business in any privileged class. If religion is to stand, it must henceforth show an open heart and follow an open-door policy. The world is grown sick of the familiar distinction between the Aryan and the Mleccha, the chosen people and the cursed, the Hellene and the Barbarian, the Christian and the Pagan, the Muslim and the Kāfir which is born of an arrogant feeling of superiority and deep-rooted hatred for others who pass as outsiders to a particular religion and the social and other institutions cherished by it.

"The ultimate result of keen contests through ages for supremacy, numerical, cultural and spiritual, is that we have now three world religions in Buddhism, Christianity and Islam, each with its dominant hold over certain nations and regions, while the rest of the historical religions have become clannish or exclusively communal. As for Hinduism with Vaiṣṇavism, Śaivism and

Śāktism as its three main forms, with Buddhism, Jainism and Zoroastrianism as the three lingering sister faiths, with Islam and Christianity as the two powerful rival faiths, and with Śikhism, Neo-Vaiṣṇavism, Brāhmoism, Ārya Samāj and Rāmkrishna Mission as the few counteracting forces, its influence remains confined to India proper between the Himalayas and the Indian Ocean".[1]

We the men of the modern age are in a far more advantageous position than our ancestors. We are far less handicapped in several respects. The Tower of Babel creating the confusion of human tongues stands now as a monument of the past. The immense progress made in linguistic studies and researches has rendered all forms of human speech sufficiently intelligible to us. The man has ceased to be the book. No literature is altogether a sealed book to-day. The commonwealth of human thought and tradition lies no longer buried in manuscripts or unrecognized in inscriptions and monuments. The pre-historic and historical data collected from all parts of the earth enable us to visualise the evolutionary process of the human race through the successive stages of growth in culture and civilization, religious beliefs and philosophic thoughts. With increased facilities in travels and communication it has been possible to freely interchange our thoughts and ideas. The time is come when with the imparting of liberal education in all parts of the globe we may proudly figure as inheritors not of a single heritage but of all the heritages of mankind.

---

1 Barua, *Asoka and His Inscriptions*, Pt. I, ch IX.

Whilst arguing for the need and importance in the process of evolution of co-operation among the members of the more advanced races, Julien Huxley, a modern biologist, acutely observes : "Biologically speaking, it is perfectly clear that some co-operative system, involving federation in one form or another, is the proper system to adopt ; and that the world-state—not necessarily organized after the plan of our present highly specialized nationalist industrialist states, which appear happily to represent only a temporary phase of evolution but none the less an organic reality, a co-operative unit—that the 'world-state' is not merely a figment of unpractical dreamers, but an obviously desirable aim of humanity. Kant, a century and a half ago even, had seen clearly enough some universal society was a necessity for the full unfolding of human possibility, and had gone further and pointed out that there were indications of a movement of civilization in that direction. In the present world, this movement has been retarded by the extraordinary and mushroom growth of Nationalism, in which his 'country' (really *Nation)* has become for the average his most real God. In the last hundred years, Nationalism has usurped the place of Religion as the most important super-individual interest of individuals —has indeed become a religion. It is leading the world into an *impasse,* as do all incomplete and partial conceptions."[1]

The same writer concludes his essay on Religion and Science with these pregnant words : "A chapter in

1 *Essays of a Biologist,* p. 39.

the history of Earth closed with the appearance of man. In man, the *Weltstaff* had been made able to think and feel, to love beauty and truth—the cosmos had generated soul. A new chapter then began, a chapter in which we are all characters. Matter had flowered in soul. Soul has now to mould matter. That moulding of matter by spirit is, under one aspect, science ; under another, art ; under still another, religion. Let us be careful not to allow the moulding forces to counteract each other when they might be made to co-operate."[1]

Speaking not as a thinker in terms of matter and mind as substances but as a confirmed believer in the reality of the life-movement presenting alternately its two phases, vital and reflective, each an infinity,—in the one, when it prevails, whatever we conceive as mind or mental functions are subservient to the vital needs, and partake, as such, of the nature of the living body, and in the other, whatever we conceive as matter or bodily functions are subservient to the reflective needs, and partake, as such, of the nature of mind, I find that just as in the one phase sound sleep, uncrossed by dreams and unworried by cares and anxieties, is naturally a culmination of prolonged drifting in the life-current, so in the other, religious ecstasy marks the natural consummation of the prolonged indwelling of consciousness on itself, its experience and vision. Just as the first is a necessity not merely for relieving the bodily fatigue and exhaustion of energy after stimulation into activity but also for rejuvenating the system for fresh work and creation, so the

1 *Ibid*, p. 236.

second is a necessity not merely for rationalizing the experience gained but also for fitting consciousness for fresh intuition and vision. I call each phase an infinity simply because when one prevails, the other is absent, and I am entirely at one with the trend of Buddha's thought when I affirm that neither in the vital series nor in the reflective the same phase recurs, although each successive phase may show certain similar features reminding us of those noted in previous ones, the alternation of two infinities presenting a series, which may be represented as—$v\ r\ v^1\ r^1\ v^2\ r^2\ \ldots\ v^n\ r^n$.

If progress is assumed as the real trend of life as a whole, we can think of unlikeness, conflict, harmony, unity and individuality as its five possible successive conditions. By birth we are likely to find ourselves in a group or association of people which tends to be unlike in the sense that it endeavours to be self-reliant, self-subsistent and self-sufficient. When they fail to be so, each by itself, they begin to invade each other's domain, the result whereof is some form of conflict of which the inner motive is the participation in certain common interests of life, while the modes of approach remain hostile and apparently irreconcilable. The state of conflict enabling each belligerent group to be conscious of the strength and weakness of itself and of its rival is likely to be followed by a state of harmony in which the groups of people, nations or communities, may find themselves either in a passive or an active order of existence. If in a passive order, they begin just to co-exist without any co-operation, and if in an active order, they go to form a co-operative system or federation of some kind without losing their individualities. When such a state of harmony is found to be ponderous and ineffective, it is likely to be followed by a state of unity in which all groups and individuals are required to merge their individualities in a regimental order where creed and discipline become the be-all and end-all of life. When the creed becomes obsolete, as is bound to be so in time, and the discipline imposed renders the course of life mechanical and dull, unity is likely to disintegrate and the individuals forming it pine for the state of singularity in and through which they seek to find their true selves and to be alive to their higher potentialities and possibilities. Whereas in all the four previous conditions the gregarious instinct and group interest guide and mould individual life, henceforth the visions and thoughts, ideals and examples of individuals begin to guide and mould the life of nations and communities. Society, state, guild or community is to exist and function only to allow the widest possible scope to each individual member of it for self-development, self-realization and self-expression. Thus the religious interest, meaning the development of personality, the fulness of knowledge, the perfection of character, and the highest enjoyment of the underlying truth, beauty and goodness of life, becomes supreme.

Conservatism, reformation, rebellion and revolution are easily recognizable as the four modes of progress. Each of these modes tried in history has its advantages and disadvantages. The dialectic movement of thought can proceed to yet another mode which, for want of a better term, be called *meeting*, and which implies the full preparedness of all, whether individuals, nations or communities, to meet each other and one another not only for healthy co-operation but also for healthy rivalry in the furtherance of the common cause of humanity.[1]

In some vital points the ways and claims of an institutional religion differ from those of science. Broadly speaking, the traditional ways of an institutional religion are to accept a Book as the most authoritative and to believe that it contains words through which the whole of truth and wisdom, good and beauty, law and discipline has been revealed by God or uttered by a Gifted Master of infallible authority. If it encourages study and interpretation, inquiry and examination, that is intended only to render explicit what is implicit in the Book and its appendices. If it enjoins practices or experiments, that, too, are intended not to arrive at any new results but only at those which are confirmatory of the results or experiences already gained. To say anything, even inadvertently, against the Book is to be construed as blasphemy, arrogance and infidelity. Its main claim is that the Book which guides its course contains the last word of truth and wisdom, or that the godliness or greatness of human personality and character reached in its founder is the last attainment of man in history, the last (*carama*) being accounted as the very best (*parama*).

1 Barua, The *Philosophy of Progress* (in the Press).

The ways of science, on the other hand, are not to accept any such authority, whether God-made or man-made. It may seek guidance from all records of the past or from none. It stands for a comparative study of all things. Some hypothesis may guide its course for the time being but not for all times to come. There is no last word to say or defend. It does not entertain the idea of finality or any infallible authority.[1] If it encourages fresh observations and new experiments, it does so either to arrive at new results or to test again and again the results so far obtained. It seeks to profit by suggestions and criticisms. It stands for readjustments of human relations to new truths and new ideas that are born of new discoveries made.

As for religion, Dean Inge claims, "Spiritual progress must be within the sphere of a reality which is not itself progressing, or for which in Milton's grand words progresses the dateless and irrevoluble circle of its own perfection, joining inseparable hands with joy and bliss in over-measure for ever."

And as for science, Julien Huxley opines, "The greatest experiences of human life, those in which the mind appears to touch the Absolute and the Infinite—what of their relation to the notion of progress? They are realized in many forms—in love, in intellectual discovery, in art, in religion: but the salient fact about all

1 As Sir Muhammad Iqbal observes, "......there is no such thing as finality in philosophical thinking. As knowledge advances and fresh avenues of thought are opened, other views, and probably sounder views......are possible"—*Religious Thought in Islam,* Preface, p. vi.

is that they are felt as of intensest value, and that they seem to leave no more to be desired. Doubtless when we say that at such moment we touch the Infinite or the Absolute we mean only that we touch what is infinite and absolute in comparison with our ordinary selves. None the less, the sense of finality and utter reality attendant on them is difficult to bring into line with our idea of progress."[1]

If such broadly be the relative positions of science and institutional religion, and the growing tendency of our youths be to discard all religions whose creeds and methods are incompatible with directions to progress and freedom from science and philosophy, it may be pertinent here to ask—will any aspects of Buddhism have an appeal to modern youth? If so, what are these aspects? This is the important question the Buddhists of Ceylon will be expected, more than others, to face and answer.

Weighing the arguments for and against Buddhism, I am inclined to think that if it will have any appeal to the present changing world of ours, that will be for such special aspects as I may humbly place before you for your consideration.

1. The aspect which strikes me most is that Buddism, I mean, the religion which is known to have been propounded by Buddha, is the only religion of which the express motto is *Ehi Passa*, "Come and See". If, like a scientist, Buddha had not a demonstrable truth

1. *Essays of a Biologist*, p. 39.

to present, he could not have proposed this as the motto for his system. But what is it?

We have from Buddha and his followers a sound ethical system which is broadbased on analytical psychology. A highly methodical system of psychology is presented in the first book of the *Abhidhamma Piṭaka,* and this has been further developed in later Abhidhamma literature in Pali as well as in Sanskrit. The psycho-ethical concepts have been carefully catatogued, classified and defined. A workable chart has been held before us, indicating the mechanism of mind, its various operations and bearings on thought, speech and action, in short, on human conduct. The levels of consciousness and planes of experience have been graded and differentiated. The types of consciousness and the corresponding mental complexes have been distinguished and explained. The mental complexes themselves have been carefully analysed into their component elements or factors. The rūpa or bodily aspect of the self has been studied and analysed from the physical, anatomical and physiological points of view in so far as matter and material qualities, body and bodily functions come within the scope of psychological ethics. A philosophy of relations *(paccayas, pratyayas),* is developed in the book of *Paṭṭhāna* and its various commentaries. These relations are intended to guide the students in understanding and discriminating the connections between mind and mental states, between one mental state and another, between mind and body and body and mind, between the motives or springs of action and the mental complexes with their outward expressions, between the organs of sense and their objects, so on and so forth. The psycho-ethical concepts are arranged according to different mental levels and planes of experience. Attempts are made to clearly indicate how one mental state counteracts another, how one helps and strengthens another, where one being present, the other is absent, and the like. The results are stated and presented for investigation and testing, examination and revision, comparison and valuation, fresh experiment and verification There is no hide-and-seek policy. The whole card of experience and results of study and instrospection is laid on the table for inspection and opinion. Study the chart or manual and you know how and where you exactly stand, on what level of mind, in which plane of experience, what makes for the elevation of your nature and the formation of your character, and what for their retardation or degradation, what is the play of motives and how to check or purify them, and the like.

2. Having accepted "Come and See" once for all as the motto of his teachings, Buddha could not but advise others not to accept anything as authoritative for their guidance along the right path of thought and of action but that which accords with their own inner experience and scientifice reason, that which is or can be tested and verified. It is not good then, according to him, to be nowhere, being easy preys to all manner of opinion, and it is no wonder that he would advise us all, as he did the Kālāmas of old, not to accept anything as reasonable and good on mere study of any or all of the texts of divine

authority handed down by tradition, or because it is a received instruction from generation to generation, or because thus hath it been held through all times, or because it may be shown to tally with the trend of teaching of the Books of authority, or because of its logical argument, or because of its mere fairness in method, or because of its nice formulation, or because it is offered as a belief held after careful introspection and going through much hardship, or beacuse it comes from a good-looking person, or because, after all, it is said by our own accredited teacher."[1]

3. As a further logical step from the above position, Buddha could not but disapprove all such dogmatic tendencies of human mind, all such exclusive mental make-up and self-complacency as lead men to extol and glorify only their own doctrines and things, and decry and condemn those which are known to be of others,—all such obstinate spirit of human character as finds its signal expression in and through the utterance—"All that is our own is the only thing true, correct, good or acceptable, and the rest are all false, incorrect, bad or rejectable" (*idam eva saccaṃ, mogham aññaṁ*).[2] This noble teaching of Buddha was indeed at the back of

---

1 Anguttara, i, p. 188f. : *mā anussavena, mā paramparāya, mā itikirāya, mā piṭakasampadānena, mā takkahetu, mā nayahetu, mā ākāraparivitakkena, mā diṭṭhinijjhānakhantiyā, mā bhabbarūpatāya, mā samaṇo no garū ti.* In translating these precious word, I have sought guidance not only from Buddhaghosa's commentary but also from the Amarakoṣa, *e.g.*, from Brahmavarga, verse 30 :

pāramparyapadeśe syād aitihyam itihāvyayam.

2 Anguttara, i, pp. 88, 188f.

Aśoka's mind when he promulgated his famous toleration edict

It is well said that Aśoka "destroyed the barriers which detached one sect from another, by teaching them tolerance and respect for one another's principles and tenets, and thus promoted the essence of religion which they all shared in common, or that this, in fact, was the message of Buddha to all lay people, and it was this universal character of Buddhism that Aśoka clearly perceived and emphasized."[1]

4. The elevation of human nature and the stoppage of its course towards degradation, the formation of human character on a strong rational foundation, the improvement of the general form and tone of society, race and civilization, the cordiality of human relations, the refinement and dignity in human behaviour, the liberal and sound education of all, the right direction given to the states for the proper discharge of their duties to the subjects, the release of all higher energies towards the cause of culture and humanity, in short, the propounding of higher ideals of life and the showing of the ways of their realisation are held out by Buddha as the true mission of all religions instead of creating sects and committing themselves to certain set creeds and practices and forms. The reluctance of Buddha to any commitment to creeds and practices and forms is indeed a remarkable feature of his religion which cannot but appeal to modern mind. It is only in the common pursuit of knowledge, the development of humna facul-

1 D. R. Bhandarkar, *Aśoka*, revised edition, p. 250,

ties, and the general ethical principles of life that there can be an agreement reached, and not certainly in the matter of the acceptance of any set of beliefs, laws, formalities, conventions, customs and usages. Let the forms evolve in accordance with the growing ideas and ideals and according to convenience, subject to revision, amendment and annulment, these being always intended for men and not men for them. Thus one may understand and appreciate why Buddha had not prescribed any social code for the householders.

5. It is no less important to observe that although *ipso facto* a Buddhist Fraternity, imbued with the missionary zeal, came to be formed, and a code of law and a system of discipline surpassing even the German military discipline came to be promulgated and enforced, Buddha never thought that he was the founder of that order and no one knew better the mischief of the law than he. Thus no laws were made in advance and there were no laws or rules that were not intended to be amended or repealed. All that he did was just to set his seal of approval to a rule of conduct which was necessitated by circumstances of the time and the need of which was keenly felt by the members of the order to whom it was applicable. While his followers as members of that order conformed to the formalities and conventions evolved by them, the simple call of "Come ye" (*Ehi, Etha*) sufficed for Buddha to gather unto him a comrade or fellow wayfarer.

6. Last but not least is that although in the Bodhisattvanaya Mahāyāna the accepted ideal was that of a

dedicated life with the resolve not to attain slavation until the rest of beings were brought up into the state of salvation or until the great cause of the world espoused was fulfilled, Buddha never promised salvation to any person, nor did he desire that any man or woman should care for any reward which was not self-earned. Although he spoke of the eternal urge of life as being towards evolving into better and still better forms, he nowhere claimed that the influence of the way of truth and of life shown by him would last through eternity, that, in other words, the religion propounded by him would not be followed by another.

I have detained you long, ladies and gentlemen, over the matters which are to me of supreme importance at the present moment when the world is passing through a grave crisis, when all our inherited ideas and beliefs are shaken to their very foundation, and when, as the urge of life would have it, we are hoping against hope to find ourselves in a new world. It is imperative to all thinking men and women to discuss what this new world is going to be, whether one founded on the provisions of the Atlantic Charter will be a fit habitat of us all, or another built on the collective wisdom of the best of men.

CEYLON LECTURES

NOTES

P. 171, l. 21 : Aśvaghoṣa Sanskritises the Pali term *idappaccayatā* as *idampratyayatā* instead of as *ihapratyayatā*, which is not, however, philologically explicable.

Pp. 266-67 : According to the Vijñānavāda as enunciated by Vasubandhu in his *Triṁśikā*, the attainment of Arhatship means the death of the *ālaya-vijñāna*, while the *ālaya-vijñāna* itself is the first resultant *(vipāka)* of the process of transformation or maturation *(pariṇāma)* undergone by *citta* or consciousness in the past existence of the individual under the influence of *avidyā*, etc. Behind his *cittamātratā* or *vijñapti-mātratā* was the Upaniṣadic idea of *cinmātratā* as the fundamental attribute of soul.

INDEX